European Higher Education, Social Responsibility, and the Local Democratic Mission

In the series *Higher Education, Place, and Social Responsibility*, edited by Ira Harkavy, John L. Puckett, and Rita A. Hodges

SJUR BERGAN

European Higher Education, Social Responsibility, and the Local Democratic Mission

TEMPLE UNIVERSITY PRESS
Philadelphia • *Rome* • *Tokyo*

TEMPLE UNIVERSITY PRESS
Philadelphia, Pennsylvania 19122
tupress.temple.edu

Library of Congress Cataloging-in-Publication Data

Names: Bergan, Sjur, author.
Title: European higher education, social responsibility, and the local
democratic mission / Sjur Bergan.
Other titles: Higher education, place, and social responsibility.
Description: Philadelphia : Temple University Press, 2025. | Series: Higher
education, place, and social responsibility | Includes bibliographical
references and index. | Summary: "Contributes to a global conversation
on the democratic mission of higher education, with an examination of
the specific case of higher education in Europe"— Provided by
publisher.
Identifiers: LCCN 2024039567 (print) | LCCN 2024039568 (ebook) | ISBN
9781439924600 (cloth) | ISBN 9781439924617 (paperback) | ISBN
9781439924624 (pdf)
Subjects: LCSH: Higher education and state—Europe. | Democracy and
education—Europe. | Democracy—Social aspects—Study and teaching
(Higher)—Europe.
Classification: LCC LC177.2 .B38 2025 (print) | LCC LC177.2 (ebook) | DDC
379.4—dc23/eng/20241211
LC record available at https://lccn.loc.gov/2024039567
LC ebook record available at https://lccn.loc.gov/2024039568

The manufacturer's authorized representative in the EU for product safety is
Temple University Rome, Via di San Sebastianello, 16, 00187 Rome RM, Italy
(https://rome.temple.edu/).
tempress@temple.edu

9 8 7 6 5 4 3 2 1

Contents

Preface

The local democratic mission of higher education as it has developed and as it could develop further in Europe is the main focus of this book. However, this mission cannot be divorced from other issues, including how we see Europe, how we look at democracy, and whether and to what extent we see education and higher education as essential to building a culture of democracy locally, nationally, and across Europe.

The author of this book is European. I cannot claim to know all parts of Europe equally well or to be unbiased toward any parts of the continent, but my perspective is also not that of a single country. That perspective is dictated by my own background.

This book is the result of my work in higher education policy for more years than I care to count or remember. It started when I was elected, in 1981, as a student representative to the Academic Senate of my alma mater, the University of Oslo, and it continued in administrative positions there in 1983–1991, as a policymaker working closely with the university leadership.

The step onto the European scene came in 1991, when I moved from Norway to France to take up a position in the Council of Europe's Education Department. The Council of Europe is an intergovernmental organization working for democracy, human rights, and the rule of law, and I took up my position at a time when Europe was seeing great changes and great opportunities. The Berlin Wall had just fallen, and, over the next decade and a half, many new countries joined the Council.[1] I worked in the Education Department during my whole career in the Council, and as the head of department from 2011 until my retirement in February 2022. I could hardly have had a better vantage point from which not only to observe but also to contribute to the development of higher education policy in Europe. Two contexts were particularly important: the European Higher Education Area and the democratic mission of higher education.

The opportunity to develop cooperation with U.S. higher education was a very welcome aspect of my job. Norway has a strong Atlantic orientation. France also looks to North America, albeit with less enthusiasm. My first direct experience of the United States came in high school, when I was an AFS[2] exchange student for a year, lived with the Yoder family in Alton, Illinois, and went to Alton Senior High School.

The Council of Europe's work on the democratic mission of higher education would not have come about had it not been for our cooperation with U.S. higher education, more specifically the International Consortium for Higher Education, Civic Responsibility, and Democracy and its longtime chair Dr. Ira Harkavy, the founding director of the Netter Center for Community Partnerships at the University of Pennsylvania. This cooperation developed from the late 1990s onward, at a time when the Council of Europe began to realize that its traditional view of democracy as institutions, laws, and elections needed to be supplemented with an emphasis on the attitudes and behaviors of those who elect and legislate. This was apparent to those of us who worked in the Council's Education Department, and it was a view held by many members of our Higher Education Committee. It was not apparent to all, however, and some committee members saw a focus on the democratic mission of higher education as an unwelcome departure from what "higher education is really about." The transatlantic cooperation was important for several reasons explored in the book, but one was that, in both the United States and Europe, higher education has different strengths and weaknesses for the countries in their approach to their contributions to building democracy. U.S. universities often have a better-developed view of their civic and societal missions than their European counterparts. European higher education, on the other hand, has more democratic governance with strong roles for the elected representatives of faculty, students, and staff.

One important aspect of the experience of working with the International Consortium is its emphasis on the need for democracy to start locally. Universities have an obligation to their local communities, and they are themselves strengthened by local cooperation. The Anchor Institutions Task Force (AITF), which is a part of the International Consortium, provides a forum for both sharing and developing good practices for local institutional-community partnerships. The experience of AITF convinced us that Europe also needs a forum—we landed on the term "platform"—to promote the local mission of higher education and that this mission needs to extend well beyond the economic cooperation that is already quite well developed in Europe. That is how we devised the local democratic mission of higher education as a European undertaking and why we are convinced that the Council of Europe is the right organization to develop and promote it.

The focus on the local democratic mission of higher education in this book is accompanied by a narrative showing:

- How I see Europe in cultural and political terms.
- What the Council of Europe's role is.
- How the democratic mission of higher education is strengthened through what started as a transatlantic cooperation and has now "gone global."
- How ensuring opportunities for refugees to use their talents and put them at the service of their new communities is both a local and a global higher education mission to strengthen democracy.

Throughout the book, I seek to provide examples from a fairly broad selection of European countries and universities, and I try to maintain a critical distance. I can, nevertheless, not pretend to be entirely objective or neutral in the discussion of events with which I have had a close personal involvement, such as the development of the Global Cooperation for the Democratic Mission of Higher Education, the proposal for a Council of Europe Platform on the Local Democratic Mission of Higher Education, the Council of Europe Reference Framework of Competences for Democratic Culture, or several aspects of the development of the European Higher Education Area.

Welcome to exploring the local democratic mission of higher education as it has developed in Europe but also how it could continue to develop and why it is important it does so.

Acknowledgments

I
f we follow John Donne in saying that "no Man is an Island unto Himself,"[1] this is true also when human beings put pen to paper. This book would not have been written without the advice and encouragement of Ira Harkavy, my friend and longtime partner in developing the Global Cooperation for the Democratic Mission of Higher Education. It was Ira who suggested that the series he is editing on the local democratic mission of higher education would benefit from a volume on how this mission is perceived and implemented in Europe. It was Ira who asked me to take charge of this volume, who convinced me it should be a monograph rather than an edited volume, and who has accompanied me through the relatively accelerated writing process. The book has also greatly benefited from the encouragement and advice of Aaron M. Javsicas at Temple University Press as well as very valuable input by Rita A. Hodges.

Beyond the work on this book, I express my sincere gratitude to friends and colleagues who have accompanied me at various stages of my career as a higher education policymaker. In addition to Ira and Rita, they include those who have been most intimately involved in the Global Cooperation: Tony Gallagher, David John Lock, Gabriele Mazza, Brian Murphy, Ronaldo Munck, Caryn McTighe Musil, Hilligje van't Land, and Joann Weeks, as well as Krzysztof Ostrowski and Henry Teune, who are regrettably no longer with us. I also thank my longtime director general at the Council of Europe, Snežana Samardžić-Marković; my director Matjaž Gruden; Mireille Wendling and Joana Kashi, the best assistants anyone could possibly have; Christopher

Reynolds, who worked with me on the Reference Framework of Competences for Democratic Culture; Margareta Platon, who did the same with the education response to COVID-19; Sarah Keating, Samir Hećo and others who worked on the European Qualifications Passport for Refugees; Sarah Breslin and others at the European Centre for Modern Languages; Aurora Ailincai, Yuliya Kochneva, and others at the Observatory on History Teaching; their counterpart in the intergovernmental program, Jean-Philippe Restoueix, and other colleagues too numerous to mention by name. Not least, I thank Liv Else Sannung, without a doubt the best teacher I have ever had. In junior high school, she taught me English, motivated me to apply for an AFS scholarship, and not least to look beyond the confines of my hometown and my home country. I also thank the Yoder family, whose life I shared during my AFS year in Alton, Illinois.

The European and international education and higher education policy community is an area where professionals also become friends. Again, the professionals and friends who have stimulated and helped me along the road are far too numerous to mention, but some in particular cannot be forgotten: Stephen Adam, Staša Babić, the late Yves Beaudin, Fr. Friedrich Bechina FSO, Carita Blomqvist, David Crosier, Que Anh Dang, Ligia Deca, the late Germain Dondelinger, Maria Fassari, Lusine Fljyan, Michael Gaebel, Irina Geantă, Peter Greisler, Cezar Mihaj Hâj, the late E. Stephen Hunt, Maija Innola, Michal Karpíšek, Maria Kelo, Manja Klemenčič, Kees Kouwenaar, Øystein Lund, Marina Malgina, Liviu Matei, Ina Mitskevich, the late Per Nyborg, Klara Engels Perenyi, Milica Popović, Lewis Purser, Ivana Radonova, Andrejs Rauhvargers, Alexandra Sandru, Stig Arne Skjerven, Athanassia Spyropulou, Tone Flood Strøm, Svein Stølen, the late Srbijanka Turajlić, Adam Tyson, Stamenka Uvalić-Trumbić, Nadežda Uzelac, Una Strand Viðarsdóttir, Claudia Zambra, and Pavel Zgaga.

My work over the years has not always favored family time. A very special debt of gratitude is owed to my wife, Margarita Riveaux, to my daughters, Gabriela and Catalina, and, of course, to my late parents, Astrid and Oddvar Bergan as well as to my son-in-law William Ramon—Catalina's husband—and my granddaughters Charlotte and Sophie.

I dedicate this book to Gabriela and Catalina. They have chosen different paths—Catalina as an events' organizer and Gabriela with a career of humanitarian work that has so far taken her to live in Georgia, Turkey, Iraq, Pakistan, and currently Kenya, with frequent work visits to Somalia. I am intensely proud of them both.

A Note on Language

E urope is a unique blend of and balance between what makes us European and what constitutes our national and local cultures. Language is an important part of this equation. I grew up as a monolingual Norwegian speaker whose first contact with foreign languages was through summers spent in Sweden and English classes in school, starting in sixth grade. In my school days, German (in junior high school) and French (in senior high school) were also mandatory subjects, even if the level most students reached was not particularly advanced. For the past three decades, I have been living in Strasbourg, on a border you cross more easily if you speak both French and German, my home language is Spanish (spoken with the Chilean accent of my wife's home country), and English and French are the official languages of the Council of Europe. Once you have contracted the language virus, there is no cure, and I have acquired other languages at lower levels of proficiency, including Italian, Portuguese, Romanian, Dutch, Russian, and Serbian. At the time of writing, I am cooperating with the Andorran Ministry of Education in a project where all documents are in Catalan.

Living life through a single language is, therefore, inconceivable to me, and plurilingualism is an important part not only of who I am but also of what Europe is. To give at least a small impression of the linguistic diversity of Europe, names are as much as possible given in their original form, sometimes with letters and diacritical marks that may be unfamiliar to some readers. This extends to the names of cities and regions, even where English uses Anglicized forms. After all, such usage evolves and may be developed in ways respectful of those who live in the cities or regions described and the languages they speak. Who would now insist on using Leghorn rather than Livorno? Why should we then use Cracow rather than Kraków or Gothenburg rather than Göteborg? Anglicizing names betrays both our inability to cope with foreign sounds and the limits of our knowledge, since we can only Anglicize the names of places we know. That is why the phonetically straightforward Roma is (too) often Anglicized as Rome, whereas the considerably more challenging name of the Alsatian village Breuschwickersheim is left untransformed. Transliteration is, of course, another story: it is the act of converting a text from one script to another. All names in this book are given in Latin script, so that the Serbian Cyrillic Београд is rendered as Beograd (rather than Belgrade, which is a transformation of the name rather than a transliteration of it), the Greek Αθήνα as Athinai, and the Armenian Գյումրի as Gyumri. However, I make exceptions where the Anglicized form is part of the official name of a document, such as the Lisbon Recognition Convention, as well as for the names of countries and languages. Hence, it is Estonia and Luxemburgish rather than Eesti and Lëtzebuergesch. The government of Turkey has now demanded that Turkey be referred to by its Turkish name—Türkiye—in international organizations. I continue to refer to the country as Turkey, even if I use the Turkish spelling in any reference to its cities and provinces, such as İstanbul.

The adjectives "American" and "U.S." also warrant a note. "U.S.," when used as an adjective, refers to that or those pertaining to the United States of America. "American" refers to that or those pertaining to the whole American continent, as Latin American friends are quick to point out.

This book uses the U.S. variety of English, which is the one I personally prefer, but quotes are given in the original spelling if the British variety of English is the language of the quote. Translations are mine unless marked otherwise.

European Higher Education,
Social Responsibility, and the
Local Democratic Mission

Introduction

Why Higher Education?

If we ask the proverbial man in the street why someone should go to college or university, the answer is likely to be "to get a good job." If we explore further and ask what a "good job" is, the answer is likely to include good pay, social prestige, and possibly good working conditions. These conditions are more likely to be white collar than blue collar and will probably involve working regular office hours rather than shifts or the typical working hours of cooks, waiters, and security guards. Job security may also be a criterion, even if in many European countries the prospect of lifetime or even long-term employment is less bright than it was for the generation to which this author belongs.

At least some respondents would hopefully emphasize that the job should be interesting. Would respondents also say the job should be meaningful in terms of what it enables the job holder to do for others? That, alas, seems less likely. The discourse of both business and public authorities has emphasized the economic importance of higher education. In many cases, higher education leaders use the same arguments. Vocations exist but do not seem to be the rule.

Education is, however, about much more than preparing students for the labor market, even if the importance of this objective needs to be acknowledged. The Council of Europe has defined four major purposes of education:

- Preparation for the labor market
- Preparation for life as active citizens in democratic societies

- Personal development
- Development and maintenance of a broad, advanced knowledge base (Council of Europe 2007: para. 5)

These missions are equally important, and they complement rather than compete with each other. Many of the competences that will make someone attractive on the labor market will also help them become an active citizen and further their personal development.

In Europe, public discourse still gives primacy to the economic importance of higher education. Public funding is more important in Europe than in the United States. If you want to secure public funding for a study program, few if any arguments can beat those that focus on its economic benefits. Immediate or short-term benefits are likely to win out over long-term benefits.

At the same time, however, European public authorities also recognize the role of education in developing democratic citizenship. Many education laws recognize this broader purpose. By way of example, the Norwegian Law on Education stipulates that the education offered in Norwegian schools should further "democracy, equality, and a scientific way of thinking"[1] (LOV-1998-07-17-6: para. 1.1). The Norwegian law on universities and colleges stipulates that higher education "contribute to an environmentally, socially, and economically sustainable development" (LOV-2005-04-01-15: para. 1.1).

In the development of the European Higher Education Area (EHEA),[2] which is discussed in Chapter 1, the multiple purposes of higher education were first mentioned in a ministerial communiqué in 2007 (Bologna Process 2007: para. 1.4). In 2015, the European ministers[3] responsible for higher education emphasized another aspect of democracy—social inclusion—by stating:

Making our systems more inclusive is an essential aim for the EHEA as our populations become more and more diversified, also due to immigration and demographic changes. We undertake to widen participation in higher education and support institutions that provide relevant learning activities in appropriate contexts for different types of learners, including lifelong learning. We will improve permeability and articulation between different education sectors. We will enhance the social dimension of higher education, improve gender balance and widen opportunities for access and completion, including international mobility, for students from disadvantaged backgrounds. We will provide mobility opportunities for students and staff from conflict areas, while working to make it possible for them to return home once conditions allow. (Bologna Process 2015d: 2–3)

Even if both public authorities and the higher education community recognize the importance of universities in developing and maintaining a culture of democracy, it cannot be taken for granted that this recognition will translate into practical support. Advocacy is required to ensure that when the time comes to set priorities for policies and funding, the democratic mission of higher education is given its due. The U.S. higher education community has long highlighted its democratic mission, and its European counterpart is now following suit.

The Democratic Mission of Higher Education

This book, then, explores the democratic mission of higher education. That is a broad and ambitious project, and I try to make it more manageable by focusing in particular on two approaches, one of which is thematic and the other geographic.

Thematically, this is a book about how the democratic mission of higher education plays out—or at least *can* play out—at the local level in Europe. Even if I do not subscribe to the view expressed by legendary U.S. politician Tip O'Neill that "all politics is local,"[4] countries cannot be considered democratic if their local communities are not governed democratically, with strong involvement by its citizens. A neighborhood, village, or city is where most of us live our daily lives, and that applies even to those who travel frequently and spend much of our working lives in online meetings with participants from other cities and countries working on issues that far transcend the local context. In the same way that countries cannot be fully democratic if their local communities are not governed democratically, higher education cannot be a credible guide to democracy if its internal practice is undemocratic.

The university—which I use interchangeably with "higher education institution," unless the context requires specification—is a preeminent example of how the local, national, and global intertwine. Some higher education institutions cater primarily to a local or regional population. The U.S. community colleges offer opportunities to many who would otherwise not have considered higher education. In my view, they could serve as models to other countries.

Most universities, including those in Europe, aim beyond the local. That applies not only to the "world-class universities" but also to the many traditionally seen as less prestigious—those with good teaching institutions that recruit nationally, with a fair share of international students, and whose faculty conduct research at least at some stages of their career. Yet, these universities are also place bound. They are located in specific communities, and they are unlikely to move from there. In the United States, this has given rise to the notion of anchor institutions, because the universities are anchored in their communities. The Anchor Institutions Task Force (AITF) now has nearly one thousand members and describes the anchor concept thus:

> Anchor institutions are enduring organizations that are rooted in their localities. It is difficult for them to leave their surroundings even in the midst of substantial capital flight. The challenge to a growing movement is to encourage these stable local assets to harness their resources in order to address critical issues such as education, economic opportunity, and health. It is difficult to imagine fragile local economies and widening social disparities changing without leveraging stable institutions, especially amidst a decline in government resources. These dynamics have given rise to the concept "anchors" as agents of community and economic development.[5]

Not all AITF members head universities, but many do, and they represent all kinds of universities. The University of Pennsylvania (Penn) is one of the world-class universities and is very active in international cooperation. It also works very closely with, and not only *in*, its immediate neighborhood in West Philadelphia (Benson et al. 2017: 92–111) and has established a specific unit—the Netter Center for Community Partnerships[6]—to coordinate this work (Benson et al. 2017: 97–123).

The earlier examples are from the United States, but the geographic focus of this book is Europe. The continent from which I hail has a credible claim to having invented the university, but it has no monopoly on the institution, nor can Europe claim credit for all or even most of the ways in which the university has developed. Europe has much to learn from other parts of the world. When it comes to the local democratic mission of higher education, Europe has much to learn from the United States. There are different interpretations of the democratic and/or civic mission of higher education, as there are different interpretations of what democracy means in practice. Some higher education leaders are inherently skeptical of engaging politically, while others see political engagement as part of their role and mission. They may also interpret the term "political" differently. As used in this book, "political" transcends party politics and refers to how universities may influence the development of society on the basis of their values and their research-based knowledge and understanding. We should keep in mind that the roots of "politics" and "political" lie in the Greek πόλις—*polis*—which means "city," so the link between democracy and community is more than that between democracy and parties. In this sense, the local dimension of democracy dates to antiquity.

Like their counterparts in other parts of the world, whatever their ambitions of being "world class," European universities are located in specific communities. Some of these communities are "university towns." They are often small- or medium-sized towns where the university is the dominant social and economic actor, and where students are a prominent part of community life. Oxford and Cambridge, both in the United Kingdom, are well-known examples, but "university towns" can be found in most parts of Europe, from Coimbra in Portugal to Uppsala in Sweden. In countless other cities, the university may not be as prominent in the community as it would be in a "university town," but it may nevertheless be the community's largest employer and also otherwise be a key actor economically, socially, and culturally. While the typical European university is necessarily *in* a community, it does not always see itself as being *of* the community. There is, however, an increasing awareness in Europe both of the university's role in developing and maintaining democracy and of the importance of the university working not only *in* but *with* its local community.

Europe is a diverse continent, and describing the different ways in which the local democratic mission of higher education is fulfilled but sometimes also rejected requires an understanding of the continent. It may well be argued that both Asia and Africa are more diverse than Europe. What is unique to Europe is perhaps its specific blend of diversity and unity: what makes us all European, and what at the same time makes us Armenian, Finnish, French, German, Greek, Maltese, Serbian, or Swiss.

Part of the diversity of Europe is its rich linguistic heritage. More than fifty official languages are spoken throughout Europe, as are many more languages or language varieties that are not official. German is a language with official status. In contrast, Alsatian—the Alemannic variety of German spoken alongside French in France's Alsace region (where the author resides)—shows how difficult it can be to decide what is a variety of a language and what is a language of its own [7] Perhaps for this reason, Alsatian is also an example of a language or a language variety that lacks official status. The language of this book is English, which is widely learned as a foreign language in Europe, but which is the native language of few Europeans except for those growing up in Ireland, Malta, or the United Kingdom. It is also not my native language, but it is the medium through which I live a considerable part of my life.

The Political Context

Europe is not only a geographic but also a political reality. It is, however, not a single or even simple political reality. Chapter 1 outlines the political and institutional complexity of Europe, organized around a narrower but deeper political and economic cooperation through the European Union (EU) and a geographically broader cooperation through the Council of Europe. While the EU is supranational, the Council of Europe is a classic intergovernmental organization focusing on democracy, human rights, and the rule of law.

It is worth noting that this double political framework does not correspond to the Cold War political division of Europe into a Western and an Eastern bloc, broadly organized around the North Atlantic Treaty Organization (NATO) and the Warsaw Pact, with some countries like Finland, Sweden, and Switzerland but also Albania and Yugoslavia remaining outside of the blocs. Today, several former Warsaw Pact members like Bulgaria, Poland, and Romania as well as the Baltic states of Estonia, Latvia, and Lithuania (until 1990 part of the Soviet Union) have joined both NATO and the EU. At the same time, some long-standing NATO members like Iceland and Norway but also Turkey have either decided not to join the EU or have tried to do so without success. The formerly nonaligned Austria, Finland, and Sweden joined the EU in 1994. Finland joined NATO in April 2023, and Sweden did so in March 2024. On the other hand, the United Kingdom withdrew from the EU, effective as of early 2020, but remains in NATO.

The political reality of Europe is, of course, not only institutional. Europe is experiencing many of the same developments seen in other parts of the world, including in the United States. Populism is on the rise and, with it, attitudes that reject the need for research-based knowledge and understanding. Saying that "everybody is entitled to his own opinion but not to his own facts"[8] may once have seemed like stating the obvious, but Europe has not been spared verbal distortions like "alternative facts" or "illiberal democracy." Countries that were previously considered examples of progressive societies, like Denmark, the Netherlands, and Sweden, have in recent years elected hard-right and extreme-right representatives to their national parliaments. France presents the particularity of having a strong populist right as well as a strong populist left, with the neoliberal movement of President Macron currently the main political alternative.

These developments challenge higher education. In fact, they challenge the very ideas on which higher education builds, and they make the local democratic mission of universities even more urgent, as does the development toward stronger and more violent international conflicts.

For Europe, the period since the end of World War II was largely characterized by an absence of armed conflicts in spite of the strong tensions between the two major blocs during the Cold War.[9] Nonetheless, Europe has seen more of these conflicts over the past generation. The disintegration of former Yugoslavia led to war in the 1990s, with Bosnia and Herzegovina and Kosovo as the most violent examples. Within the area of the former Soviet Union, the armed conflict between Armenia and Azerbaijan over Nagorno-Karabakh[10] as well as the Chechen wars were the best-known examples until February 2022. Then, Russia launched a full-scale invasion of Ukraine, which is a game changer and has led to very strong reactions from most other European countries. The Russian invasion of Ukraine was taken a significant step further on September 30, 2022, when Russia declared it had annexed four occupied areas of Ukraine and that these would henceforth be part of Russia. This land grab is not internationally recognized, and it came at a time when Ukraine had regained parts of the territory occupied by Russia. The illegal Russian annexation, while a sign of weakness rather than strength, will probably make finding a negotiated end to the war even more difficult. At the time of writing, two and a half years after the start of the invasion, Russia is far from achieving its stated war goals, and Ukraine enjoys strong support from both Europe and the United States, even if there is regrettably some signs of this support weakening, at least in parts of the European population if less so among governments, and also signs that the Ukrainian position on the battlefield is weakening.[11] In the elections in the Slovak Republic at the very end of September 2023, the populist right party, relatively friendly to Russia, headed by former premier Robert Fico, became the strongest force and formed a new government.[12] Germany has seen a significant strengthening of the far-right Alternative für Deutschland (AfD)[13] and a corresponding weakening of the tripartite governing coalition (Social Democrats, Greens, Liberals) in both local and regional elections[14] over the summer and in the early fall of 2023 and some signs that the determination of all democratic parties against cooperation with the AfD may be weakening in some local and regional contexts.[15] These developments are not due to the war on Ukraine alone—or even primarily. At the time of writing, there is, however, no end to the war in sight that would allow Ukraine to recover its territorial integrity.

One consequence of the war on Ukraine is that academic cooperation with Russia is no longer possible. Cooperation with and assistance to Ukrainian higher education has been substantially strengthened, but, at the same time, the infrastructure of many Ukrainian universities has been destroyed.[16] In parts of Ukraine occupied by Russia, the leaders of universities as well as schools have been replaced by people "loyal" to Russia and curricula have been Russified. While it may be too early to describe the full impact of the war on Ukraine on higher education in Europe, it is already clear that it is extensive. Both institutional and individual research cooperation has largely been broken, and student exchanges to and from Russia and Belarus are now almost nonexistent. It is difficult to see how they could be reestablished in the foreseeable future. This also implies that students and staff working on issues related to Russia and Belarus will have few if any opportunities to pursue research in situ and that, if and when Russia may again become a bona fide actor in international affairs, some of the academic competence on the country may have been lost. One consequence of the war is, incidentally, that students wishing to learn Russian—whose numbers may well diminish—are now increasingly seeking admission to programs for foreign students at universities in Kazakhstan, where Russian is the native language of many residents.[17] Ukrainian universities have suffered extensive damage and will require very substantial aid from the EU and from individual European countries to rebuild their infrastructure[18] as well as to continue to support student and staff exchange and competence building.[19] Among the millions who have left Ukraine as refugees, many are higher education graduates, staff, or students—mostly women because of the restrictions on men of military age leaving the country. Even if the motivation of many refugees to return to help rebuild Ukraine once the war ends remains strong, and even if many refugees have already returned, it is likely Ukraine will suffer a brain drain that will probably increase the longer the war lasts.

Higher education operates within this political reality, but it also has a political reality of its own. The same political changes that made an expansion of the EU and the Council of Europe as well as NATO possible and consigned the Warsaw Pact and its economic cooperation counterpart COMECON[20] to what their founders would undoubtedly have referred to as the trash heap of history[21] also did away with many restrictions on pan-European academic exchange and cooperation. With an impeccable sense of timing, the EU launched the ERASMUS[22] program in 1987, shortly before the fall of the Berlin Wall. This student exchange scheme has turned out to be one of the most successful EU programs ever. Today, I suspect more Europeans have heard about the ERASMUS program than about its namesake, Erasmus of Rotterdam.

The most important development, however, came some twelve years later, with the launch of the Bologna Process in 1999. In 2010, it evolved into the EHEA, and it provides the framework not only for extensive structural reforms but for much of Europe's higher education cooperation. From its initial twenty-nine members, all participants in EU education programs, the EHEA has expanded to forty-nine member states. Not all have a relationship with the EU, but all are parties to the Council of Europe's European Cultural Convention.[23] The EHEA is described in greater detail in Chapter 1, and its importance to the development of higher education in Europe is substantial. I have had the privilege of being a participant in the development of the EHEA since its beginning.

What Europeans Have in Common and
What Is Specific to Each Country

With the EHEA and the European Cultural Convention, we move toward the cultural reality of Europe, which is the subject of Chapter 2. In this book, culture is understood in the anthropological sense of ideas, customs, language, and social behavior. Europeans have much in common, and, without this feeling of cultural belonging, the political cooperation that has developed would hardly have been possible.

At the same time, like most other people, Europeans have several overlapping identities. In a poll conducted in the fall of 2020, 73 percent stated that they identify with their nationality (Eurobarometer 2021: 76), and 69 percent indicated they identify with their local area or region (Eurobarometer 2021: 74). There is, of course, no contradiction in possessing multiple identities. We may identify as Europeans, Irish, Dubliners; residents of a specific neighborhood like Ballymun; English and/or Irish speakers; Catholic, Protestant, Jewish, Muslim, or atheist; supporters of a specific sports team; graduates of a given university, or members of a given professional group all at once. Which identities are stronger may depend on circumstances, but the Eurobarometer survey confirms the instinctive impression most Europeans have that nationality remains important. If asked, most Europeans will say they are Armenian, Finnish, French, Irish, or Italian before they will say they are European. Identity may also depend on where we are. It is said that Alsatians[24] identify with a specific neighborhood when they are in their village or city, with their village when they are elsewhere in the same *département* (French administrative division), with their *département* when they are elsewhere in Alsace, with Alsace when they are elsewhere in France, and with France when they are elsewhere in Europe. When they are outside of Europe, they may identify as either French or European, or both.

European countries are vastly different in size and location. Russia spans eleven time zones spread over 17 million square kilometers with a population of approximately 145 million. By way of comparison, the United States has a population of approximately 337 million spread over approximately 9.8 million square kilometers, and, unlike that of Russia, the U.S. population is increasing. Contrast this with the smallest European countries. Liechtenstein, Monaco, and San Marino all have fewer than forty thousand inhabitants each, and Andorra is home to a little fewer than eighty thousand people. Approximately 20 percent of Russia's territory lies north of the Arctic Circle, whereas the northernmost tips of Cyprus and Malta are located at around thirty-six degrees north. Compare this to the United States, where only a part of Alaska lies north of the Arctic Circle—its capital, Juneau, lies to the south of the European capitals of Stockholm, Helsinki, Tallinn, Reykjavík, and

Oslo—and where both Florida and Hawaii are well south of the southern-most European countries.

Historically, universities have played an important role in developing national identities. Whereas the earliest universities were global institutions (insofar as the term made sense at the time) linked to the Catholic Church, the Reformation brought universities whose scope was national. The consciousness of state and nationality was not well developed in the decades following the Reformation, but the link to the political power was strong. Not least in the Protestant parts of what is now Germany, universities were founded by local rulers who carried titles like dukes or *Kurfürsten* and whose authority extended over territories of quite different size and resource base.

As of the nineteenth century, universities were an important part of nation building in smaller countries that felt the need to develop a cultural identity distinct from that of their former colonial powers. Norwegians do not tend to think of Denmark as a former colonial power, but there is consciousness of Norway having had a culturally distinct identity also during the almost five centuries commonly referred to as "the Union" (1319–1814) and that nationalist Norwegian historians of an earlier age referred to as the "five centuries long night." The University of Oslo, established in 1811, played an important role in developing Norwegian identity, at a time when Norway went from being a suzerain of Denmark to coming under Swedish rule, in 1814, and developed a constitution of its own , adopted on May 17, 1814. Academics also contributed to making national romanticism one of the predominant intellectual currents in many parts of Europe. A century and a half later, the University of Malta, whose roots go back to the late sixteenth century, played a similar role leading up to and after independence from the United Kingdom in 1964. Universities that played a role in developing national identity, of course, also played other roles. As with other universities, they contributed to economic development as well as to the need for an "enlightened public." Today, they are important in developing a culture of democracy.

The Council of Europe: A Pan-European Voice for Democracy, Human Rights, and the Rule of Law

The Council of Europe is a product of conflict, reconciliation, and reconstruction. It is devoted to democracy, human rights, and the rule of law. The organization was established in May 1949, some three and a half years after the United Nations (UN) and a month after NATO. It preceded the European Coal and Steel Community, which eventually developed into the EU, by two years and was the first purely European intergovernmental organization set up in the aftermath of World War II. The Council of Europe was established in the logic of "never again," but, unlike NATO, its purpose was not military defense and, unlike the Coal and Steel Community, its purpose was not economic cooperation. Even today, neither is included in the Council's competences.

The Council of Europe is primarily an organization for legal cooperation, perhaps with the European Convention and Court on Human Rights as its main achievement. Any resident of Europe can bring a suit against the government of his or her country of residence before the European Court of Human Rights, broadly subject to two conditions: that the matter be covered by the European Convention on Human Rights and that the possibilities of appeal within the national legal system have been exhausted.[25] While member states are free to decide whether to adhere to most of the Council of Europe's more than two hundred conventions, no country can be a Council member without ratifying the Human Rights Convention, nor is this Convention open to accession by nonmembers. When Russia was excluded from the Council of Europe in March 2022 in response to its invasion of Ukraine, one of the consequences was that, after a brief transition period, residents of Russia were no longer protected by the European Convention on Human Rights.[26]

Chapter 3 presents the Council of Europe, with a focus on the Council's education program. From the outset, education and culture were seen as important factors in building a post–World War II Europe built on democracy, human rights, and the rule of law as well as on cooperation rather than conflict. The Council of Europe's founders believed that people(s) who knew each other's history and culture would be less likely to go to war than those who knew little about each other. In 1954, the Council's activities in education and culture were given a legal basis through the European Cultural Convention (Council of Europe 1954) Today, fifty states have acceded to the Cultural Convention, of which forty-six are members of the Council. Especially after the fall of the Berlin Wall, so throughout the 1990s, new member states typically ratified the Cultural Convention before they became Council members.

The Council's education program furthers the role of education in developing and maintaining democracy and human rights. One notable achievement is the development of a Reference Framework of Competences for Democratic Culture (RFCDC; Council of Europe 2018a, 2018b, 2018c). The RFCDC builds on the conviction that while fair elections, good laws, and solid institutions are important to democracy, they cannot function democratically unless they build on what is variously referred to as democratic culture or a culture of democracy. These terms designate a set of attitudes and behaviors that recognize that conflicts are best settled through dialogue rather than violence, that diversity strengthens rather than weakens societies, and that, as citizens, we should be willing and able to look at issues from various points of view.

The RFCDC aims to describe the main competences[27] that European education systems, schools, and universities should develop in students in order to further democracy. The twenty competences in the model are divided into four categories: values, attitudes, skills, and knowledge and critical understanding. For each competence, a set of descriptors has been developed and categorized as basic, intermediate, or advanced. The RFCDC also improves on the traditional understanding of competences, expressed as learning outcomes. These are generally seen as a description of what a student knows, understands, and is able to do on completion of a study program. From the Council of Europe's view, however, this is insufficient. There are things we may be *able* to do but should not, for ethical and other reasons. For example, we may have the technical ability to conduct research experiments that for ethical reasons we should refrain from conducting, or we may have the technical ability to manipulate public opinion in a local community on a key issue, which, for equally clear ethical reasons, we should refrain from doing. The *will* to do—which includes the will to abstain from doing something that is ethically or morally wrong—is, therefore, an essential fourth element of the understanding of competences and learning outcomes.

The RFCDC can be used as it stands, or it can be adapted to the context of each education system. There is a set of guides to implementation for different purposes such as curriculum development or assessment or for specific strands or levels of education, including a guidance document for higher education. The RFCDC is highly relevant to both the Global Cooperation for the Democratic Mission of Higher Education, which is described in Chapter 5, and the new European Platform on the Local Democratic Mission of Higher Education, which is the subject of Chapter 6.

The Multiple Purposes of and Public Responsibility for Higher Education

Traditionally, higher education in Europe has been public, and this is one of the features that distinguishes the situation in Europe from that in the United States. Europe also has a long-standing tradition of universities that are formally private but that are very similar to public universities. This is the case notably with the traditional Catholic universities.

Europe also has a long-standing tradition of public financing of higher education. Financing has traditionally been provided primarily as block grants to institutions, often specified according to broad purposes such as staff, operational funding, or infrastructure. Increasingly, public funding comes with more detailed specifications and/or is tied to specific projects. Private funding is, of course, not new to higher education in Europe, and areas such as medical and pharmaceutical research have had a high proportion of non-public funding for a long time. Nevertheless, the share of public funding is, in the best of cases, stable but decreasing in many countries (European Education and Culture Executive Agency, Eurydice 2018: 37–38), and private funding is increasing and is often project specific (Chevaillier and Eicher 2021: 2). Large parts of the higher education community are, therefore, concerned that the funding model may increasingly favor areas that are economically important, while longer-term research as well as academic disciplines that are culturally important or that further the broader societal and democratic role of higher education but that may not provide sufficient economic return on investment could suffer. Public responsibility for higher education (Weber and Bergan 2005) is an important part of European higher education policy (Bologna Process 2001, 2003) and is considered one of the fundamental values of higher education (Bologna Process 2018). A statement on the public responsibility for higher education was adopted by the 2024 Ministerial Conference of the EHEA (Bologna Process 2024a). This, again, is a point at which the situation in Europe differs from that in the United States, perhaps with the United Kingdom as a partial exception.

Another traditional feature of higher education in Europe is a governance model that is essentially internal to the university. Academic senates are made up of representatives elected by the various groups that form the academic community. Tenured faculty have more representatives on the governance bodies than students, who have more than technical and administrative staff. This model balances representation and competence in the key missions of the university. All groups are represented, but those with the highest competence in research and teaching are better represented. In this model, rectors[28] and deans are elected from within the institution by the governing body or by an electoral college in which the various groups of the academic community are represented proportionally. In recent years, however, an alternative model has emerged, in which there is considerable external representation on university governing bodies and/or in which rectors and, in some cases, deans are hired rather than elected and as often as not come from outside the institution. It may be too early to say to what extent the choice of governance model influences the local democratic mission of a university, but the case for greater interaction with the local community is important to make.

Chapter 4 explores the concept of public responsibility for and of higher education as seen from a European perspective. The starting point is the statement by the European ministers responsible for higher education at two successive conferences to the effect that higher education is a public good and a public responsibility (Bologna Process 2001: 1, 2003: 1). The Council of

Europe took this as an indication that ministers were not stating the obvious but rather expressing concern that what had been an important feature of European higher education could no longer be taken for granted. Our view was that to defend the public responsibility for higher education, we need to have a clearer view of what this responsibility actually means. The Council's work included developing a more nuanced view of different aspects of public responsibility as well as of the multiple missions of higher education (Weber and Bergan 2005; Council of Europe 2007), as I explore in Chapter 4. In this view, public authorities have exclusive responsibility for the framework within which higher education and research are conducted, the leading responsibility for ensuring both effective equal opportunities to higher education for all citizens and that basic research remain a public good; and substantial responsibility for financing higher education and research, the provision of higher education and research, and for stimulating and facilitating financing and provision by other sources within the framework developed by public authorities. The main missions of higher education are seen as preparation for the labor market, preparation for life as active citizens in democratic societies, personal development, and the development and maintenance of a broad and advanced knowledge base. Chapter 4 describes the considerations around this work as well as its influence on the development of the EHEA. As already noted, the first mention of the multiple purposes of higher education came two years later (Bologna Process 2007). The chapter also considers the implications of the European view of the public responsibility for education for the democratic and local democratic mission of higher education.

The Development of a Global Cooperation for the Democratic Mission of Higher Education

What is today the Global Cooperation for the Democratic Mission of Higher Education started more modestly in 1999 as a transatlantic project spearheaded by colleagues at Penn and comprising several U.S. higher education organizations and almost fifty European countries through the Council of Europe.[29] From 2006, the cooperation focused on a series of large-scale conferences, known as Global Fora, each of which gave rise to a book in the Council of Europe Higher Education Series. The cooperation became truly global in 2018–2019, when both the Organization of American States (OAS) and the International Association of Universities (IAU) joined.

Chapter 5 describes the evolution and the current state of the global cooperation. While today, this cooperation enjoys the full support of the Council of Europe's Education Committee, it was not uncontested in 1999 or even 2006. Some committee members felt that making the democratic mission of higher education one of the Council of Europe's main projects would politicize higher education and remove the Council's program from what should be the main concerns of the higher education community: structural reforms and the quality of education. These objections were overcome partly through the success of the cooperation and partly also by developments within the Council of Europe, where the representatives of member states in the Committee of Ministers underlined that projects and programs would be judged according to the extent to which they contributed to the Council of Europe's overarching goals of furthering democracy, human rights, and the rule of law.

Toward a European Platform for the Local Democratic Mission of Higher Education

The successive Global Fora on the Democratic Mission of Higher Education addressed various aspects of this mission, always from a broad thematic perspective. The contributions to the Global Fora and the publications presented views from both the United States and Europe, and increasingly also from other parts of the world. However, the role of universities in their local communities was not among the primary topics covered.

Nevertheless, we were conscious of the fact that democracy needs to be practiced locally. This conviction was strengthened by our U.S. partners—notably Penn's Netter Center for Community Partnerships[30] and the AITF—as well as by some of the European participants and some others, in particular those from South Africa. From the very beginning, Penn was the main U.S. partner in the cooperation through the Netter Center and its founding director Dr. Ira Harkavy, who also chairs the International Consortium. Penn presented the particularity of being a recognized elite research university located in West Philadelphia, in what may safely be described as an underprivileged neighborhood. In the 1980s, this contradiction led the university leadership to decide that Penn could no longer remain aloof from its local community. Among other things, Penn's growing engagement with its local community led to the establishment of the Netter Center in 1992. One important feature of Penn's community engagement is enabling students to earn credits toward their degree by enrolling in courses with a community engagement component.

Harkavy is also the founding chair of the AITF,[31] whose director David Maurrasse is a frequent contributor to the Global Fora. The AITF's almost one thousand members, to a large part, come from the world of higher education, and there is also interest in the AITF in other parts of the world, in particular in South Africa. After discussions with Harkavy and Maurrasse, we concluded that Europe also needed to work on the local mission of higher education. There were, of course, extensive contacts between universities and their local communities in Europe, but, to a large extent, these focused on the economic role of universities rather than on their broader societal and democratic mission. The discussions also took place on the background of the 2014 Global Forum, which was held at Queen's University Belfast (Queen's) and innovated in that it included a preconference day with visits to community centers working with Queen's, and the conference program itself included a powerful session presented by leaders from one of the community centers (McDonald et al. 2015).

The next step was a series of three small-scale invitational seminars between 2017 and 2019. To each, we invited some twenty higher education leaders from different parts of Europe, and the Council made sure that Harkavy and Maurrasse had important roles in the program. These three seminars led both the organizers and most participants to conclude that if the local mission of higher education were to become a priority in Europe, a cooperation structure was required. The Council of Europe established a working group— this is how intergovernmental organizations tend to function—and out of this group came a proposal that a European platform[32] be established.

One important suggestion was that a focus on the local mission of higher education would be insufficient—the focus needed to be specifically on the local *democratic* mission. This would distinguish the platform from other initiatives, and it would link it directly to the broader cooperation for the democratic mission of higher education, of which the platform will be a part. At the time of writing, the platform is still in its inception phase, and it has been slowed down by changes in the Council of Europe. There is, however, interest in representative organizations like the IAU,[33] the EUA,[34] and EURASHE—the European Association of Institutions in Higher Education,[35] which organizes professionally oriented institutions—as well as in the Council's Education Committee. While it may seem paradoxical that a European platform would be needed to further the local democratic mission of higher education, the paradox is only superficial. The platform will be a forum for exchange of experience and mutual learning as well as advocacy, all of which are required both to convince public authorities of the importance of the local democratic mission of higher education and to convince the higher education community itself and its leaders. The development of the platform is described in Chapter 6.

European Universities Working with Their Local Communities

European universities work with their local communities in numerous ways and in many different contexts. Chapter 7 explores this complex reality without any pretense of providing a complete overview. In selecting the examples presented in this chapter, I have been guided not only by a concern for thematic and geographic diversity but also by the understanding of the local mission that underlies the Council of Europe platform described in the previous chapter (i.e., that universities work not only *in* but *with* their local communities). The examples are organized thematically and analytically rather than geographically.

Economic cooperation between a university and its local community is important even if it is not the main focus of the book. The example chosen is that of a university with long and proud academic traditions—the Jagiellonian University of Kraków in the southeast of Poland—which was able to develop this role only after the political changes around 1990 that made democracy possible.

The broader societal mission of higher education is illustrated by examples from Iceland, the Czech Republic, and San Marino. Together, they illustrate how the university can serve its local community through societal outreach, student engagement, and a comprehensive organization of university-community cooperation. All three countries illustrate various ways in which universities can improve opportunities for local people by putting academic knowledge and understanding at the service of the community.

Some universities are spread out over different campuses, so that a single institution serves several local communities. The University of the Aegean is an unusual example in that it is located in six different islands in a strategically important but peripheral part of Greece in which higher education helps provide its communities with the same opportunities other parts of the country enjoy. Among other things, the university works to assist refugees arriving across the sea from Turkey, often in makeshift vessels, and to make the local population more accepting of them.

An engaged university embeds public engagement into its work. Dublin City University (DCU) is a relatively new university located in a disadvantaged part of northern Dublin, and it demonstrates several ways in which universities help improve access to education for disadvantaged populations, alleviate social divisions, and equip the local population with competences that help them have a greater say in local affairs. So does Queen's, with the added dimension that it makes a determined effort to serve both major communities in Northern Ireland's conflictual society: Catholics and Protestants.

Europe has many ethnic, linguistic, or religious minorities, some of which are indigenous and some of relatively recent origin. Providing minorities with fair access to higher education is part of the democratic mission of higher education, and this can mean providing study programs in minority languages. A small higher education institution in the far north of Norway—Samisk høgskole/Sámi allaskuvla—where teaching and research is entirely in Sámi illustrates the importance of this mission in the case of a small and historically marginalized minority. The Swedish-speaking minority in Finland has historically been elite rather than marginalized, but its numbers are falling relatively rapidly, mostly through assimilation. Åbo Akademi University, with campuses in two parts of Finland where the Swedish-speaking minority is strong, illustrates the importance of higher education provision in a minority language even when this minority is well connected to a broader language community in its neighboring country.

Malta is a de facto bilingual or even plurilingual country with a strong English language heritage in addition to Maltese. Even if most of its teaching is in English, the University of Malta plays a key role in developing Maltese language and culture as well as in the broader development of a small island society with a strong international orientation. It also runs outreach activities aimed at disadvantaged populations, including immigrants with low education levels. Taken together, the examples included in Chapter 7 describe at least a cross-section of the very diverse ways in which higher education institutions seek to carry out their local democratic mission in Europe.

European and Local: The European Qualifications Passport for Refugees

In the summer of 2015, much of Europe saw a rapid increase in the number of people seeking refuge from war and persecution. The immediate backdrop was the war in Syria and, more broadly, the situation in the Middle East. Reactions in Europe were highly diverse both at a government level and among individual citizens, ranging from German chancellor Merkel's assurance that "we'll manage this" (*wir schaffen das*) and individuals and local authorities organizing to receive refugees to the rejection by the Hungarian premier Viktor Orbán and citizens in many parts of Europe.

The world of higher education was to a large extent prepared to receive and help refugees. The EUA set up a Refugees Welcome Map[36] that brought together initiatives by individual institutions to help refugees. The website helped individual refugees looking for appropriate assistance, and it also served as inspiration for universities who could see what others were doing and devise measures adapted to their own circumstances.

Far from all refugees have higher education qualifications, but many do. However, those who have to flee their homes in a hurry and just have time to take the most necessary things may not think of taking their education diplomas. Once they have fled, they are unlikely to get much help from home in retrieving the documents. Public officials in their home countries are often reluctant to help those who have fled and whom officials may, therefore, consider traitors to their countries. Even if officials were willing to help, establishing contacts may be difficult, with ordinary mail interrupted and electronic mail uncertain and possibly surveilled. If, as in Syria, the refugees' country suffered war or civil war, the files from which the refugees' diplomas could be retrieved may well have been destroyed. On my first visit to Kosovo, just after the cessation of hostilities in July 1999, I saw countless "student books"—the document that at the time proved and registered student status and achievements in what was left of Yugoslavia—spread out across the floor in a large room at the University of Prishtina. The books belonged to students at the former Serbian university in what had just become an independent Albanian-speaking country, and nobody at the new Kosovar University of Prishtina thought it was worth saving and keeping them.

Many refugees, therefore, arrived with qualifications they could not document. Refugees' lives are difficult in the best of circumstances. Without documents to prove their qualifications, however, the refugees would easily be condemned to passivity, they would lose hope, and they would ultimately lose the qualifications they once had because a skill or a qualification that is not used, kept up to date, and developed will no longer exist. It was, therefore, important to find ways to assess refugees' qualifications even when they could not be documented.

Based on the Lisbon Recognition Convention, which was developed by the Council of Europe and UNESCO and provides the legal framework for the recognition of qualifications in Europe, the Council of Europe and partners developed the European Qualifications Passport for Refugees (EQPR), which was launched with four countries and the UN High Commissioner for Refugees (UNHCR) in 2017 and now encompasses more than twenty countries. The EQPR has a double purpose: to develop a method for assessing refugees' qualifications even in the absence of adequate documentation and to describe the assessment in a format that can be used if and when the refugees relocate to a new country. Repeating the assessment would be a waste of public resources as well as of refugees' time and could, in the worst of cases, mean that refugees miss opportunities to work or enroll in further studies while waiting for their qualifications to be assessed yet again.

Chapter 8 describes the EQPR as well as the process through which it was developed. It recounts some of the individual success stories and also points to challenges that have to be met to make the EQPR an even more broadly accepted instrument to help refugees. The chapter underlines the importance of universities engaging in cooperation with their local communities. More than eighty students have been admitted to higher education in part because universities were directly involved in the assessment. The EQPR helps refugees become integrated in their host societies by enabling them to use the qualifications they have but may not be able to document.

The ultimate goal is twofold. First, the aim is to help EQPR holders do what the holder of the first EQPR ever issued, Anwar al-Hasani, has achieved. A trained physical therapist, she was first admitted to further studies and now works in an organization whose work is closely related to her professional qualifications.[37] Second, the aim is to make assessing refugees' qualifications for the EQPR a normal part of what credentials evaluators do. In this way, what could be a vicious circle can be turned into a virtuous circle where refugees' worth and potential are recognized, where they contribute their knowledge and skills to their new societies. The difference between the vicious and virtuous circles is important also to the refugees' home countries. Refugees who can use their competences in their new homes will develop them further. Rather than returning demotivated with diminished competence, they will come back, if and when conditions allow, with improved competences and motivation that will be sorely needed in reconstructing their home countries. Chapter 8 also examines challenges that must still be met for the EQPR to become a fully integrated part of credentials evaluation in Europe and to be better accepted by both public and private employers.

Looking Ahead

Chapter 9 summarizes the highly diverse European experience with, and approach to, the local democratic mission of higher education and suggests some ways in which the Council of Europe, the Global Cooperation for the Democratic Mission of Higher Education, individual universities as well as the European and international organizations representing them, students and faculty, and not least local authorities and communities can cooperate to fulfill the four major purposes of higher education, as they were presented at the outset of this introductory chapter.

1

Europe

The Political and Educational Context

Faces of Europe

A Norwegian saying claims that a well-loved child has many names. Judging by this standard, Europeans are not particularly fond of their continent. All European languages for which I have been able to verify use a variety of Europe/Europa/Evropa/Europi as the name for the continent to which they are indigenous. Latvian and Turkish deviate somewhat but not so much that you would need a dictionary: Eiropā and Avrupa.

If, however, rather than ask what Europe is called, we ask what it actually means, the responses will be more varied, both in terms of the area it encompasses and the reactions it elicits. The narrower concept is that of the EU. It has stronger competences than any other international or supranational institution, even if its twenty-seven member countries have preserved their national identity and considerable decision-making powers. As its name implies, the European Commission, which is the executive branch of the EU, tends to use "Europe" to denote what is otherwise called "the EU" or even "the EU 27." Many otherwise well-informed people also do. I remember a meeting in one of the Commission buildings in Brussels with representatives of both EU members and other European countries for a project the Council of Europe ran jointly with UNESCO and the European Commission when the Italian representative disagreed with something the representative of Armenia had said and ended by saying, "But you are not in Europe."

Since I was next in line to speak, I took the opportunity to say a few words about the difference between the EU and Europe.

The EU should not be equated with Europe, but it has an enormous—and in my view mostly positive—impact on the whole continent. All of Europe would look very different today had we not had the EU. In higher education, we would have had much less academic exchange both within the EU and between the EU and other parts of the world, we would not have a system for credit transfer—the European Credit Transfer and Accumulation System (ECTS)[1]—that is used well outside of the EU, and we would not have a European strategy for universities.[2] Joining the EU was an important goal for most of the countries of Central and Eastern Europe after the political changes in the early 1990s that both led to and followed from the collapse of the Soviet Union. Joining the EU is now a priority for Ukraine and Moldova, as it is for Albania and the countries of former Yugoslavia that are not yet members. The regional newspaper in Alsace, which is unsurprisingly strongly pro-EU, suggests the EU could theoretically grow to include thirty-six countries but also indicates such an expansion would be very challenging.[3] However, in view of the resistance of many EU members to the long-standing previous Turkish goal of joining the EU, as well as the development of more authoritarian policies under the Erdoğan government, Turkey no longer aims to accede to the EU.

The attraction of the EU is therefore obvious, but it is accompanied by skepticism. My home country, Norway, is an exception to the general trend toward joining the EU. In two bitterly fought referendums in 1972 and 1994, Norwegian voters decided to remain outside of the EU. In each referendum, the margin was the same—roughly 53 percent against joining and 47 percent in favor—but the composition of the vote was quite different. The 1972 referendum was particularly bitter, in some cases splitting families and destroying marriages. I was squarely in the "yes" camp in both referendums, even if too young to vote in the first, and my family was indeed divided even if it remained unbroken. The United Kingdom joined the EU in 1972 but left it again in 2020 after a protracted and bitter process known as Brexit. As a whole, the U.K. voted to leave but in Scotland and Northern Ireland, as well as in the greater London area, a majority of voters wished to remain.[4] In the current EU member states, overall attitudes to the EU are more favorable than negative, but even if a clear majority of those polled are positive, a substantial minority opinion is not (Pew Research Center 2020). There is also a tendency among political decision-makers to take credit for what goes well and blame problems on the EU. In this case, they often do not blame "Europe" but rather use the other shorthand for the EU: Bruxelles. It sounds more distant and bureaucratic, much to the chagrin of the people who actually live there.

There is also a broader Europe. The French president Charles de Gaulle famously spoke of a "Europe from the Atlantic to the Urals,"[5] but the exact borders of Europe are not easy to identify. Setting its western borders on the Atlantic shore of the continent would leave out not only the United Kingdom and Ireland (something one could suspect de Gaulle of wanting to do) but also Iceland and the Faeroes. Greenland, like the Faeroes, belongs to Denmark politically but is not a member of the EU. It is closer to the North American continent and developing an identity of its own. If and when Greenland becomes independent, will it be European, North American, or rather "Arctic"?

The eastern borders of Europe are also not easy to identify. The Urals run through Russia and are certainly not a cultural border. Armenia and Georgia, while east of the Urals, have a clear European identity. The Bosporus is another geographic landmark that is often seen as the border between Europe and Asia, to the point where it is said you can cross between the two continents by a Bosporus ferry, and we readily refer to the "European" and "Asian" parts of İstanbul. But the Bosporus runs straight through Turkey, which is one of the Council of Europe's founding members. Cyprus—well to the southeast of the Bosporus—is not only a Council of Europe but also an EU member. Since the Turkish invasion in July 1974, Cyprus is also de facto a divided country.

The northern and southern borders are easier to identify. To the north of Europe, there is little but sea and ice on the way to the North Pole, and to the south there is Africa and the Mediterranean even if the European country of Malta is located further south than the northern tip of Tunisia, and Spain maintains two enclaves—Ceuta and Melilla—on the Mediterranean coast of Africa, to the considerable irritation of Morocco. Some European countries still have colonies in other parts of the world, but the colonies, even when disguised under names indicating a more benign affiliation with the metropolitan power,[6] are not considered as belonging to Europe.

Politically and institutionally, this broader Europe is incarnated by the Council of Europe, which was established in 1949 to promote democracy, human rights, and the rule of law. Of course, 1949 was both the immediate aftermath of World War II and the outset of the division of Europe into a Western and an Eastern bloc.[7] The Council of Europe was founded by and with ten members and now has forty-six.[8] About half of its members joined the organization after the political changes in 1989–1990 often referred to as "the fall of the (Berlin) Wall." Even Finland, which is a long-standing democracy but which maintained a studied East-West neutrality, joined only in 1989. Almost every European country that could legitimately aspire to Council of Europe membership has now achieved it, with three important exceptions. Belarus was on its way to membership in the late 1990s, but the repressive policies of the regime of Alyeksandar Lukashenka,[9] elected president for the first time in July 1994, put the process on hold. It is unlikely to resume as long as the current regime is in power. Russia became a Council of Europe member in 1996 but was excluded in March 2022 in response to its war of aggression on Ukraine. We have an opportunity to return to this issue later in the chapter. There are also some territories whose status is disputed. The main example is Kosovo, which is recognized as an independent country by some one hundred governments[10] but whose status remains contested by Serbia and some other European countries. Kosovo membership in the Council of Europe will most likely depend on progress in the status negotiations, and that progress is exceedingly slow.

So, there is a smaller (EU) and larger (Council of Europe) concept of Europe. Democracy is essential to both concepts, even if the democratic ideal is all too often violated. The EU is by far the more powerful of the two, with large budgets and strong supranational powers in many areas, including economic policy and the regulation of its internal market. The Council of Europe is much less powerful but nevertheless has important achievements in areas related to democracy, human rights, and the rule of law, and several of these achievements are to be found in education. Whereas the Council of Europe has been labeled "the conscience of Europe" (Coleman 1999), the EU is in many ways the powerhouse of Europe. The terminology of both institutions can be confusing, which is why Appendix 1 provides a brief glossary of the main organizations and frameworks.

I happily acknowledge the important achievements of the EU, but this book refers to Europe in the true sense of the word, and I refer to the EU as such. But even this is not entirely straightforward. The Council of Europe now has forty-six members but fifty states are parties to the European Cultural Convention,[11] which was adopted in December 1954 and is the legal framework for the Council of Europe's activities in education and culture. The four Cultural Convention states that are not Council of Europe members are Belarus, the Holy See, Kazakhstan, and Russia. Because of the war on Ukraine, Belarus and Russia are currently (August 2024) not invited to participate in meetings and activities under this convention. The Cultural Convention underlines that education and culture are important bridge builders and, historically, aspiring Council members first ratified the Cultural Convention. That is why Belarus is a Cultural Convention state but not a Council member, all the more so as there is no exclusion mechanism from the Cultural Convention.

Europe represents a unique mix of what we have in common as Europeans and what makes each of our countries and cultures specific, of what makes us European and what makes us Armenian, Finnish, Greek, Romanian, or Spanish. Europe is also a mix of international and local. In many areas, ranging from security policy through trade and industry and cultural performance to higher education, Europe has ambitions on the world stage. At the same time, the everyday reality of most Europeans, both those who travel widely and those who rarely leave their community, is above all local. The mix of what is international and what is local complements the mix of what Europeans have in common and what is unique to each country and community. This unique mixture influences how we work together as a European higher education community as well as how higher education works in and with its local community.

Few areas are as international as higher education and research. This was already true when the first universities were established in Europe in the mid- to late Middle Ages. Both students and teachers at the early universities like Bologna and Paris came from many parts of at least western and central Europe. A major intellectual like the Dominican St. Albertus Magnus, who was born in Bayern (Bavaria), probably around or just before 1200, was educated mainly in Padova but also in Bologna, both in Italy. He taught in Köln (Cologne), Freiburg, and Strasbourg—all at the time within the German cultural area even if Germany did not yet exist as a political construct—and then in Paris. His best-known student in Paris was Italian: St. Thomas Aquinas. At all European universities, Latin was the language of learning and teaching as well as of academic publications. Latin was a language of great prestige but by then had few, if any, native speakers. The situation students and staff faced then was perhaps not unlike the one that those who are not native English speakers face today: learning, teaching, reading, and writing in a language that is not their first language. However, without a solid knowledge of that language many opportunities will remain closed. Some would see the existence of a single academic language as an advantage. I would personally point to the lack of linguistic diversity as a drawback, and not because I am rarely able to work in my native language.

Even if they were international, the early universities were also rooted locally. The term "anchor institutions" had not yet been invented, but the University of Bologna has been anchored in the same community since 1088. Travel was, of course, infinitely more cumbersome in those days, but border formalities were easier. It is precisely this blend of the local and the international that this book sets out to explore, describe, and analyze.

The Europe of Higher Education

European contacts and cooperation have been a reality for as long as it is meaningful to talk about higher education. In the twentieth century, many Europeans studied in countries other than their own for longer and shorter periods, and many of them took their entire degree in a foreign country. This led to a need to recognize their qualifications. Later, governments encouraged more students to take at least a part of their degrees in foreign countries. Some countries had their own programs, perhaps with the U.S. Fulbright program—from which many Europeans benefited—as the most emblematic. In the late 1980s, the European Commission, acting on behalf of EU member states, launched its ERASMUS program preceding the dramatic political changes in Central and Eastern Europe by only two or three years. In turn, these changes as well as the need felt in many countries to reform their higher education systems led to the Bologna Process, which started with twenty-nine countries in 1999, led to the launch of the EHEA in 2010, and now provides the framework for a cooperation between forty-nine countries[12] with diverse traditions and histories of a kind that cannot quite be found in any other part of the world. I look at each of these developments in turn and close this chapter with a consideration of how democratic values underpin the EHEA but also present serious dilemmas as to which countries should be included and how possible exclusions affect the academic community in the countries concerned.

Recognition of Qualifications

The fact that Europeans needed to be able to use the qualifications they had earned abroad when they returned home led to the first Council of Europe conventions on education, more specifically on the recognition of qualifications. The first was adopted in 1953, only four years after the Council of Europe had come into existence, and it was followed a good year later by the European Cultural Convention. It is significant that less than ten years had passed since the end of World War II. Cooperation in education and culture, with a view to developing greater understanding among the peoples of Europe, was very much part of the efforts to reconstruct Europe and try to avoid another major war.

These conventions took a piecemeal approach to recognition and addressed specific issues. They did not provide an overall coherent approach, and they reflected their time and age. In the early post–World War II years, learning the language of the host country was seen as the most obvious reason to study abroad. More importantly, however, all these conventions refer to "equivalence" rather than "recognition." This is far more than a semantic difference. If credentials evaluators look for "equivalence," they will require a high degree of similarity between a foreign qualification and the corresponding qualification in their own system. There is plenty of anecdotal evidence that this could be a very detailed examination. When I was a student representative in the Academic Senate of the University of Oslo in the early 1980s, older colleagues told me that a few years earlier, a very well renowned professor of English literature had made sure no application for "equivalence" was approved unless the applicant could demonstrate that his or her curriculum included at least one literary work from the sixteenth century or earlier.

In the 1990s, there was still little reference to learning outcomes in European higher education, but there was a feeling that both the old conventions and the methods used in implementing them required a serious update. Reviewing the existing recognition conventions was one of my major early tasks in the Council of Europe. However, simply updating the existing texts would not be the best option: there were too many of them, updating an existing convention is technically difficult, and my colleagues and I believed it would be better to start from scratch. Add to this that many European countries were also parties to two UNESCO conventions. These were more modern in terminology in that they refer to "recognition" rather than "equivalence." They were nevertheless quite general in their wording, without strong obligations on and commitments by the states party.

For all of these reasons, the Council of Europe suggested, and UNESCO accepted, that the two organizations develop a new recognition convention for all of Europe—or rather, for the UNESCO Europe region, which, in addition to Europe proper, also includes the United States, Canada, and Israel. Australia, New Zealand, Kazakhstan, Kyrgyzstan, and Tajikistan were also parties to the UNESCO European convention—as what in UNESCO parlance is called "out of region" states—and were, therefore, invited to participate in the development of the new convention.

I had the honor of being the Council of Europe official working on the convention, with Stamenka Uvalić-Trumbić[13] as my UNESCO counterpart. The choice was logical, since we were the two individuals responsible for recognition issues in the two organizations. We conducted a feasibility study in 1994, after which we launched work on the convention proper with the help of an expert group chaired by Kees Kouwenaar of NUFFIC,[14] the Dutch national information center on the recognition of qualifications.

Developing a legal text in four languages—English, French, Russian, and Spanish—was something of a challenge, with Russian as a particular challenge since none of us was truly fluent in the language even if both Uvalić-Trumbić and I had a reasonable understanding of it. Nevertheless, work progressed fast as far as international legal treaties go. In the fall of 1996, we organized a conference of all potential parties to the convention in Den Haag, thanks to Kouwenaar, and, in the spring of 1997, we went to Lisboa for the diplomatic conference that we hoped would adopt the convention. The conference did, so that on April 11, 1997, the Council of Europe/UNESCO Lisbon Recognition Convention[15] came into being.

We were surprised at how rapidly the convention gained traction. It took less than two years to come into effect, with the fifth ratification on February 1, 1999. In most countries, ratification of an international treaty requires a parliamentary procedure, so the convention competed with all other issues that national assemblies need to deal with. As of August 2024, the Lisbon Recognition Convention had been ratified by fifty-six states, while one country—the United States—had signed but not ratified.[16] The Lisbon Recognition Convention is also the only international legal treaty underpinning the EHEA.

Academic Mobility and Exchange

Academic mobility had been an important feature of higher education in Europe since the medieval universities. Some students went abroad on their own account, but many were supported by exchange programs like the Fulbright program. Many students had also had an exchange experience in high school thanks to AFS (originally American Field Service) or similar organizations. My own AFS exchange was to Alton, Illinois, and it marked the start of what developed into an international career, an international family, a very international set of friends, and a lifelong passion for languages.

Nevertheless, there was a desire in many European countries to increase and also to diversify academic mobility and exchange. That is the background for the launch of what I believe is the most successful academic mobility program ever: the ERASMUS program,[17] which the European Commission launched in 1987. So far, more than nine million students have studied for at least one semester abroad with the ERASMUS program. Even if the EHEA still struggles to achieve the goal of 20 percent mobility decided by ministers in 2009 (Bologna Process 2009: para. 18)[18] and originally set for 2020, it would be difficult to exaggerate the impact of the ERASMUS program, whether in terms of numbers, its cultural impact, or the way it has changed the student experience or higher education in Europe more broadly.

The ERASMUS program is financed by the EU to the tune of some 26 billion euros for the seven-year period 2021–2027[19] and run by the European Commission with National Agencies (in EU member states as well as associate countries)[20] or National ERASMUS+ offices (in other participating countries).[21] The general objective of the program is "to support, through lifelong learning, the educational, professional and personal development of people in education, training, youth and sport, in Europe and beyond, thereby contributing to sustainable growth, quality jobs and social cohesion, to driving innovation, and to strengthening European identity and active citizenship."[22]

The ERASMUS budget is impressive, and its program objectives and administrative arrangements well developed. Two of the particularities that give the program its flavor, however, are the strong student involvement as well as the commitment of universities. The ERASMUS Student Network

(ESN)[23] came to be only a couple of years after the program was established, and it is now a legally registered NGO with 513 sections in forty-four countries as well as an international board and secretariat. The ESN illustrates that students are often the best advocates for a program among other students. Official and legally binding information is best obtained through the commission's website for the program, but the ESN blog,[24] which claims to speak with the voice of the ERASMUS generation, provides very practical tips for exchange students and also recounts the experience of individuals. Désirée Majoor, who was the first president of ESN, underlines the importance of the individual student experience and not least of languages.[25] Language is important because many European universities and students are torn between teaching and studying in English and helping international students and staff develop a working knowledge of the local language.[26]

Two other exchange programs deserve special mention. In 1988–1989, the Nordic Council of Ministers—an intergovernmental organization of the five Nordic countries—established the NORDPLUS program to stimulate higher education exchange between Denmark, Finland, Iceland, Norway, and Sweden. The program was seen as a Nordic response to the ERASMUS program, to provide an exchange opportunity to students who did not want to, or were unable to, venture too far away from home, but also to help develop a Nordic identity. In 2008, Estonia, Latvia, and Lithuania became full members of NORDPLUS,[27] building on the strong cooperation developed between Nordic and Baltic universities since the early 1990s.

NORDPLUS is a very minor player compared to the ERASMUS program, with an annual budget of approximately 10 million Euros for five subprograms, of which higher education is the largest. While the NORDPLUS program continues to fill an important niche and plays a role in furthering Nordic cooperation, it seems to struggle to find an identity and a mission of its own faced with the success of the ERASMUS program. Denmark was the lone Nordic EU member when NORDPLUS was launched, but now three of the five Nordic countries and all three Baltic countries are EU members, while the two remaining Nordic countries—Iceland and Norway—are members of the European Economic Area.[28]

The Central European Exchange Program for University Studies (CEEPUS) was established in 1995 to promote exchange and cooperation in the Danube region, with Austria as the initiator and main sponsor. At its outset, when none of its member states except Austria[29] were EU members, CEEPUS played an important role in promoting academic exchange and cooperation in an area that had traditionally had strong bonds, but which had seen these bonds weaken after World War II. With the fall of the Berlin Wall and developments in Yugoslavia, the founders of CEEPUS saw an opportunity to reestablish and strengthen this cooperation, even if the disintegration of Yugoslavia also presented the program with particular challenges that led it to see part of its role as working toward cooperation and reconciliation between the countries emanating from former Yugoslavia.

Currently, CEEPUS lists fifteen member states: Albania, Austria, Bosnia and Herzegovina, Bulgaria, Croatia, the Czech Republic, Hungary, Moldova, Montenegro, North Macedonia, Poland, Romania, Serbia, the Slovak Republic, and Slovenia. The participation of Serbia, in particular, and the issues around recognition of Kosovo's independence[30] prevent CEEPUS from including Kosovo as the sixteenth country in its list of members, but its website indicates that the "Universities of Pristina, Prizren, Peja et al."—all in Kosovo—"are also participating."[31]

CEEPUS should especially be singled out for its innovative approach to promoting exchange between countries with highly disparate levels of income and prices. Had it operated with uniform scholarships, this would have worked beautifully for Austrians going to, say, Montenegro or North Macedonia but much less well for those going in the other direction. Instead, CEEPUS devised a financial strategy whereby the sending country covers travel expenses and the receiving country local expenses like housing and a subsistence grant, adjusted to the local price level. Austrian students going to Bulgaria, for example, get their travel tickets from Austria and their housing and food allowance from Bulgaria, according to Bulgarian standards. This arrangement helps ensure a reasonable balance in the exchange between the different CEEPUS member countries.

The European Higher Education Area

The increased cooperation, including academic exchange, and the need for recognition of qualifications led to a desire for broader cooperation at the level of higher education systems. Here, I give a brief account of the development of the EHEA before turning to issues of democracy within this cooperation.

In the 1990s, there was a feeling that something was amiss in higher education in Europe. The business sector, for one, often alleged that universities did not prepare students for the labor market, or—as the business sector often put it—for "real life," as if business would be the measure of the purpose of life. Also, the number of Europeans leaving to study in other parts of the world surpassed that of students from elsewhere coming to Europe. The sense of urgency was underlined by a report presented to the French minister of education Claude Allègre in the spring of 1998 by Jacques Attali as chair of an ad hoc committee made up of fifteen prominent representatives of French academic life as well as the world of business (Attali 1998). The report described a "system in danger" and outlined a series of reforms, including a new degree system modeled on the bachelor–masters–doctorate structure in the United States and the United Kingdom.

The Attali report was published shortly before the 800th anniversary of the Sorbonne University in May 1998, to which Minister Allègre[32] invited his colleagues from Germany, Italy, and the United Kingdom. Together, they adopted the Sorbonne Declaration, in which they made the point that "Europe is not only that of the Euro,[33] of the banks and the economy: it must be a Europe of knowledge as well" and calling for "an open European area for higher learning" (Bologna Process 1998: 1).

The Attali report and the Sorbonne Declaration strengthened the feeling among many European ministers of education that they needed to reform higher education. The Sorbonne Declaration, in particular, convinced many ministers that they would be better served if they reformed their systems together than if they each did so separately. At the same time, ministers from several smaller EU member states felt that they had missed an important opportunity by not being invited to the Sorbonne anniversary.

These factors together led the Italian minister of education Luigi Berlinguer to invite his counterparts from all EU countries, all countries in the European Free Trade Association, and countries that seemed to be on the path toward EU membership to a large meeting at the University of Bologna, Europe's—and the world's—oldest university, in June 1999. I can testify to the impressive settings, with a conference dinner in an inner courtyard. Bologna is known not only for its university but also for its culinary prowess. After a gathering of representatives of the academic world, ministers met separately to discuss and adopt the Bologna Declaration (Bologna Process 1999), which is the real starting point for the Bologna Process and the development of the EHEA. As with the Sorbonne Declaration, the Bologna Declaration gave a prominent place to the reform of education systems and structures, introduced a commitment to establishing a bachelor's and master's degree system in all signatory countries as well as a system of credits (such as the ECTS), and emphasized free mobility.[34]

The space available here does not allow me to trace the history and development of the EHEA. Therefore, I only point to some important trends. The EHEA is no longer limited to an EU framework. In 2003, the criteria for membership were changed so that members now need to have ratified the European Cultural Convention (Council of Europe 1954) as well as to commit in writing to implementing the principles and objectives agreed to between the ministers at their meetings every two to three years (Bologna Process 2003). From the original twenty-nine countries, the EHEA expanded quite quickly, so that by 2005 it had forty-five member states and today it has forty-nine.[35] Of the countries that have currently ratified the European Cultural Convention, only Monaco is not an EHEA member. Working with many of the newer EHEA member countries to advise them on how best to implement higher education reform has been one of my most rewarding professional experiences.

Even if the EHEA is an intergovernmental process, higher education cannot be reformed and developed through ministerial decisions alone. Therefore, the voice of higher education institutions, students, and staff as well as of other stakeholders is heard very clearly in the EHEA. Eight organizations[36] are consultative members, and those that represent institutions, students, and staff as well as the Council of Europe are particularly active in the discussions. They also contribute in no small measure to the work of the thematic groups that prepare much of the discussion in the formal decision-making bodies. They make up for the inability of consultative members to vote—which is anyway a rare occurrence—by contributing strongly to the preparation and conduct of most policy discussions. I chaired several working groups on structural reforms on behalf of the Council of Europe between 2007 and 2015, and the European Students Union cochairs the one on the social dimension of higher education. The cooperation and partnership between public authorities, universities, and students and staff is an important characteristic of the EHEA and, more broadly, of higher education in Europe. I represented the Council of Europe in both the Bologna Follow Up Group (BFUG), which oversees the development of the EHEA between the ministerial conferences, and several working groups from the very start until April 2022 and enjoyed almost every minute of it.

The EHEA provides a forum in which ministers agree on policies and priorities that they undertake to put into practice within their respective education systems. In many countries, there are regular consultations between the ministry responsible for higher education and the Rectors' Conference as well as student and staff organizations. Even if each country is ultimately responsible for its own education system, at each conference, ministers are presented with a report detailing the level of implementation of their agreed on goals. The first stocktaking report was presented in 2005,[37] and the current version presents a quite detailed overview in which the state of implementation in each country is detailed (European Education and Culture Executive Agency, Eurydice 2018).[38] Even if ministers for obvious reasons seek to interpret the report to their advantage, the fact that they accept that official information on their performance is produced outside of their control is noteworthy.

Thematically, the reform of education systems and structures remains a strong point of the EHEA. This focus has led to the adoption of an overarching qualifications framework[39] for the EHEA and standards and guidelines for quality assurance (Bologna Process 2005b, 2015c) as well as the use of the Lisbon Recognition Convention (Council of Europe and UNESCO 1997) as the standard for the recognition of qualifications within the EHEA. The focus on structural reform has, however, been supplemented by work and policies in a good number of other areas, including a mobility strategy (Bologna Process 2012c, 2015b) and "Principles and Guidelines to Strengthen the Social Dimension of Higher Education" (Bologna Process 2020a). There is some discussion within the BFUG between those who would want the EHEA to focus on what they consider its core areas, in particular structural reforms, and those who would like to see the EHEA develop policies for all or most of the issues facing higher education in Europe. There is also concern about a possible decline in the interest in the EHEA on the part of ministers (Bergan and Deca 2018).

Dilemmas of Democracy and Higher Education Cooperation

From its outset, the EHEA built on a set of values. The Bologna Declaration refers to the "fundamental principles laid down in the Bologna Magna Charta Universitatum of 1988"[40] (Bologna Process 1999: 2). In 2004, the BFUG decided that autonomous universities, student participation in the governance of higher education, and public responsibility for higher education were among the principles underpinning the Bologna Process and that applicant states should confirm their adherence to these principles (Bologna Process 2004: 2). The point about student participation had also been made by ministers in their Prague Communiqué, where they affirmed that "students should participate in and influence the organisation and content of education at universities and other higher education institutions" (Bologna Process 2001: 3).

In the early years of the EHEA, the values on which it was built were, however, largely taken for granted. They were occasionally referred to but rarely discussed, with one exception. When Belarus indicated it would apply for accession to the EHEA in 2005, its representatives were told informally but in no uncertain terms that such an application would be rejected because of concerns about the lack of democracy in the country, including lack of academic freedom, university autonomy, and student representation. After this, Belarus refrained from applying for membership on this occasion.

While there was little reference to fundamental values when ministers met in 2012 (Bologna Process 2012a), sometime between then and 2015, the fundamental values of higher education turned into a much more pressing concern. In 2015, ministers stated that the EHEA is based on public responsibility for higher education, academic freedom, institutional autonomy, and commitment to integrity (Bologna Process 2015d: 1). Ministers further said that they were determined to achieve an EHEA "where higher education is contributing effectively to build inclusive societies, founded on democratic values and human rights; and where educational opportunities provide the competences and skills required for European citizenship, innovation and employment. We will support and protect students and staff in exercising their right to academic freedom and ensure their representation as full partners in the governance of autonomous higher education institutions. We will support higher education institutions in enhancing their efforts to promote intercultural understanding, critical thinking, political and religious tolerance, gender equality, and democratic and civic values, in order to strengthen European and global citizenship and lay the foundations for inclusive societies" (Bologna Process 2015d: 1–2).

There were several reasons for this change. Belarus had lodged a formal application for membership of the EHEA in 2011, but its application was turned down by the BFUG in January 2012 and not brought to the attention of the ministerial conference[41] because of the oppressive measures taken against those who protested the highly flawed presidential election in December 2010 (Bologna Process 2012b: 24–25). Following the developments in Belarus and a renewed application, ministers then admitted Belarus to the EHEA in 2015, but with a roadmap (Bologna Process 2015a) outlining the obligations the country undertook on becoming an EHEA member, to be followed up by an ad hoc group working with the Belarusian authorities in 2015–2018.

The official argument for the roadmap was that Belarus was the first country admitted after the EHEA had been formally established, in 2010, and, therefore, that it required assistance in implementing reforms that other EHEA members had had much longer to achieve. Nevertheless, the fact that the fundamental values of higher education were in a precarious position in Belarus was an important part of the reason why we proposed a roadmap. This was also the reason why there were difficult discussions in the BFUG as well as at the ministerial conference of whether to accept Belarus in the EHEA or not. I was one of four drafters of the Yerevan Communiqué, the lead drafter of the Belarus Roadmap, and a member of the ad hoc group appointed to follow up on the roadmap, and I can testify to the challenge of the exercise.

The case of Belarus illustrates the dilemmas of democracy and cooperation. I was among those who argued in favor of accepting Belarus, not because I had any illusions about the state of democracy in the country but because we received very clear signals from contacts in Belarus that, if the country were not accepted then, those members of its academic community who were working for democratic changes in Belarus, and trying to stake out a road toward Europe that would not lead through Russia, felt they would be cut off from the contacts that motivated them to work under very difficult circumstances. This concern not to isolate those in Belarus whom both this country and the rest of Europe will need once there is a new political regime in the country was, in my view, a valid argument until the repression that followed the failed presidential election in August 2020 made it almost impossible for civil society to continue to exist in the country.[42] Conditions have not improved since then, and Belarus was the only country to join Russia in providing direct military support for the invasion of Ukraine in February 2022. What remains of Belarusian civil society is extremely tenuous, with most of the main opposition leaders either in exile or in prison.

Concerns at the precarious state of democracy in general and of the fundamental values of higher education in particular were not limited to Belarus, however. In March 2017, the Hungarian government proposed changes to the country's higher education law that were presented as a general measure but that concerned only the Central European University (CEU) and were, therefore, seen as an attempt to restrict and even close the activities of this institution. The CEU has a very international body of faculty and students and a good academic reputation, and it receives substantial financial support from the Open Society Foundation. The campaign against the CEU was run in parallel to a crude government campaign against George Soros, with clear anti-Semitic overtones. The proposed legislation led to large protests both in Hungary and internationally, but the Hungarian government did not back down, and the law came into force in April 2017. In October 2020, the European Court of Justice[43] ruled that the "lex CEU" infringed the provisions of the Charter of Fundamental Rights of the EU relating to academic freedom. In the absence of specific EU legislation on academic freedom and institutional autonomy, however, the Court ruled that the legislation violated Hungary's commitments under the World Trade Organization. The legal ruling, therefore, concerned an infringement of free trade rather than an infringement of fundamental academic values. In practice, this made no difference, and neither argument moved the Hungarian government to change its legislation. In the meantime, and in the face of threats to close the institution, the CEU moved most of its activities and all of its teaching from Budapest to Wien, where it received its first cohort of undergraduate students in September 2020, shortly before the ruling of the European Court of Justice.[44]

Meanwhile, even before the failed military coup in Turkey in July 2016, the pressure on the country's academic community was very considerable (O'Malley 2021). Academics for Peace,[45] which protested against the government's treatment of the Kurdish community, was particularly exposed and nineteen members of the association were detained in January 2016.[46] The crackdown on Turkish civil society, including many in the academic community, was reinforced after the failed coup, and it was clear that it went well beyond any search for Gülenists[47] that may have been involved with the coup. By early 2018, more than 50,000 people had been arrested, 150,000—including many academics—had been sacked or suspended from their jobs,[48] and many university leaders had been replaced by people who were loyal to the Erdoğan government.

These and other concerns led to a renewed focus on the fundamental values of higher education within the EHEA, reflected in the work of the BFUG as well as in ministerial communiqués. In 2018, the ministers defined the fundamental values of the EHEA as academic freedom and integrity, institutional autonomy, participation of students and staff in higher education governance, and public responsibility for and of higher education (Bologna Process 2018: 1). In 2020, they adopted a statement on academic freedom (Bologna Process 2020b). A working group on fundamental values developed a statement on the remaining fundamental values, which was adopted by the Tirana ministerial conference in May 2024 (Bologna Process 2024a). The Tirana ministerial conference also decided to prolong the suspension of Russia and Belarus from the EHEA governing bodies and work program (Bologna Process 2024b).

As noted, the renewed focus on the fundamental values of the EHEA coincides with broader concerns about the state of democracy in Europe, often referred to as the backsliding of democracy (Council of Europe 2021). Academic freedom and institutional autonomy and their importance for the future of democracy was the focus of the Global Forum on the Democratic Mission of Higher Education held in 2020 (Bergan, Gallagher, and Harkavy 2020), as part of the global cooperation to further the democratic mission of higher education, which we explore in Chapter 5.

The backsliding of democracy is seen both nationally and locally. In countries like Hungary and Poland, the nationalist right has been in power for several years and is implementing policies that seek to increase what is presented as national independence, reduce what is presented as dependence on the EU, and target immigrants. The election in Poland in October 2023 offers some hope, as it provided a parliamentary majority for a liberal pro-European government that was sworn in just before the crucial European Council meeting in December 2023 that decided to open membership negotiations with Ukraine and Moldova.[49] The new prime minister is Donald Tusk, who served in the same role from 2007 until 2014 and was then the president of the European Council until 2019. National independence and restrictions on immigration were also among the main arguments that led the United Kingdom to leave the EU, but events since then do not provide arguments for saying Brexit led to greater prosperity or political stability. These policies are accompanied by a rhetoric that undermines democracy, seeks to divide the world into "us" and "them," and pretends there can be such a thing as "illiberal democracy," a favorite expression of Hungary's prime minister Orbán. In 2022–2023 alone, the populist right scored highly in elections in France, Sweden, Italy, and the Netherlands; in France, this score was almost matched by that of the populist left. The result of the election in late September 2022 left Italy with a populist right government.[50] Similar tendencies are found in many local communities.

Later in the book, we look at the implications for higher education and its work in and with local communities of the backsliding of democracy and the prominence of populist attitudes that question the need for or even legitimacy of academic research, knowledge, and understanding. First, however, we supplement our exploration of the political context of Europe with a look at Europe from a cultural perspective and in terms of what Europeans have in common and what distinguishes them as belonging to a specific national and cultural background.

The European Education Area and the European Universities Initiative

In late 2017, at the initiative of French president Emmanuel Macron, EU Heads of State and Government decided to launch the European Education Area (EEA),[51] with the first policy measures adopted in 2018 and 2019. The EEA spans all education levels, from early childhood to higher education, and it also includes adult learning. It is an EU initiative that concerns EU member states as well as Iceland, Liechtenstein, and Norway as members of the European Economic Area.

The EEA is, therefore, distinct from and independent of the European *Higher* Education Area (EHEA), but the higher education component of the EEA will nevertheless have considerable impact on the EHEA. This is further underlined in the 2022 European Council Recommendation on building bridges for effective European higher education cooperation, which underlines the importance of the instruments developed with the EHEA, with specific reference to qualifications framework, the Standards and Guidelines for Quality Assurance in the EHEA (ESG), the Database of External Quality Assurance Results[52] developed by the European Quality Assurance Register for higher education, and automatic recognition.

The European Strategy for Universities aims to support higher education institutions and assist them in helping European societies meet the major challenges these are facing. As one would expect from an EU initiative, there is considerable emphasis on the role of higher education in economic development, including its contribution to Europe's "resilience and recovery." Its four main objectives are also expressed in terms that are not atypical of EU language: "Strengthen the European dimension in higher education and research, . . . support universities as lighthouses of our European way of life, . . . empower universities as actors of change in the twin green and digital transitions, . . . [and] reinforce universities as drivers of the EU's global role and leadership."[53]

One of the key initiatives within the European Strategy for Universities is the European Universities alliances, which provides support for alliances between higher institutions from all parts of the EU as well as other countries participating in relevant EU programs. In general terms, each alliance should have no more than one member per country, and all countries are not represented in all alliances. One example among many of an alliance of classic universities is the Arqus alliance, with the participation of the universities of Leipzig, Maynooth, Granada, Graz, Lyon 1, Minho, Padova, Wrocław, and Vilnius, while the E3UDRES2 alliance includes Fulda University of Applied Sciences, the Hungarian University of Agriculture and Life Sciences, Jamk University of Applied Sciences (Finland), Politehnica Timişoara, the Polytechnic Institute of Setúbal, the Saxion University of Applied Sciences (the Netherlands), St. Pölten University of Applied Sciences, UC Leuven-Limburg University of Applied Sciences, and Vidzeme University of Applied Sciences (Latvia).

To what extent do these EU initiatives complement and enhance the EHEA, and to what extent could they develop initiatives in a narrower geographic framework at the expense of EHEA initiatives? There is no easy answer to this question, beyond "a bit of both." There is genuine concern that resources that could otherwise have been deployed across the EHEA will rather be focused on the EEA, and that some policy development that could have been undertaken within the EHEA will instead be done within the EEA. At the same time, however, the EHEA could not have developed as it has without the very substantial support of the European Commission, in terms of both funding and intellectual input. Some overlap and shift in priorities between the two frameworks cannot be excluded and even seems likely. At the same time, my impression from discussions in the BFUG and other contexts is that both the European Commission and representatives of member states are well aware of the need to further develop these initiatives. There is also awareness that policies and initiatives affecting all forty-nine members of the EHEA cannot be developed exclusively within a framework in which some of them have no voice. There are clear indications that the Commission is seeking to avoid overlap and develop EEA initiatives in higher education as complementary to, rather than as duplicating or overriding, policies with the EHEA. In addition to the reference to EHEA tools in the 2022 Recommendation outlined earlier, one could point to the Commission's intention to develop the guiding principles on protecting fundamental academic values, stated in the European Strategy for Universities. In this work, care is taken to respect the work on fundamental values in the EHEA, and the definition of fundamental academic values used is the one found in the Paris and Rome Communiqués (see earlier).[54]

At the same time, there is frustration within the Commission at what it sees as relatively slow progress in several areas of the EHEA, and it is possible that one of the functions of the EEA will be to develop policies in areas where the Commission sees the EHEA as acting too slowly. For the EEA to develop policy, however, a majority of member states need to share this view and consider the EEA an appropriate framework.

Lessons Learned

I suggest that the major lessons to learn from this chapter are the following:

- The EHEA was a comprehensive political and policy response to the specific circumstances of the democratic revolution in Central and Eastern Europe and the ensuing possibility to establish truly European cooperation in higher education for the first time in at least two generations. It was also a response to concerns about whether European higher education had lost some of its attractiveness and whether it fully played its role in preparing highly qualified graduates for the labor market.
- The broad political response of creating the EHEA was possible because key political decision-makers saw higher education as an important part of the response to significant political challenges, and also because they saw no alternative to higher education playing this role. They believed that their concerns about the ability of higher education to prepare graduates for the labor market could be addressed through systemic reforms in higher education, and they saw no other actors who could fulfill this role.
- Key political actors understood that these issues could not be addressed by each country on its own but that a European response was required. The flip side of this understanding was also important: launching the reforms as part of a European response—even in a policy area where national competence is well rooted in law as well as in public opinion—to an extent, provided cover for political decision-makers who could underline that all European countries needed to move in the same direction. These were not reforms imposed within a single national context only.
- The higher education community rose to the challenge, and the cooperation developed between the higher education community and public authorities proved crucial.

- The importance of respecting democratic values in higher education cooperation has been brought closer to the top of the education policy agenda. This is largely for an unfortunate reason, as infringements have increased since at least 2012, but these issues have also not been shoved aside. The dilemma of how to further democratic values through education and how to further the fundamental values of higher education in a situation characterized by what the Council of Europe has come to call "democratic backlash" has not been resolved, and there is no easy answer. Keeping this issue on the agenda remains essential.

2

What Makes Us European and What Makes Each Country and Culture Unique?

Setting the Scene

The previous chapter ended with an expression of concern about the backsliding of democracy. That is partly an issue of institutions and governance, which were covered by the previous chapter, but it is also an issue of how public attitudes evolve. If nondemocratic governance has support from those who should benefit from democracy, the problem goes well beyond institutions. Here we touch on one of the basic problems of democracy: how do we deal with those who would use democracy to destroy it?

The attitudes that Europeans display toward Europe and their national as well as regional or minority cultures are complex and, of course, influence policy and politics.[1] Therefore, a clear-cut distinction between the aspects of Europe described in Chapter 1 and the aspects described in this chapter is difficult to make. Nevertheless, in this chapter, I focus on attitudes, on the way Europeans think and feel about their continent, their country, and their community. This chapter, then, focuses on the cultural context, and with culture understood in the anthropological sense of ideas, customs, language, and social behavior rather than in the "fine arts" sense of the term.

Language, Identity, and Cooperation

Culture is linked to language. Most Europeans speak an Indo-European language, and moreover a language that belongs to one of three major families within this group: Germanic (to which English[2] and German belong), Romance (also called Latin languages, including French, Spanish, and Italian), and Slavic (including Russian, Ukrainian, and Polish). Some speak Indo-European languages belonging to smaller families, like Celtic (Irish, Welsh) or Baltic (Latvian, Lithuanian) or that are isolates within the Indo-European group, such as Albanian, Armenian, or Greek. Some Europeans speak languages that are not Indo-European at all. Estonian, Finnish, and Hungarian are Uralic languages, Turkish, Kazakh, and Azeri are Turkic, and Georgian is a Kartvelian language, spoken in the South Caucasus. Basque, spoken in northern-eastern Spain and the southwest of France, is generally considered a language isolate; that is, a language with no known relatives.

With the exception of Basque, all the languages listed in the preceding paragraph are official state languages, and Basque has official status in a region of Spain. However, many Europeans speak a minority or regional language, whether an indigenous one or a language that has come to Europe with recent immigration. Sámi, spoken in the far north of Europe, Galician, spoken on the Iberian peninsula, and Kurdish, spoken in parts of Turkey, are examples of the former, while Urdu and Somali are examples of recent arrivals.

The status of a language may even differ from one country to another. Turkish is the official language of one European country and a language of immigration in several others, while German is the official langue of two countries (Germany and Austria), one of several official languages in three others (Switzerland, Luxembourg, and Belgium), and a recognized minority language in the north of Italy. In specific regional varieties, it is an official language of Luxembourg (along with standard German and French) and also spoken in the French region of Alsace. There is also a good argument for considering the variety of German spoken as an official language in a large part of Switzerland as a distinct variety, in fact, so much so that German television tends to provide subtitles when Swiss German is spoken on screen.

Most of those who are native speakers of a regional or minority language are also fully proficient in the official language of the country in which they live. Minority and regional languages are under sufficient pressure for the Council of Europe to have developed a Charter for Regional or Minority Languages to protect and promote them and to enable speakers to use them in both private and public life.[3] As of August 2024, twenty-five countries have ratified the charter, while a further nine have signed it pending ratification.[4]

Many Europeans, whether they belong to linguistic minorities or majorities within their own countries, speak at least one foreign language, but not all do. A survey conducted in 2016[5] among the then twenty-eight member states of the EU[6] reported that over one-third of the working age adults know no foreign language. On the other hand, this means that almost two-thirds do, even if this figure is still quite some way from the ambitions of international organizations as well as many national governments. The EU, the Council of Europe, and many national governments seek to stimulate the learning of foreign languages, including but not limited to English, in schools and universities as well as through nonformal learning for both children and adults. The EU has stipulated a goal of "native plus two," so that every EU resident should speak at least two foreign languages, whereas the Council of Europe promotes multilingualism without limiting ambitions to a specific number of foreign languages. Together, the EU and the Council of Europe promote multilingualism through the European Day of Languages, celebrated annually on September 26.[7]

The situation varies greatly from one country to another. More than half of those surveyed in Luxembourg reported that they know three or more foreign languages, with respondents from Finland and Slovenia also indicating a good share of plurilingualism.[8] Few Europeans would be surprised to find the United Kingdom at the other end of the scale, with some 65 percent of respondents saying that they do not know any foreign language. This contrasts with the situation in eight EU member states, where less than 10 percent of respondents said they know no foreign language. In Sweden, only 4 percent reported they are monolingual. It is also not surprising that younger people tend to be more proficient in foreign languages than older EU residents.

Very often, the foreign language Europeans speak, or in which they feel most at home if they speak several foreign languages, is English. It has de facto become the language of communication across borders in Europe even if it is native only to the United Kingdom and Ireland, with the Maltese and people from Gibraltar generally being bilingual or at least near native speakers of English. Incidentally, the variety of English used by nonnative speakers in Europe is as likely to be inspired by American as by British English, even if schools tend to persist in teaching the British variety. In some regions, Russian, French, or German are spoken quite widely as foreign languages, often in addition to and not at the expense of English. Foreign language proficiency may also depend on age: in the Baltic countries, for example, Russian is widely spoken by those old enough to have gone to school before independence in the early 1990s and largely repudiated by the younger generations. Within the EU, English is by far the most widely studied foreign language in school. In 2019, some 96 percent of all upper secondary school[9] students studied English as a foreign language, while about 26 percent studied Spanish, 22 percent French, and 20 percent German. Italian and Russian came far behind, both with around 3 percent.[10]

Even if it would be desirable that more Europeans be highly proficient in foreign languages, also in languages other than English, the fact that foreign

language proficiency is reasonably good in Europe greatly facilitates cooperation and contacts across borders. A Europe of monolinguals would have
been very different from the Europe we know today, and higher education
cooperation would have been far less extensive, as would contacts between
local communities. Cooperation between the latter has been institutional-
ized through the Council of Europe's Congress of Local and Regional Authorities.[11]

Countries and Borders

As we explore later, most Europeans identify more strongly with their country than with Europe. The country is felt to be concrete, whereas Europe is
often felt to be more abstract or diffuse. As we saw in the previous chapter,
Europe can mean different things to different people. We also saw that the
borders of Europe are not easy to establish in every direction. On the other
hand, with the exception of some disputed territories and some territories
where a substantial part of the population works for greater autonomy or
independence, the borders between European countries are fairly clear and
undisputed.

This does not necessarily mean they have been stable throughout history.
Portugal is often considered to have the oldest unchanged borders in Europe,
although San Marino must be a close contender for the title. Germany and
Italy both came into being in the nineteenth century in their current form,
even though much earlier there were German-speaking and Italian-speaking cultural communities. They were, however, divided into different states,
and it was Luther's translation of the Bible and Dante's literary works rather
than any political decision that set the norms for standard German and Italian. France has taken on its current shape gradually, with Savoie and Nice[12]
as the last major additions in 1860. Corsica became French shortly before
the birth of Napoléon Bonaparte in 1769, whereas Alsace, where I have lived
for the past three decades, became part of France (but not thereby French
speaking[13]) in 1648 and was again under German sovereignty in 1871–1918
and 1940–1945. All five changes of sovereignty were the result of war and the
peace treaties that followed. A person who was born before 1870 and lived
beyond 1945 could have changed nationality five times without ever changing residences.

Two regions of Sweden—Bohuslän[14] (in the southwest) and Jämtland and
Härjedalen (in central Sweden)—were parts of Norway (and hence Denmark-
Norway) until the mid-seventeenth century. Even if most Norwegians and
Swedes are conscious of this, there is no serious movement on either side of
the border to change affiliation. Bohuslän, where I spent my childhood sum-
mers, is a peripheral region of Sweden, and, in my childhood, people would

sometimes say they wanted the region to return to Norway when they complained about the policies of the Swedish government. This was, however, said jokingly and perhaps also because they were speaking to my parents, who were of course Norwegian. I have never heard a Swede or a Norwegian make a serious argument for changing the current border even if views on the dissolution of the union between the two countries in 1905 still differ considerably. It was only in the 1980s that Norwegian and Swedish historians could sit down to discuss the issue with a degree of dispassion.

Kosovo is the most recent independent country in Europe, even if its independence is contested by Serbia and several other countries. Its independence is recognized by some one hundred governments,[15] but because of the opposition of Serbia, Russia (a veto power in the UN), and some other countries, Kosovo is not (yet) a member of the UN or of the Council of Europe. Kosovo is, however, a member of the International Monetary Fund,[16] of the World Bank,[17] and of two entities under the Council of Europe: the Venice Commission[18] and the Development Bank.[19]

Catalunya[20] and Scotland are examples of territories that have recently held referendums on independence. The referendum in Catalunya was declared illegal by the Spanish authorities, and some of the leaders of the independence movement were sentenced to prison. An amnesty was part of the discussions leading to the formation of a government after the Spanish parliamentary elections in July 2023, as the Socialist-led government needed the support of regionalist and autonomist parties to remain in power.[21] In the referendum held in October 2017—in spite of the strong resistance of the Spanish authorities—some 90 percent of those who voted were in favor of independence but only some 43 percent of voters participated in the referendum.[22] The Scottish referendum in 2014, held with the approval of the U.K. government, gave a 55–45 margin against independence, with an 84 percent participation rate.[23] The United Kingdom's leaving of the EU, known as Brexit, has, however, raised questions about a new referendum on Scottish independence. Scotland voted against Brexit,[24] and polls in the fall of 2022 indicated there would be a majority in favor of independence. The U.K. Supreme Court has ruled that such a referendum cannot be held without the agreement of the U.K. government, which looks unlikely. The Scottish prime minister Nicola Sturgeon declared she was determined to hold a new referendum,[25] but she resigned in late March 2023, and, at the time of writing, it seems unlikely another referendum will be held in the foreseeable future.

Rivers and mountains are often considered natural borders, and there are numerous examples where European borders follow these. Whether they are natural is nevertheless questionable. Konstanz is the only German city located to the south of the Rhine, and the border between Germany and Switzerland runs not on its Rhine bank, but just on the other side of the city. Today, the Rhine marks the border between France and Germany, but the Germanic dialects spoken on either side of the border, in Alsace and Baden-Württemberg, are very similar except for the relatively high number of French loanwords in Alsatian. In medieval times, the Bishops of Strasbourg as well as the early medieval monastery of the Honau had extensive landholdings on both sides of the Rhine, which was at the time neither a de facto nor de iure border. In spite of the relatively strong current in the Rhine, which in Roman times diverted much civilian river traffic to its quieter tributary the Ill, the Rhine never impeded what would today be cross-border traffic and contacts.[26]

If national borders sometimes change, the same is true of those of local communities. Nevertheless, many European local communities have roots far back in time, when transportation was primitive and travel was seldom undertaken for pleasure. Therefore, communities were more isolated and travel between them relatively rare, even if merchants, warriors, and academics traveled far and wide. In some areas, mountains were real obstacles to contact, and they may, at least in part, explain the rich variation in dialects found in, for example, German and Norwegian. Even in less mountainous parts, people were acutely aware of relatively minor linguistic variations. I remember a TV series that my parents used to watch, in part because it was set in the part of the Swedish West Coast where we spent our summers. When we returned to our summer quarters, my parents asked their local friends about the series and commented that its location must have been very close to there. Their friends, however, were adamant that because of the dialect used in the series, the action must have been located closer to the next community down the coast, some 10 or 15 kilometers away. Their concept of local was, indeed, *very* local.

Distance was not the only impediment to travel and contact. In a religiously mixed area such as Alsace, there were Catholic and Protestant villages and contacts between them were characterized by mutual suspicion. My own village of La Wantzenau, just north of Strasbourg, is traditionally Catholic, whereas Hoerdt, some 6 or 7 kilometers away, is traditionally Protestant. Older people from La Wantzenau have many stories about rivalry rather than cooperation, and, in an age that was hardly imbued with a spirit of ecumenism, mixed couples met serious opposition from both families and the two villages. Today, my Catholic parish leaves its church to the relatively small Protestant community on a Sunday morning once a year for confirmation and a provides a smaller chapel on a regular basis, so we have made quite some progress.

For many people today, both professional and personal mobility reduce allegiances to a specific place and soften local accents and dialects, but many people nevertheless feel a strong attachment to place. This attachment may be double, to both the place where they grew up and their current place of residence, especially if they have not lived elsewhere in between. Immigrants may likewise feel attachment to both their country of origin and their new country of residence. For example, most of the proverbial "hyphenated Americans" feel American first but also retain a strong affinity for the country from which their forefathers migrated to the United States. Similar phenomena can be found in Europe. In France, the far right uses the fact that some North African immigrant communities cheer for Algeria, Morocco, or Tunisia when these national teams play France in soccer as an argument against immigration and in favor of enforcing what they call national unity, a concept that seems to leave little room for variation and diversity.

Identity, Nationality, and Location

In the villages of both Alsace and Bohuslän, many people have strong local identities. At the same time, they also feel French and Swedish. There is, of course, no contradiction in possessing multiple identities. Rather, this is a normal state of affairs. We identify with our country, region, city, neighborhood, sports team, profession, religion, and/or language, all at once. Which identities are stronger may depend on circumstances, but a recent survey (Eurobarometer 2021) confirms the instinctive impression most Europeans will have that nationality remains paramount.

The Eurobarometer survey just referred to, which was conducted in the fall of 2020 and published the following year, explored the values and identities of EU citizens. Even if this survey was limited to respondents in EU member states, there is little reason to assume national identity is less strong in other European countries, and I am not aware of any similar survey with a broader European scope.

As we see later, the sense of identity is quite strong, and, if we add up the numbers, it is quite evident that many Europeans have overlapping identities: 73 percent of those asked stated that they identify with their nationality (Eurobarometer 2021: 76) and 69 percent indicated that they identify with their local area or region (Eurobarometer 2021: 74). There are clear differences between countries, but in only one country—Luxembourg—did less than half of those asked say they identify with their nationality. There is no information in the survey on why this is so, but it may be noted that, in spite of its small size and distinct national culture, Luxembourg has played an important role in developing the EU. Narrow nationalism has so far not been a viable way to power for Luxembourg politicians, nor has the national scene been big enough for the most ambitious among them. The country has provided several politicians of European scope, including three former presidents of the European Commission,[27] it hosts several EU institutions, and its economy is highly international. Close to half of its current population is of immigrant origin, hailing from some 170 different countries, and close to 200,000 people live across the border in France, Germany, or Belgium and work in Luxembourg, adding a sizable daily influx to a total population of approximately 650,000.[28]

The same survey (Eurobarometer 2021: 79) reports that 56 percent of those asked identified with being "European" (here used in the sense of the EU), with extremes ranging between 76 percent and 42 percent. Somewhat surprisingly in view of the fact that several elections have given a clear majority to nationalist politicians, respondents in Hungary identified as "Europeans" to a greater extent than those in any other EU country. It is certainly not a sentiment the present Hungarian government is prepared to encourage or even consider.

Overall, residents of cities are more likely to identify as Europeans than residents of rural areas, but the difference at an aggregate level is only five percentage points. Overall, the survey concludes that "family ... was the item respondents identified with most strongly (81 percent), followed by nationality (73 percent)." In order of decreasing importance, the elements included in the survey with which Europeans identify the most are: one's family, nationality, gender, age and state of life, one's area or region, sexual orientation, occupation, ethnic or racial background, "being European," political orientation, and religion or beliefs (Eurobarometer 2021: 48). For our purposes, it is important to note that nationality is considered a more important element of self-identification than one's local area or region and that both are considered more important than identifying with Europe. On the other hand, only slightly more than half of the respondents said they identified with being European (56 percent), political orientation (54 percent), and religion or beliefs (53 percent). Significantly, in view of the surge of populist political parties, the survey also concludes that "most Europeans (56 percent) do not feel like their identity is under threat" (Eurobarometer 2021: 133).

It may also be interesting to note that the two countries in which a particularly high number of respondents state that ethnic or racial background is important are Belgium and Cyprus, with 84 percent and 83 percent, respectively. These figures should not be taken to indicate that Belgians and Cypriots are more racist than other Europeans. In both countries, rivalries between indigenous ethnic or linguistic groups are, however, important in national politics, in Belgium between Flemish speakers and French speakers, and in Cyprus between Greek Cypriots and Turkish Cypriots. In Cyprus, it seems reasonable to assume that this divide, which has long roots, has been reinforced by the de facto division of the country following the Turkish invasion in July 1974.

The same survey explored the extent to which EU citizens identify with a set of values: 64 percent of those surveyed gave importance to tolerance, expressed as "listening to others and understanding those who are different from them," while 29 percent agreed "somewhat," and only 4 percent disagreed entirely. There is some but not enormous variety between countries, and much of the difference is between those who "agree" and those who "agree somewhat." Cyprus and Spain show the highest level of agreement, combined with most of the remaining 20 percent or so agreeing "somewhat." In Finland, the Czech Republic, and Lithuania, slightly more than 40 percent agreed entirely but some 50 percent agreed "somewhat." Seventy percent of those surveyed indicated that they consider equality of opportunity to be important, with a further 24 percent considering equality of opportunity to be somewhat important. Only 4 percent considered it of little or no importance (Eurobarometer 2021: 45).

These findings, however, contrast with those of a Romanian survey, which, rather than asking whether respondents believed tolerance is important, asked whether they trust members of a broad range of groups. It turned out, they did not. The following are the percentages of distrust for the subject groups: 74 percent, homosexuals; 72 percent, Roma; 69 percent, immigrants; 68 percent, Muslims; and 58 percent, those suffering from AIDS/HIV. Also, 58 percent distrusted people of other religions, 58 percent, Hungarians,[29] and 46 percent, Jews (all figures from Naumescu 2019: 259). I have no good explanation for why the figures from the two surveys are that different, even if a part of the explanation may lie in the difference between asking what people consider positive or important and asking whom they trust. I do not, certainly, believe attitudes in Romania are fundamentally different from other EU member states, and the Eurobarometer survey shows no such large differences for any of the parameters included. Even in the absence of similar surveys for Europe beyond the EU, I do not believe other Europeans would have significantly different attitudes. These results are, of course, deeply disturbing, and they underline the importance of education at all levels, including higher education, playing a key role in developing attitudes of citizenship and tolerance. The results, alas, constitute a pungent argument for the need for higher education to contribute to building democratic, inclusive, diverse societies marked by mutual respect. That commitment needs to be translated into action and activities at the local level, including the local communities of which higher education is a part.

For our purposes, it may be worth looking at the extent to which the respondents' level of education influences their answers. This is not entirely straightforward, because the Eurobarometer survey does not distinguish between levels of education but rather uses three categories: those who left education when they were aged twenty years or over, those who left school between the ages of sixteen and nineteen, and those who left aged fifteen years or younger.[30] Even if we must assume there is a link between the age at which people leave the education system and the level of education they reach, there is no indication of whether the older "education leavers" undertook higher education and, if they did, what level they reached. We can safely assume that those aged nineteen years or younger who left education did not achieve a higher education degree, but we cannot conversely assume that all of those aged twenty years or older who left education did.

With these caveats, it does seem that the level of education has some impact on identity and values: 68 percent of those who left education when they were aged twenty years or over agreed that tolerance is very important compared to 63 percent of those who left school between the ages of sixteen and nineteen and 61 percent of those who left aged fifteen years or younger (Eurobarometer 2021: 39). On the one hand, we could have wished for the effect of education to be greater, but, on the other hand, we should be satisfied that the level of tolerance is relatively high for all levels of education. Likewise, it is worth noting that 75 percent of students[31] considered the equality of opportunity to be important, a score that is somewhat higher than the average for all groups surveyed (Eurobarometer 2021: 45).

The effect of education is far greater on identification with one's ethnic or racial background: 69 percent of the respondents who left school by the age of fifteen identify with their ethnic or racial background, whereas 56 percent of those who continued studying beyond the age of twenty do. The survey does not allow us to draw conclusions about the political attitudes of those who so identify, but, in several countries, the populist right political parties are strengthening their position.[32] At least for these currents of thought, identifying with one's ethnic or racial background is far from innocuous. Such identification coincides with political programs seeking to limit the rights and position of those with different—nonnational, immigrant—backgrounds. From my point of view, the percentage of those who identify on the basis of ethnicity is high for both groups, but, to the extent the responses to this question give an indication of how likely Europeans are to be racist, the effect of education is encouraging. We should, however, treat the responses with some care. As noted previously, race is a much less salient concept in Europe than it is in the United States, so that where Americans think in terms of race, Europeans think in terms of immigration and ethnic, linguistic, and religious minorities. These can be indigenous as well as recent migrants, and they may coincide, as when Muslim immigrants speak a different language and have a darker skin color. Likewise, the more highly educated respondents in the survey expressed stronger support for the freedom of thought, expression, and religion (Eurobarometer 2021: 98).

Interestingly, 64 percent of the respondents say they identify with their level of education (Eurobarometer 2021: 61), with respondents with the highest education level—or at least the longest schooling—identifying most strongly with their education. However, it seems unclear whether education is an independent factor here and to what extent it is linked to factors like employment, income, and socioeconomic background and class.

Commitment to Democracy and to Europe

The Romanian political scientist Valentin Naumescu says that "if we seek the formula that best characterizes the new tendencies in Central and Eastern Europe, none can better summarize this than the crises of liberal values and the European Idea" (Naumescu 2019: 234). He also says that in Central and Eastern Europe, the development toward Euroskepticism and populist nationalism started some ten years after the countries in question joined the EU (Naumescu 2019: 235).

These tendencies are not limited to Central and Eastern Europe, even if they may be particularly evident in countries like Hungary and Poland. My country of residence, France, is unusual in that it has a strong populist right as well as a strong populist left, neither of which is pro-EU. In the French system, the first round of the presidential election gives a better impression of how preferences are distributed than the second round, in which only the two candidates who got the highest number of votes in the first round still compete. In the first round of the 2022 presidential election, Macron—the incumbent—got 27.85 percent of the vote. Far-right candidates[33] got a total of 32.28 percent, whereas far-left candidates[34] got 25.56 percent. Between them, antisystem candidates thus got almost 58 percent of the vote, whereas the representative of the traditional right, Valérie Pécresse (a former minister of education), got 4.78 percent and the representative of the mainstream Socialist party, Anne Hidalgo—who is the elected mayor of Paris—got 1.75 percent. In both cases, the traditional center right and center left parties scored their worst ever. In the second round, President Macron won reelection with a clear margin against Marine Le Pen: roughly 58.5 percent against 41.5 percent.[35]

The current government of President Macron *is* pro-EU and aims to strengthen French leadership within the EU. At the same time, it must carry at least a part of the blame for the development of strong populist parties. President Macron is essentially a neoliberal, and while he set out by proclaiming that he was neither left nor right, he is increasingly considered as being firmly of the right. That is, of course, fair enough but he has managed to weaken the traditional right as well as the traditional left.[36] The classic French left, the Socialist party, has declined to a level of near insignificance. The party's social democrat wing has largely joined Macron's movement, while its left wing has joined the populist left coalition around Mélenchon. A similar division has occurred on the classic right, les Républicains, which has also declined very significantly. Many of those prominent in President Macron's government and movement come from the moderate part of the classic right, while those further to the right have moved rightward, albeit in most cases without joining the far right of Le Pen. Whether the relatively new hard-right leadership can rebuild the party remains to be seen. The current leadership seems to believe that the best way to counter Le Pen is to move further to the right but not quite as far right as her party, the Rassemblement National, and it is far from obvious that this strategy of "almost Le Pen, but not quite" will find favor with voters who self-define as being quite far to the right of the political center or who are unhappy about the current government without having a clear ideological position.

Climate change presents European societies with difficult choices and challenges, as it does elsewhere in the world. According to a Eurobarometer survey conducted in the spring of 2021, 93 percent of those surveyed consider climate change to be a serious problem, and 78 percent consider it to be "very serious."[37] But, even if relatively few Europeans seem to doubt the reality of climate change, the will to take action is less than stellar. This applies, in particular, to the kind of measures that would require serious lifestyle modifications.[38] The political complexities of the need to take firm action in the face of climate change, which, at an intellectual level, seems to be relatively well accepted, and the political strife arising from the cost of doing so, may be illustrated by the discussions in Germany around the so-called *Heizungsgesetz*, a law that entered into force on January 1, 2024,[39] which aims to further the use of renewable over traditional forms of energy. The law led to bitter discussions within the government coalition,[40] with the FDP (Freie Demokratische Partei; neoliberal) more reluctant to try to raise the price of energy than the SPD (Sozialdemokratische Partei Deutschlands; Social Democrat) or Green Party, and then to bitter discussions in parliament with the CDU (Christlich Demokratische Union Deutschlands; classic right) and the AfD (far right), both of which maintained that increasing the cost of heating would hurt consumers badly, which was a graver concern than longer-term concerns about climate change.

The French *gilets jaunes* ("yellow vests") movement, which started in the fall of 2018, was a reaction by people in low-income groups, especially in rural areas and smaller cities, against increased energy taxes on gasoline that would be particularly difficult for those with modest incomes in areas with inadequate public transportation who rely on their private car to go to and from work as well as to do shopping, get to doctor's appointments, and so on. What was in origin a protest against a transportation tax then transformed into a broad social protest alleging that the government and the elites were insufficiently attentive to the concerns of broad parts of the population. Unlike previous protests in France, the *gilets jaunes* were spontaneous and did not arise from any organized opposition (Duhamel 2023: 108). The labor unions neither controlled the movement nor did they quite know what to do in the face of it. Even if far from all participants were unemployed or marginalized, they also did not feel fully integrated into French society, whether socially, politically, or geographically. Groups that may not have had a feeling of belonging together developed a strong sense of solidarity over the duration of the protests and developed shared demands that extended to what it saw as the rights of citizens (Paugam 2020). The political climate in France deteriorated further with the heated discussions about the new retirement regime adopted in the spring of 2023. What many observers considered a necessary measure,[41] increasing the retirement age from sixty-two to sixty-four years, was opposed by almost all political parties outside of the government coalition—including a part of the classic right Les Républicains, whose program had nevertheless claimed the retirement age should be sixty-five[42]—as well as all trade unions and a considerable part of civil society. In the words of one astute observer of French politics, the French furiously rejected reforms that their neighbors had accepted with fatalism (Duhamel 2023: 76). This time, the labor unions were on the front line rather than on the sidelines.

Immigration is a hot topic in many European countries, and a considerable part of the shift of voters toward the populist right is due to concerns about immigration, both because, in particular, many Europeans with lower skill levels fear immigration will marginalize them further on the labor market and because, regardless of what polls may say, many Europeans seem uncomfortable with cultural and religious diversity. Sweden is a particularly poignant example, for at least two reasons. On the one hand, the strong electoral performance by the anti-immigration Sweden Democrats has led the current center-right government to rely on tacit support and a measure of informal coordination with the Sweden Democrats, whereas, until recently, all other Swedish parties had declared they would not cooperate with this party. The party identifies Muslim immigrants as a strong danger to Sweden and has even declared that it wants to stop the building of all mosques as well as tear down some of the mosques that have already been built,[43] a measure that would be difficult to reconcile with the freedom of religion. On the other hand, Sweden is currently facing the most violent criminal gang warfare anywhere in Europe—and among the most serious in the world.[44] The gang warfare, which is carried out by arson, shootings, and bombings and also hits innocent bystanders, escalated over the summer of 2023, and the gangs are largely rooted in immigrant groups. As an example, the assumed leader of the most prominent gang is an Iraqi Kurd, nicknamed the Kurdish Fox,[45] who came to Sweden as a young man and who now also holds Turkish citizenship. One important challenge of addressing immigration as a major societal issue is to acknowledge that there are reasons for concern without closing our borders. Democratic societies need to be open to impulses and ideas from elsewhere, and they also have to fulfill their humane obligation toward those in need.

Politics evolves, but there is a good argument for saying that democracies need a strong center right and a strong center left as viable alternatives. If a substantial portion of society feels one or more realistic electoral outcomes would be disastrous, it is a sign that this society faces severe challenges. In Norway, the compromise reached between left and right in the mid-1930s has been crucial to building a political culture that is reasonably consensual, even if clear cleavages persist, and generally marked by mutual respect (Olstad 2019: 242–267). An important part of that challenge, and one that is highly relevant to the concerns in this book, is the implication of this divide for the culture of democracy and the ability of European societies to (re)develop and maintain societal dialogue as well as to seek the compromises that are often required to govern, not least in Europe, where few parliaments provide a majority for a single party.[46]

Strong democracies need strong civil societies, so that citizens can engage on issues of concern to them and provide continuous input to the elected political bodies. In Europe, however, the space for civil society is shrinking in many countries, peaceful public events are too often treated as being dangerous, and legislation restricting civil society organizations and actors has been introduced in recent years, for example, in Hungary and Russia. In a number of countries, government-led campaigns have been observed against selected associations, human rights defenders, and civil society leaders, while discrimination, notably on grounds such as political views, religion, ethnic background, or sexual orientation, is being inflicted on minorities and vulnerable groups on the pretext of protecting society at large. At the same time, electoral turnout continues to fall, while public protest—sometimes leading to violence and unrest—has increased. All of the elements listed here are among the main findings of the 2021 annual report by the Secretary General of the Council of Europe on the state of democracy, human rights, and the rule of law (Council of Europe 2021: 6–8).

Even if the situation varies considerably between countries, there is reason for serious concern about the state and prospects of democracy throughout the continent. The Council of Europe report on the state of democracy, human rights, and the rule of law points out that while lack of trust is a serious concern, people tend to trust local more than central governments. It is, therefore, encouraging to see both that many Council of Europe member states have undertaken reforms leading to increased decentralization and that governments are giving higher priority to involving citizens and civil society at large in public decision-making (Council of Europe 2021: 65–66).

My History Is My Own—or Is It?

Europeans' identification with their country is strengthened by the way schools teach history. This is hardly specific to Europe, but the balance of what we have in common and what makes us French, German, Italian, or Spanish, which I argue is unique to Europe, is not well reflected in history as taught in our schools.

In part, this is because the perspective in history teaching is mostly national. There is relatively little emphasis on a broader European perspective, and Europe is mostly seen as the development of the EU. Hence, the perspective is political and institutional rather than cultural and social, and depending on the period covered, the emphasis is on six, nine, or twenty-something countries. To my knowledge, there is little place in school curricula for considering how the idea of Europe as a cultural community has developed over time, even if there is some emphasis on the heritage of ancient Greece and Rome.

In part, the issue is also that the history teaching in schools takes today's states as their starting point, or perhaps ending point, so that it turns into an explanation of how country A or B was formed, with a tendency toward teleological views. That country A ended up with today's borders is taken for granted and as a natural state of affairs rather than as a development that requires explanation and that may have had a different result.

Not least, the problem is a lack of what the Council of Europe labels multiperspectivity (Council of Europe 2001b; Stradling 2001, 2003; Bergan 2016). In somewhat simplified form, multiperspectivity expresses the notion that history can and needs to be considered from different angles. My history is not only mine but also yours, and your view of it may be very different from mine. In caricatural terms, my heroes may be your villains and vice versa. To a large extent, France and Germany—to take the examples of two neighboring countries whose borders have shifted considerably through time—share a history but national views of that history are very different. Where the French would see victory, the Germans would see defeat, and vice versa. The same is true if we add the United Kingdom to our group of countries. A common joke has it that a French tourist goes to London and sees names like Trafalgar Square and Waterloo Station, whereupon he wonders aloud why the English name their stations, streets, and squares for military defeats. From a French perspective, they were, of course, but to the British, they were victories.[47]

Our view of history, even as taught in schools, can and should evolve. When I was in school in Norway, Vikings were still considered national heroes, and there was little emphasis on their role in spreading violence across large parts of Europe. Now, there is a much more nuanced view of the Vikings both as perpetrators of unjust wars and as traders and agents of cultural change (Titlestad 2012). The German public TV station ZDF went one step further and commissioned a six-part TV series on German history from the well-known foreign historian Christopher Clarke, who studied in Germany and speaks almost unaccented German. He is, however, Australian by origin and now teaches in the United Kingdom.[48]

The issue, then, is not primarily one of giving stronger emphasis to teaching the history of European institutions like the Council of Europe or the EU, even if an improved understanding of these would already help Europeans gain a better understanding of their continent and its place in the world. It is above all making history teaching less national and introducing a measure of multiperspectivity. Seeing one's own history from different points of view does not mean that one's own view is wrong or unimportant. It does mean, however, that one's own view is not the only one possible and that we need to understand why others view our history differently.

Making the difference between understanding and acceptance is crucial but also very difficult. We need to understand why slavery developed and was abolished, and we need to understand why and how the Holocaust came about, otherwise we cannot prevent similar phenomena from developing in the future. But, in these and many other cases, understanding cannot mean acceptance. No amount of multiperspectivity can justify or legitimize the kind of monstrosity of which our history has no shortage of examples. Multiperspectivity helps us interpret history. No interpretation can replace or dispense with a reliance on historical facts, which is the basis of any valid interpretation.

This is an underlying premise of the Council of Europe's program in history education,[49] and it is the main motivation behind the establishment of the Council of Europe Observatory on History Teaching in late 2020 to provide "a clear picture of the state of history teaching in its member states, based on reliable data and facts on how history is taught, through regular and thematic reports."[50] The Observatory aims to document how the focus of history education in schools varies between countries, which can again give rise to policy recommendations at the European level. The Observatory is still in an initial phase, and its first comprehensive report was published at the end of 2023 (Council of Europe 2024). Also, through conferences and activities as well as a first thematic report (Council of Europe 2023b), it has given rise to interesting discussions and considerable media coverage.[51] It is perhaps indicative of how sensitive a topic history teaching is in many European countries that the first thematic report focused on the presumably neutral topic of how pandemics and natural disasters are reflected in history teaching. Even a topic such as this, though, obliges us to look at how certain groups, such as Jews, were made into scapegoats for disasters that befell local communities in various parts of Europe.

Even if the focus of the Observatory, and traditionally also of the Council of Europe's broader program on history education, is primary and secondary education, higher education is, of course, also an important factor. Few universities are without a study program in history, many of them educate the history teachers of tomorrow, and academic research is key to determining how European societies will see their own history and that of others a decade or a generation from now. European history is certainly not one of a straight road to democracy, but learning from history, from our failures as well as our successes, is an integral part of the democratic mission of higher education, at a global, European, and local level.

Looking at Ourselves through the Eyes of Others

Beyond history education, the concept of multiperspectivity is essential to developing the democratic mission of higher education, be it at a global, European, national, or local level. Democracy depends on open minds, the will and ability to dialogue, and the courage to accept that there are different ways of looking at ourselves and issues that matter deeply to us.

It also requires being able to identify and deal with paradoxes. Most European countries at some points in their history "exported" parts of their population to other continents. In other words, they were sources of emigration, but one country's emigrants are another country's immigrants. Few have illustrated this better than the Argentinian artist Joaquín Salvador Lavado Tejón, better known as Quino, the creator of the comic strip Mafalda. Its main, eponymous, character is a perennially six- or seven-year-old girl from Buenos Aires whose comments wonderfully illustrate the complexity of adult life. One of her friends, Manolo, is the son of Galician immigrants, from the northwest of Spain. In one strip, Mafalda deplores the fate of those who have to settle in a foreign country. When Manolo comments that this was the fate of his father, Mafalda's reaction is an outraged "but Argentina is not a foreign country." It is, in fact, the only country she knows.

Europeans tend to be proud that Italian, Norwegian, German, or French immigrants to North America have to some extent kept the language and culture of their ancestors, but public opinion in those same countries is deeply skeptical of the proposition that Pakistani, Somali, or other immigrants to Europe not only can but should be bilingual and bicultural. French speakers in Canada should keep their linguistic heritage alive, but, in France, Arabic and Berber speakers from North Africa are expected to teach their children French only. Unfortunately, this kind of attitude is not a caricature. Too many Europeans see proficiency in and identification with another language as a threat rather than as an advantage.

High-quality education and research depends on the ability to ask critical questions and to find answers to these questions. So does democracy. That ability depends on being able and willing to think outside the box—on exercising multiperspectivity. As we saw earlier, multiperspectivity does not imply accepting the views of others uncritically. It does not mean giving up one's culture and convictions, and it does not mean that those who settle in a new country or community do not need to adapt to their new environment and learn its language, even if, historically, this has not been a prominent virtue of European migrants to Africa and Asia. It does, however, mean that we need to be open to the possibility that we may learn from others and that we may even be convinced by their arguments. To be credible, a "never again," heard after so many conflicts, not least in Europe after both world wars, needs to be accompanied by an understanding of the circumstances that led to the conflicts we need to avoid in the future.

An important part of the mission of higher education is to develop this ability to look at issues from different angles, even when it is painful. Today's Danes, Norwegians, and Swedes cannot be held responsible for the devastation spread by Vikings, but the reevaluation of history that we see is currently underway and that has already led to more nuanced views of a key period of Nordic history is a good sign that higher education and research matter to the development of a culture of mutual respect. The age of the Vikings is distant, and exercising multiperspectivity in its regard should, therefore, not be too painful. Nevertheless, part of the heritage of nineteenth-century national romanticism is giving Vikings an outsize place in modern national identity, perhaps, in particular, in Norway, which had no history as an independent country between 1319 and 1905. It was not a coincidence that Quisling[52] and his collaborators harked back to the Vikings to illustrate their idea of national greatness.

Likewise, academic history can help a local community confront its own past, as when the history of the Bavarian village of Oberstdorf turns out to be one of both courage and cowardice, collaboration and at least quiet resistance, human cruelty as well as human decency when faced with life under an authoritarian regime and ultimately war (Boyd and Patel 2022) or when exploring the reasons that led an artist to be a fervent admirer of Hitler even if his art was considered degenerate.[53] Similar exercises in multiperspectivity can help Spain face its civil war and Serbs, Croats, Bosnians, Slovenes, Macedonians, Montenegrins, and Kosovars understand the disintegration of Yugoslavia, parts of which—in particular in Bosnia and Herzegovina and Kosovo—were very violent and others much less so. One day it will hopefully help both Russians come to terms with the cruelty perpetrated in their name and seemingly largely with their at least tacit support (Volkov and Kolesnikov 2022) as this book is being written and Ukrainian and Russian historians to explore the causes and the consequences of Russia's war on Ukraine. That day may well be far off even in the best of cases, but it will not come about unless higher education contributes decisively.

From a consideration of the cultural diversity of Europe and its communities, of what makes us European and what makes us citizens of a part of Europe, we now turn to the role of the Council of Europe as a voice for democracy, human rights, and the rule of law, and how this role colors its education program.

Lessons Learned

In Chapter 2, the following lessons stand out:

- Proficiency in several languages is essential to European cooperation in higher education as well as to the European notion of what it means to be an educated person.
- The de facto development of English as a lingua franca has practical advantages but cannot replace the importance of language to understanding other cultures. As the saying goes, those who only know their mother's tongue are limited to their mother's world. Therefore, proficiency in several languages is, ultimately, also an issue of democratic competences.
- Most Europeans identify strongly with their country, but nationality is not the only factor that determines one's identity. The local community, one's education and professional experience, one's religious convictions, and one's interests are other important elements.
- Education can and should contribute to developing multifaceted identities that are open to those of others and to building democratic, inclusive, and diverse societies marked by mutual respect.
- Many countries in Europe are suffering a backlash of democracy and a lack of trust in government. Local government does, however, seem to be more trusted—or less distrusted—than national government, and the local community could and should play an important part in restoring confidence in democracy. The local democratic mission of higher education is essential also in this respect.
- An understanding of history is essential to democracy. The teaching and learning of history in schools tend to be national, whereas it would need to incorporate the notion of multiperspectivity

developed by the Council of Europe. In this, making the difference between understanding and acceptance is a crucial but difficult challenge.

- More broadly, multiperspectivity is essential to developing the democratic mission of higher education at a global, European, national, or local level because democracy depends on open minds, the will and ability to dialogue, and the courage to accept that there are different ways of looking at ourselves and issues that matter deeply to us.
- Democracy as well as high-quality education and research depend on our ability to ask critical questions and find answers to these questions.

3

The Council of Europe

A Pan-European Voice for Democracy,
Human Rights, and the Rule of Law

Introduction

The Europe that emerged from World War II was in ruins, for the most part. Some countries had stayed out of the war, but all were affected by it. More than any previous war,[1] this had been a war about two radically different sets of values, ways of life, and political systems. Which of those sets of values, ways of life, and political systems prevailed had profound significance. From a western European perspective, democracy emerged victorious if shattered. From an eastern European perspective, the outcome was much less clear-cut, and the emergence of new totalitarian forms of rule became even more evident in the immediate postwar period, exemplified by the Communist coup in Czechoslovakia in 1948.

The European architecture that emerged in the late 1940s and early 1950s must be understood on this double background of destruction and division. From it emerged the conviction that democracy had to be defended. NATO[2] was established in April 1949 as a transatlantic defense alliance with the United States in the leading role. The European Coal and Steel Community was established in 1951 by six countries—Belgium, France, the Federal Republic of Germany,[3] Italy, Luxembourg, and the Netherlands—with the strong encouragement of the United States. From relatively modest beginnings, the Coal and Steel Community developed into the European Community and then the EU,[4] which encompasses most areas of public policy, with the exception of defense. The EU has an executive branch (the European Commission[5]), an intergovernmental branch (the Council of the European Union[6]), a judicial branch (the Court of Justice of the European Union[7]), and a legislative branch (the European Parliament[8]) whose members have been elected directly since 1979.[9] From its initial six members, it gradually grew to twenty-eight, to then see one of its members—the United Kingdom—leave the EU after long negotiations that were both difficult and painful.

NATO focuses on military and security cooperation, and the origins of the EU are to be found in economic cooperation and the conviction that countries that are bound together economically will find it difficult to take up arms against each other. Whether that theory is supported by historical evidence will not be the focus of consideration here. In the immediate aftermath of World War II, the need was also felt for strong political cooperation, the immediate consequence of which was the establishment of the UN in October 1945. Its values basis was codified through the adoption of the Universal Declaration of Human Rights in December 1948.[10]

In parallel, western European governments felt they needed to strengthen democracy, human rights, and the rule of law through a regional organization. This is the origin of the Council of Europe,[11] founded in May 1949. While the Council of Europe is best known for its legal work and, in particular, for the European Convention[12] and Court[13] of Human Rights, we pay particular attention to its role in education.

European Cooperation? Not on Terminology

Before we delve further into the history and role of the Council of Europe, a warning about terminology may be in order. Briefly stated, the warning is straightforward: the terminology of European cooperation is complex and confusing even to Europeans. The cooperation does not extend to agreeing on what terms and names to use. The somewhat more elaborate form of the warning points to terms and structures that are often confused, and Appendix 1 provides a brief glossary.

A crucial difference between the EU and the Council of Europe lies in their ideology and approaches, even if both institutions are ultimately governed by their member states, and all EU members are also members of the Council of Europe. The EU has developed a neoliberal ideology[14] that emphasizes open markets and gives pride of place to economic performance, whereas the Council of Europe is values oriented and promotes democracy, human rights, and the rule of law. The EU sees education first and foremost as key to ensuring that Europe will be competitive in an increasingly complex and sophisticated economic environment, even if it is also open to the importance of education in developing democracy. The Council of Europe sees education above all as critical to ensuring the future of democracy, even if it also recognizes the economic importance of education, and its Education program has gained in importance over the past decade, as democracy has been seen as threatened.

A European Organization for Democracy, Human Rights, and the Rule of Law

Defending democracy was an important priority in Europe in the late 1940s and throughout the 1950s. Nazism and Fascism had been defeated through the most devastating war ever waged in Europe, but the eastern part of the continent saw the installation of Communist regimes. The impression of democracy being in danger was strengthened by the emergence of the Cold War. Ideologically, Nazism, Fascism, and Communism are not one and the same, but the distinction between them may easily have been lost on many of those who had to live under one or more of them.

The Council of Europe, then, was set up to promote and defend the opposite of totalitarianism: democracy. The experience of World War II had shown that human rights were an indissociable part of democracy. This had already led to a UN declaration, but European governments took this declaration a step further and adopted the European Convention on Human Rights in 1950.[15] The convention came into force in September 1953, and it has since been complemented by sixteen protocols that are an integral part of the text. They show how the concept of human rights has developed over the seven decades since the convention was first adopted. For example, Protocol No. 13, adopted in 2002, bans the death penalty in all circumstances, including for crimes committed in times of war and imminent threat of war,[16] while Protocol No. 12 enlarges the principle of nondiscrimination.[17] The European Convention on Human Rights has also been supplemented by a range of other conventions covering issues that were not on the European agenda in the early 1950s, such as violence against women[18] and trafficking in human beings.[19]

The most innovative aspect of the Council of Europe's work was nevertheless the establishment of the European Court of Human Rights. Any resident of a country that has ratified the Convention on Human Rights, which is to say of any Council of Europe member state, can take the government of that country to court if he or she considers that their human rights have been violated. To do this, there are two important conditions to meet. First, the reason for the complaint has to be covered by the convention. Complaining that your local authority lets your neighbor cut the grass at an ungodly hour will not get your case to Strasbourg. Second, all possibilities for appeal within the national court system need to be exhausted. You cannot go directly from a local court to Strasbourg.[20]

In complex modern societies, there are few meaningful roles available for those either without or with only very low formal qualifications. At the same time, democracies rely on well-educated citizens to function in practice. It is, therefore, no surprise that the right to education is included in the convention.

Education and the Human Rights Convention

The right to education is stipulated in the first protocol to the convention,[21] which was adopted in 1952 and entered into force in 1954. Its article 2 states:

> No person shall be denied the right to education. In the exercise of any functions which it assumes in relation to education and to teaching, the State shall respect the right of parents to ensure such education and teaching in conformity with their own religious and philosophical convictions.

The court has issued an overview of its case law concerning the right to education and the court's interpretation of this right (European Court of Human Rights 2022).[22] The court is explicit that "in a democratic society, the right to education, which is indispensable to the furtherance of human rights, plays such a fundamental role that a restrictive interpretation of the first sentence of Article 2 of Protocol No. 1 would not be consistent with the aim or purpose of that provision" (para. 8).

Most importantly, the court considers the right to education fundamental to democracy and the enjoyment of human rights, and it has, therefore, demonstrated a relatively liberal interpretation of this right. Even if most of the cases brought before the court have concerned primary and to some extent secondary education rather than higher education, the right to education concerns all levels.[23]

The state is responsible for private as well as public schools, which I read to mean that this obligation exists as long as the private schools—and, by extension, private universities—are considered part of the national education system.[24] Importantly, the case law establishes that the public authorities are under no obligation to provide financial support for private institutions. One would assume, however, that if the public authorities do decide to provide financial support for private institutions, they need to do so fairly.

Access and admission must be fair and equitable, but public authorities may impose restrictions on access as long as these are nondiscriminatory.

Restrictions must also be foreseeable, so that students may reasonably prepare for access to higher education on the assumption that the access requirements will not change significantly at short notice. Preventing discrimination, of course, extends beyond the area of access. It is crucial to ensuring
human rights in and through education as well as in other areas. The cases
brought before the court that concern discrimination with regard to the right
to education are relatively few. The court has generally held that as much as
possible, children with disabilities should be given an opportunity to be
schooled with other children, but it has recognized that, in some cases, their
disability makes this impossible. The court has also gone relatively far in underlining the obligation of public authorities in making access to education
an effective right for Roma children. It has ruled that this obligation goes
beyond ensuring the mere absence of discrimination to encompass positive
measures taking account of the special needs of this minority, which is considered particularly vulnerable in Europe (paras. 56–58).

As important as the Convention on Human Rights and indeed the Council of Europe are, and in spite of World War II having been fought to defend
democracy against Nazism and Fascism, democracy was built only gradually over the decades following the founding of the Council of Europe in 1949.

Developing Democracy

The Council of Europe was established by ten countries: Belgium, Denmark,
France, Ireland, Italy, Luxembourg, the Netherlands, Norway, Sweden, and
the United Kingdom. As a commitment to democracy was a prerequisite for
membership, the Council of Europe was in its origin a western European organization, even if from the outset it had the hope and ambition that it would
someday cover the whole continent.

In the period from 1949 to 1970, eight additional countries joined.[25] It is
worth noting that these included Germany and Austria, who were both on
the losing side of World War II. Austria actually joined only in 1956, as it
was under allied occupation until the year before. Cyprus and Malta became
independent only in 1960 and 1964, respectively, while Switzerland's policy
of neutrality kept it out of the Council of Europe until 1963 and of the UN
until 2002. Greece and Turkey show that, even if several Council of Europe
member states have issues with democracy, serious breaches can jeopardize
membership. Greece suffered a military coup in 1967, which led to discussions about its status as a Council of Europe member. In the end, the Greek
junta withdrew from the Council in December 1969, just before the country
would have been excluded. Greece returned only in late 1974, after democracy had been restored. Turkey was excluded from representation in the Parliamentary Assembly from 1981 to 1984, again following a military coup and

until free elections had been held. The next accessions had an important democratic dimension. Portugal and Spain had been dictatorships since the 1920s and 1930s, respectively. Neither dictatorship long survived the passing of their emblematic dictators, António de Oliveira Salazar and Francisco Franco, respectively, even if the transition from dictatorship to democracy had deeper roots. As new democracies, Portugal and Spain joined the Council of Europe in 1976 and 1977, respectively.

When I joined the Council of Europe in early 1991, Hungary had just become the organization's twenty-fourth member and the first country from Central and Eastern Europe. Hungary's accession was the first in a long line following the fall of the Communist regimes generally referred to as the "fall of the (Berlin) Wall," so that the membership of the Council of Europe expanded quite rapidly in the late 1990s and early 2000s. Albania became the first member from Southeast Europe and Moldova the first from the former Soviet Union beyond the Baltic countries. As Maitland Stobart, who was the head of the Education Department when I joined the Council, used to say, we went from being the Council of half of Europe to being the Council of all of Europe. A common joke among staff at the time had it that the first duty of the Secretary General on arriving at the office every morning was to count the flags at the entrance.

Russia joined the Council of Europe in February 1996, after its membership had been postponed because of the first Chechen War.[26] Its accession was an attempt to integrate Russia within European cooperation more than an expression of any belief that democracy had taken firm roots in the country. It was to an extent also an expression of support for then president Boris Yeltsin and what European leaders saw as his efforts to move Russia in a democratic direction.

However, Russia became an increasingly difficult partner and was often out of step with the majority of member states. As just two examples, the Russian Federation prevented the Conference of Ministers responsible for Youth held in Sankt Peterburg in September 2012 from adopting a final declaration because of its opposition to any mention of sexual orientation and gender identity.[27] A recommendation[28] on passing on remembrance of the Holocaust and preventing crimes against humanity could not be adopted by the Committee of Ministers as long as Russia was a Council of Europe member because of its insistence that the role of the Red Army in liberating concentration camps be highlighted. In the end, the recommendation was adopted in March 2022.[29] Even if Russia was at odds with most member states on many issues and also ceased payment of its contribution to the Council of Europe budget for a period, it remained a Council of Europe member. However, Russia's invasion of Ukraine on February 24, 2022, made it impossible for the Council to let it remain, and Russia was excluded on March 16.[30]

As we saw, the United Kingdom left the EU, effective as of early 2020. Brexit has had no negative impact on the U.K. membership of the Council of Europe. If anything, it may even have had a slightly positive impact. In 2016, Theresa May, who was the then U.K. Home Secretary, argued that the United Kingdom should withdraw from the European Convention on Human Rights.[31] May seems to have been in a minority position on this, but, had the United Kingdom done so, it could not have remained a member of the Council of Europe. With Brexit, the U.K. government seems to feel it does not need further problems in its relationship with the rest of Europe, and even if the right wing of the Conservative Party dislikes being bound by the convention and occasionally raises the issue of withdrawal, this has so far not led to any serious initiative beyond rhetoric.[32] The British Institute of Human Rights has stated that, while the United Kingdom leaving the European Convention of Human Rights would be a development of great concern, there is so far no firm indication this will happen.[33]

The expansion of the membership of the Council of Europe followed by the exclusion of Russia is one important indication of how democracy in Europe has evolved since 1949. This expansion would not have been possible without the democratic development of Portugal and Spain, the return of democracy in Greece, and the developments in Central and Eastern Europe from the late 1980s and early 1990s onward.

A Culture of Democracy

Another indication of how democracy has developed is how Europeans' view of it has evolved from one that essentially considered formal arrangements—legislation, institutions, and elections—to a consideration of how well these arrangements work in practice It is perhaps not an entirely new observation that there is more to democracy than mere form. Peter Rhodes, a scholar of Athenian democracy, suggested that a true democracy not only has a democratic structure on paper but functions democratically; that is, with meaningful participation of the people (dēmos) (paraphrased in Cartledge 2016: 241).

There was great optimism that the political changes in Central and Eastern Europe would lead to the rapid establishment of democracy. These expectations may seem unrealistic now, but they were widely shared at the time. It is important to remember that Greece, Portugal, and Spain had shown less than two decades earlier that a rapid transition was possible. However, it soon became evident that institutions are important but not sufficient, and it may have been the financial scandal with the collapse of a pyramid scheme in Albania in 1996–1997 that drove this point home with great force.[34]

Democratic societies need to build on a culture of democracy, which is understood as a set of attitudes and behaviors that recognizes the diversity of opinion and cultural background as positive, holds that conflicts can best be resolved through dialogue rather than violence, and believes that while the majority rules, the minority has inalienable rights. The multiperspectivity that I referred to in the previous chapter can also be seen as a measure of democracy. I would argue that a society that is unwilling or unable to practice a measure of multiperspectivity cannot be fully democratic.

The concept of democratic culture was first used in a high-level official Council of Europe statement in the Action Plan adopted by the Council's Third Summit of Heads of State and Government held in Warszawa in May 2015, which says that the Council of Europe will promote a model of democratic culture, underpinning law and institutions and actively involving civil society and citizens (Council of Europe 2005b: III). The Action Plan also underlined the importance of education in building democracy (Council of Europe 2005b: III.3). The concept of democratic culture had been developed within the Council's education sector—I would even claim paternity—and we saw the inclusion of the concept in the Action Plan as a significant achievement that was to mark the further development of our Education program.

Building Democracy through Education

From the outset, the Council of Europe's Education program sought to underpin democracy, human rights, and the rule of law. It did so in part by facilitating contacts between young people in different parts of Europe. The European Cultural Convention explicitly mentions the study of languages, history, and civilization (Council of Europe 1954: article 2) as well as the importance of safeguarding and encouraging the development of national contributions to the common cultural heritage of Europe (Council of Europe 1954: article 1). Its preface underlines the importance of "a greater unity between its members for the purpose, among others, of safeguarding and realising the ideals and principles which are their common heritage" and that "the achievement of this aim would be furthered by a greater understanding of one another among the peoples of Europe."

Even before the Cultural Convention was adopted, the first convention on the recognition of qualifications had stated that "one of the objects [sic] of the Council of Europe is to pursue a policy of common action in cultural and scientific matters," that "this object [sic] would be furthered by making the intellectual resources of members freely available to European youth," and that "the university constitutes one of the principal sources of the intellectual activity of a country." Interestingly, this text, which was adopted only eight years after the end of World War II, underlines the importance of students being able to "enter a university of their choice in the territory of other members" (Council of Europe 1953: Preamble) and of the freedom of movement. At the time, freedom of movement was seen as a democratic right that had been and was impeded by dictatorships. Today, the EU has come to see the freedom of movement as part of an open market policy that emphasizes economic aspects. At the same time, this right is increasingly challenged by those who wish to limit or even stop immigration. They are found in all European countries, and, even if many of them belong to the populist right, far from all do. In December 2023, the French government's draft immigration law was defeated in the National Assembly at an early stage of consideration by a coalition of those on the right who wanted a tougher law and those on the left who wanted a less strict law.[35] Regrettably, the end result was a stricter law adopted with the votes of both what the French call the "hard right" (Républicains) and the far right (Rassemblement National) as well as with most of the votes of the government bloc. However, fifty-nine parliamentarians from the government bloc voted against the text, which they saw as violating key principles, the minister of health immediately resigned in protest,[36] and the minister for higher education reportedly wanted to resign in protest at the implications of the law for foreign students but was prevented or dissuaded from doing so.[37] Appropriately, a highly critical editorial in the leading regional newspaper in Alsace accused the French hard right and far right of engaging in "populism without borders."[38] Among the protests from civil society, we find those of a clear majority of French university presidents.[39]

Developments are of concern not only in France, however, even if the French law seems particularly restrictive and the process leading to its adoption was exceptionally messy. Also in December 2023, the European Parliament and the European Council agreed to what is labeled a "new pact on migration and asylum," which aims to speed up the process of asylum but also of rejection, and, overall, it implies more restrictive policies.[40] Migration of both refugees and those who seek a better life outside of their own country has become one of the most divisive societal issues in Europe, and solving it without renouncing our democratic and humane values is one of the main challenges we currently face (Knaus 2020).

Migration is, particularly, an education issue, in more ways than one. Partly, the issue is one of skills and competences. Many migrants are working in low-skill jobs, and this applies also to those with more advanced competences,[41] so that the recognition of their qualifications is also a challenge (see Chapter 8). Nevertheless, many migrants have low skills. According to the OECD, across the EU, the share of very low educated migrants is around three times that of the native born. Also, immigrants are more likely to work on temporary contracts in Europe, unemployment rates of the foreign born exceed those of the native born in most OECD countries, and immigrants are more likely than their native-born peers to be long-term unemployed.[42] Language competences are also a significant challenge to the integration of migrants in both the labor market and broader society, as indicated by the addition of a new lower level ("pre-A1") to the Council of Europe's CEFR (Council of Europe 2020a: 21–24). The need for this level is particularly rooted in the migration of people with low skills—including lack of literacy—even in their native language, and it includes descriptors like, "Can understand short, simple instructions for actions such as 'Stop,' 'Close the door,' etc., provided they are delivered slowly face-to-face, accompanied by pictures or manual gestures and repeated if necessary" (Council of Europe 2020a: 51). Conversely, those of the native-born population with low skills could be expected to see immigration as a threat, both because many migrants work in jobs requiring lower skills than their real qualifications would dictate and are, therefore, competitors to the low-skilled native-born population rather than to those with higher skills, and also because the low skilled have fewer employment possibilities. At least to an extent, this expectation seems to be borne out (OECD 2020: 30).

Education is, of course, important not only to developing labor market competences but also to developing attitudes (see the discussion of the Council of Europe's RFCDC, later). Overall, those with higher education qualifications seem more favorable toward immigration. Nevertheless, the difference in attitudes between those with higher and those with lower skills has little to do with the fear of losing their jobs. Instead, the differences seem linked to cultural values and beliefs, with the more educated parts of the population being less racist and more positive to cultural diversity (Hainmueller and Hiscox 2007: 401–402). Therefore, the most important factors are not whether immigrants have qualifications that can compete with those of the native born with higher education or rather fill occupations requiring only low skills. The main issues seem to be whether they lack some of the competences that could facilitate integration, such as language and cultural competences. Hainmueller and Hiscox suggest that "the results indicate that the division between more—and less—educated natives over support for immigration is primarily a distinction in values" (433).

As views of democracy as well as education evolved, so did the Council's Education program. This is reflected in the cooperation both on the democratic mission of higher education, which is the subject of the following chapters, and on a project that focused on the role of education more broadly as a site of democratic citizenship. Both were launched in the very late 1990s and anticipated the later work on the role of education in developing democratic culture. The concept of democratic citizenship is similar to that of democratic culture in underlining that institutions and laws alone do not a democracy make. The recommendation adopted at the end of the project defines education for democratic citizenship (EDC) as "education, training, awareness-raising, information, practices and activities which aim, by equipping learners with knowledge, skills and understanding and developing their attitudes and behaviour, to empower them to exercise and defend their democratic rights and responsibilities in society, to value diversity and to play an active part in democratic life, with a view to the promotion and protection of democracy and the rule of law" (Council of Europe 2010: para. 2a).

Even if the 2010 Recommendation is an important statement of principle, its wording is fairly vague and difficult to operationalize. Soon after its adoption, there were two important developments. The Committee of Ministers underlined the need for all Council programs and activities to help the Council of Europe fulfill its main goals of furthering democracy, human rights, and the rule of law. Activities that were judged insufficient in this regard would be eliminated. For the education sector, this was an incitement to accelerate a review of the program that had already been underway.

At the same time, Andorra was preparing to lead the Committee of Ministers[43] and made it clear that it wanted to make education the overall priority of its six-month presidency. My suggestion was that if we wanted the preparation for active citizenship in democratic societies to be a main purpose of education, as the Council of Europe had already claimed it is (Council of Europe 2007), we needed to be able to stipulate what students should learn at different levels of education that would help them be better citizens. Out of the discussion with the Andorran authorities grew the project that sought to outline Competences for Democratic Culture. It was launched through a conference in Andorra la Vella in February 2013 (van't Land 2013), which was crucial for gaining acceptance for the project in the Committee of Ministers.

We had thought in terms of a classic intergovernmental project over several years, but, in January 2015, a series of events in France brought home the urgency of what we had set out to achieve. Over three days, sixteen people were killed in three terrorist attacks in Paris, the most emblematic of which was the one on the satirical weekly Charlie Hebdo.[44] These attacks gave our budding work an importance and an urgency it may otherwise not have had, and we sped it up as much as we could. The model for the RFCDC was adopted by the Council of Europe Standing Conference of Ministers of Education in Bruxelles in April 2016,[45] and the full RFCDC was approved in the spring of 2018 (Council of Europe 2018b, 2018c, 2018d).

Competences for Democratic Culture

The RFCDC outlines the main competences[46] that European education systems, schools, and universities should develop in students to further democracy. The twenty competences in the model are divided into four categories: values, attitudes, skills, and knowledge and critical understanding, as out-

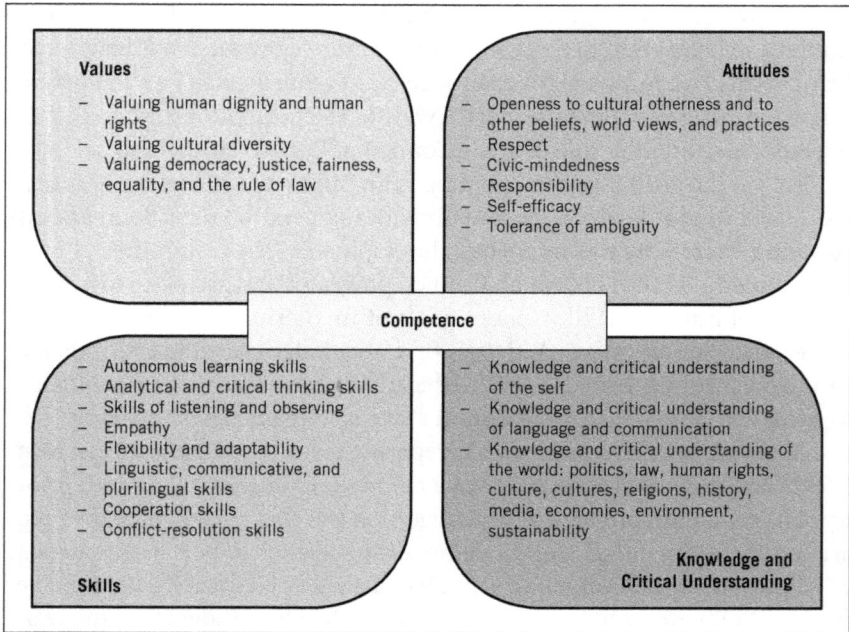

Figure 3.1 Reference Framework of Competences for Democratic Culture (RFCDC), the model. *(Source: Council of Europe [2018a]. © Council of Europe. Reproduced with permission.)*

lined in Figure 3.1. For each competence, a set of descriptors has been developed and categorized as basic, intermediate, or advanced (Council of Europe 2018c).

Learning outcomes had become an important concept in the debate about European education—particularly higher education—and were very present in the discussion of qualifications frameworks within the EHEA (Bergan 2005a). The Tuning project, which was a project coordinated by the Universities of Deusto (Spain) and Groningen (Netherlands) "to understand curricula and to make them comparable," made the important distinction between transversal and subject-specific competences. The latter are almost self-explanatory and designate competences that relate to specific disciplines: what a history graduate should know about history, a chemistry graduate about chemistry, and so on. Transversal learning outcomes are those that all higher education graduates at a certain level, for example, those holding a bachelor's degree, should have achieved. Typical examples are analytical abilities and communication skills. While the definition of learning outcomes may differ somewhat between authors (Kennedy, Hyland, and Ryan 2007: 4), the working definition adopted by the 2005 guide to the European Credit Transfer and Accumulation System (ECTS Users' Guide) provides a good summary: "Learning outcomes are statements of what a learner is expected to know, understand and/or be able to demonstrate after completion of a process of learning" (quoted in Kennedy, Hyland, and Ryan 2007: 5).

As we developed the RFCDC, it quickly became clear that an important element was missing in the classic definition of learning outcomes. Knowledge, understanding, and the ability to do are all important, but they are insufficient. You may be able to do things that you should not do, for moral, ethical, or other reasons. We, therefore, included the will to undertake a given action as the fourth element of our understanding of learning outcomes, and this includes the will to refrain from doing something you may be able to do but should not, such as manipulate an election. This fourth element of our understanding of learning outcomes is an important link to the ethical dimension of education, explored in the Council of Europe ETINED Platform, launched in 2015. Therefore, we decided to include this dimension in the RFCDC and its description of competences (see, for example, Council of Europe 2020a: 6).

We recognized that even if the model and the descriptions make up the core of the RFCDC, those who use it need guidance. Therefore, we developed a set of guidance documents assisting those who wish to explore the RFCDC in a specific context or focus on a specific aspect of it (Council of Europe 2018d). Democratic culture, for example, concerns higher education as much as any other level and strand of education, and we developed a guidance document specific to this level (Council of Europe 2020d). Higher education fosters a culture of democracy through the transversal competences it develops in all its students, the way in which institutions are run, how the members of the academic community interact, and how higher education institutions see themselves and behave as actors in society at large (Council of Europe 2020d: 6). This guidance document on higher education makes the claim that "education is to society what oxygen is to living beings: we cannot exist without it. But if society cannot thrive without education, nor [sic] can education exist meaningfully except in the context of society" (Council of Europe 2020d: 5). It also underlines that the full implementation of the RFCDC requires a whole-institution approach that makes the promotion and fostering of Competences for Democratic Culture an institutional priority for policy as well as practice.

Three Contested Issues

We appointed an ad hoc group of experts to help us develop the RFCDC. Its members were experts in different areas covered by our education program, such as history education, language education, EDC, and higher education policy. They also came from different parts of Europe. Three discussions in the expert group help illustrate some of the challenges we faced in developing the RFCDC.

One of the starting points for the RFCDC was that to be credible, the competences needed to meet three criteria. Educators need to be able to teach them, students need to be able to learn them, and the education community needs to be able to assess them. It was, in particular, the proposition that values could be assessed that met with resistance. Some of this resistance may be due to skepticism among a minority of the education community to the very notion of at least formal assessment, whereas some of it may be rooted in a view that equates assessment with testing or exams. However, assessment may be carried out in many ways, both formal and informal. The assertion, which we also heard, that values are too personal to be taught or assessed is equally unconvincing. That did not mean we did not need to have this discussion with at least one colleague within the Education Department as well as with the experts in the group. Education systems do seek to develop values. I am unaware of any society that does not seek to transmit its key values to the next generation of citizens through education, and I have yet to see a good argument for why values, unlike other competences, cannot be assessed.

A second discussion was whether competences for democratic culture should be taught in theory only or also in practice. During Communist times, many central and eastern European countries had mandatory political education or classes on the theory of Marxism. Developing competences for democratic culture through education is, however, essentially different. Political education as just described told students *what* to think, whereas the RFCDC seeks to teach *how* to think. Its aim is to develop the ability in students for ethical and independent thinking, and it also seeks to develop the ability in students to transform theoretical knowledge and understanding into action, built on due ethical consideration. Europe has a strong tradition of student participation in education governance as well as of student associations in schools and on campuses. The degree of participation and influence depends on the age of the students and the level of education, and it is most developed in secondary and higher education. Student and staff participation in higher education governance is even one of the fundamental values of the EHEA (Bologna Process 2018: 1). It would be incoherent to disallow the positive experience of Europe in this respect. In the end, a clear majority in the group was in favor of underlining that, to be learned, democracy must be practiced as well as understood theoretically, but the discussion was important because it helped clarify different aspects of what we understand as "political" as well as the mission of education in furthering democracy.

The third issue concerned critical thinking. All members of the expert group considered analytical skills as one of the most important competences education should help develop in students. Almost all saw critical thinking in the same way, but one of the experts objected. At least in part, the issue was one of language. "Critical" was understood as equivalent to "finding fault" or even "tearing down," and this was seen as entirely negative. The majority in the group underlined that the ability and will to question received wisdom is crucial to both the quality of education and research and to democracy. Neither can progress unless our convictions and the way we do things can be challenged. We also maintained that "finding fault" is the easy part of critical thinking and that the more challenging aspect is developing alternatives to the views we currently hold. This is, of course, even less appealing to some Council of Europe member states, and I suspect this was ultimately the reason the expert objected to the notion of critical thinking. The French academic Tatiana Kastouéva-Jean recently confirmed this by saying that, in Russia, there is a total absence of critical reflection on the Soviet past, on Russia's almost imperial relations with its neighbors, considered as inferior, on the failure of economic, political, and social modernization, and on the absence of democratic culture (Haque and Pluyette 2023: 21). John Aubrey Douglass, for his part, asserts the importance of universities by underlining that "universities are unique environments for educating and mentoring free thinkers, entrepreneurs, and citizens" (Douglass 2021: 35). Critical thinking remained a key element of the RFCDC.

Other Parts of the Council of Europe Education Program

The Council's Education program is multifaceted, and all parts aim to strengthen a culture of democracy, human rights, and the rule of law.[47] Space does not allow for an extensive description of the other parts of the program, except for the democratic mission of higher education, which is covered in Chapters 5 and 6, and the EQPR, which is described in Chapter 8. Along with the Council's contribution to the EHEA,[48] these are the parts most relevant to higher education. Language and history are, on the other hand, the two aspects of education explicitly mentioned in the European Cultural Convention (Council of Europe 1954), and the Council has been active in both policy areas since the 1950s. I, therefore, briefly discuss these two aspects and their importance to multiperspectivity before continuing to describe the Council's Education program.

Language Education

Over the years, attention in the language education program, which dates back to the early 1960s,[49] shifted from the teaching of foreign languages to a broader understanding of language as a tool for communication, with an emphasis on plurilingualism and intercultural communication. In 1998, the

Committee of Ministers agreed that "the needs of a multilingual and multicultural Europe can be met only by appreciably developing Europeans' ability to communicate with one other [sic] across linguistic and cultural boundaries" (Council of Europe 1998: Preamble).

Language is crucial to democracy. No idea can be described or discussed without language, and Europe could not develop democracy across the continent if it were a continent of monolinguals. The Council of Europe's most significant achievement in language education is the CEFR (Council of Europe 2001a, 2018a). Its purpose is to provide a transparent, coherent, and comprehensive basis for the development of language syllabuses and curriculum guidelines, the design of teaching and learning materials, and the assessment of foreign language proficiency.[50] The CEFR has had a significant influence on language teaching and learning in Europe, and the descriptors can be used for both formal assessment and self-assessment. Many self-teaching methods for languages now indicate the level students may reach using the method. The CEFR was an important source of inspiration for the development of the RFCDC. Nevertheless, the RFCDC is careful to underline that it is not a tool to measure whether any given individual is "sufficiently democratic."

The importance of language education to developing a culture of democracy, however, goes well beyond the CEFR. Multiperspectivity ultimately depends on language, and proficiency in several languages encourages us to look at the world from different angles. As just one example, both English and the Nordic languages state that "I *am* right," whereas German says, "I *have* right." Both turns of phrase leads one to think of the law and of having rights. Romance languages, such as Spanish and French, on the other hand, say the equivalent of "I have *reason*," emphasizing persuasion and intellect over legal rights.

In 2022, the Committee of Ministers adopted a recommendation on the importance of plurilingual and intercultural education for democratic culture, which underlines that language is essential to understanding, assessing, and formulating the arguments and opinions that are essential to democracy and that linguistic and cultural diversity within a country reflects the vitality and richness of Europe's culture. The recommendation further argues that "efficient functioning of democracies depends on social inclusion and societal integration, which in turn depend on an understanding of, respect for and engagement with linguistic and cultural diversity" (Council of Europe 2022b: para. 1).

History Education

History education was also an early focus of the Council's Education program. It has produced both standard-setting texts, such as the recommendation introducing the notion of multiperspectivity (Council of Europe 2001a), and tools for educators. The latter include an e-book on *Shared Histories for a Europe without Dividing Lines* (Council of Europe 2014) and on quality history education (Council of Europe 2018e).

History education is particularly challenging in political terms, and the multiperspectivity to which Council of Europe member states subscribed in 2001 has been much less in evidence in recent years. I personally doubt whether the 2001 Recommendation would have been adopted today. The latest indication is the discussion preceding the adoption of a recommendation on passing on remembrance of the Holocaust and preventing crimes against humanity referred to earlier in this chapter (Council of Europe 2022d). Even on a topic that should be consensual and on which the Council has done substantial work over the past twenty years, the adoption of a text that bears the marks of numerous compromises was possible only after Russia had been expelled from the Council. Before that, we spent countless hours trying to find compromise formulations that could be acceptable to member states, including Russia, without betraying the principles of democracy and human rights on which the Council is built. Another example is the fact that the Council is unable to refer to the Armenian Genocide[51] as such because of objections from Turkey and Azerbaijan. In spite of other countless hours that my colleagues and I spent trying to find an acceptable way of describing the Genocide—the reality of which cannot reasonably be denied—in the end, we had to give up publishing a book on teaching the history of the South Caucasus because we were unable to reach agreement on a formulation.

The Council's history education program has, however, been able to bring together history educators from some conflict areas. The most successful such project was in Cyprus where, in the face of considerable obstacles, the Council managed to bring together history teachers from both major communities, Greek Cypriots and Turkish Cypriots. The project had to take account of the fact that the self-styled "Turkish Republic of Northern Cyprus" is unrecognized by any country except Turkey and that the Council could not have contacts with public authorities in this part of Cyprus. We therefore worked through an NGO—the Association for Historical Dialogue and Research[52]—which brings together history educators from both communities. The project put multiperspectivity into practice and also sought to identify elements both communities felt they had in common, such as music, handicrafts, and food. In this sense the project took a "ping pong diplomacy" approach to history teaching, and, with time, it was able to address less consensual topics. The project led to reports on multiperspectivity (Council of Europe 2005a) and the use of sources in history (Council of Europe 2009a, 2009b) as well as a publication issued in English, Greek, and Turkish (Council of Europe 2011b).

Like its work on language education, the Council of Europe's work on history education was an important source of inspiration for the RFCDC. The concept of multiperspectivity has relevance far beyond history education, and the work with history educators from conflict and postconflict areas shows the potential as well as the challenges of putting the concept into practice.

Putting Theory into Practice

The examples we have looked at so far all come from the intergovernmental cooperation program, which is the part of the Education program financed by the ordinary budget[53] and in which all states party to the European Cultural Convention participate. Policy development is carried out mainly in this part of the program, which also includes many activities aimed at education practitioners. Much of the Council's work to put theory into practice is, however, done through other forms of financing.

One such form is Partial Agreements, where the budget is provided only by the countries that acceded to a specific Partial Agreement, and only these countries can participate in and benefit from its activities. At present, the Education program includes two Partial Agreements. The ECML[54] was established in 1994 at the initiative of Austria and is located in the country's second-largest city, Graz. Its purpose is to provide training for language educators or, in the words of its website, to "encourage excellence and innovation in language teaching and support its member states in the implementation of effective language education policies." In addition to its own specific program, the ECML coordinates the annual European Day of Languages.[55]

The Observatory on History Teaching in Europe[56] was established in November 2020 following an initiative by France during its presidency of the Committee of Ministers in the fall of 2019. The information gathered through the observatory will in its turn help policy development under the intergovernmental program. The observatory will produce regular reports, which will provide as complete an overview of history teaching in Europe as possible, as well as thematic reports that will address specific topics. Given the political sensitivity of history teaching, it is perhaps not surprising that the first thematic report focused on pandemics and natural disasters as reflected in history teaching (Council of Europe 2023b). The first regular report was produced in the fall of 2023 (Council of Europe 2024).

The capacity-building program in education is essentially financed through bilateral or regional projects set up for a limited time. Many projects are financed by the European Commission, and others are financed by Council of Europe member states. Capacity-building projects generally target a region or a specific country, with Southeast Europe having received the greatest support so far. When conditions in Ukraine allow projects to be run inside the country, one would expect the Council of Europe to play an important role in rebuilding its education provision. All capacity-building projects are now based on the policy work of the Council of Europe and tailored to the specific needs of each country. Most projects focus on education for democracy, and several of them play an important role in putting the RFCDC into practice, including current or past projects in Albania, Bosnia and Herzegovina, Georgia, Kosovo,[57] Moldova, Montenegro, Serbia, and Turkey.

Three capacity-building projects have a broader scope. One provides online training and resources related to education for democracy, including an extended course on the RFCDC.[58] Another seeks to identify, recognize, and disseminate relevant practices in promoting academic integrity throughout higher education institutions in Europe.[59] It builds on the ETINED Platform[60] promoting ethics, transparency, and integrity and fighting corruption in education, which is part of the intergovernmental program. The third is the EQPR, which we explore in Chapter 8.

A New Education Strategy 2024–2030

At the end of September 2023, a conference of European ministers of education adopted a new Education Strategy, which covers the period 2024–2030. The strategy sets the Council of Europe's overall priorities for education for this period, which goes beyond a single budget period. The strategy aligns the Education program with the priorities adopted by the Summit of Heads of State and Government in Reykjavík in May 2024[61] and outlines what it calls three pillars:

1. Renewing the democratic and civic mission of education
2. Enhancing the social responsibility and responsiveness of education
3. Advancing education through a human rights–based digital transformation (Council of Europe 2023a: 4).

It further stipulates that these are underpinned by five "cross-cutting principles": flexibility in curriculum and program design, learner autonomy, professional development, inclusion and participation, and democratic and participatory governance of education systems and institutions (Council of Europe 2023a: 3). All Council of Europe Education programs and activities will need to fit into these fairly broad categories, and it remains to be seen to what extent the range of activities will be renewed, including what activities will be discontinued. From the resolutions adopted by the conference,[62] it is clear that the role of Artificial Intelligence in education will be a new focus of the program.

Governance and Secretariat

The intergovernmental Education program is overseen by a committee[63] in which all states party to the European Cultural Convention are represented.[64] The committee also includes representatives of NGOs active in education, and higher education is particularly well represented among these.[65] Logically, it is called the Education Committee,[66] but it has had several incarnations. Until 2012, the Council had separate committees for higher education and research, on the one hand, and all other aspects of education, on the other. My experience with the Education Committee (and its previous incarnations) is that it provides excellent advice on and support for the Council's Education program as well as very valuable links to national authorities.

All of the Council's Education program is run by the Education Department, which I had the honor to lead until February 2022. The staff is made up of international civil servants on permanent or time-limited contracts. The staff is small and has been reduced through various cutbacks over the past fifteen to twenty years. The cuts reflect a decreasing willingness by member states to finance the Council of Europe[67]—the saying is that the Council budget is the rough equivalent of one postage stamp per European—but also an ongoing discussion among member states about how broadly or narrowly democracy and human rights should be defined. Several member states seem unable to think much beyond the European Court of Human Rights. More than half the staff in the Education Department are financed through, and work on, either capacity-building projects or the Partial Agreements, so that, in particular, the intergovernmental program is under considerable pressure. All the Council's member states are not represented among the staff in the department, but we have a fairly good mix of both nationalities and gender. Put together, we have a good understanding of most of Europe's education systems and languages.

Lessons Learned

I suggest the main lessons learned in this chapter are:

- The concept of democracy is evolving. While the focus for a long time was on institutions and laws, there is now an understanding that to function democratically, institutions and laws need to build on a set of attitudes and behaviors—on a culture of democracy.

- Education, including higher education, is essential to building a culture of democracy.
- To make the role of education in developing a culture of democracy a reality, we need to set priorities and define learning outcomes that correspond to this educational mission.
- The traditional definition of learning outcomes, at least in Europe, is that they describe what a student is expected to know, understand, and be able to do at the end of a course or—in more generic terms—at a certain level of education. This definition is, however, incomplete in that it omits the ethical dimension of education: there may be things we are able to do but should nevertheless not do, for ethical or other reasons.
- All parts of the Council of Europe's Education program further democracy, human rights, and the rule of law.
- The Council of Europe's RFCDC, completed in 2018, defines twenty competences divided into four categories: values, attitudes, skills, and knowledge and critical understanding. For each competence, a set of descriptors has been developed and categorized as basic, intermediate, or advanced.
- Language education is crucial to democracy. No idea can be described or discussed without language, and Europe could not develop democracy across the continent if it were a continent of monolinguals.
- History education is also essential to democracy but particularly challenging in political terms. The multiperspectivity to which Council of Europe member states subscribed in 2001 has been much less in evidence in recent years.

From this overview of the Council of Europe and the role the Education program plays in furthering democracy, human rights, and the rule of law, I now turn to the democratic mission of higher education.

4

The Multiple Purposes of and Public Responsibility for Higher Education

The European approach to higher education includes two concepts that may require some further exploration: the multiple purposes of and public responsibility for higher education. Both approaches are European because they have been accepted as official positions by the public authorities of all European countries in the framework of the Council of Europe and the EHEA.

Toward a View of Higher Education with Multiple Purposes

In European public debate, the role of education in furthering economic development and in preparing students for the labor market has long been and remains preponderant. The Attali report (Attali 1998), which caused quite some debate in France and was, at least indirectly, an important factor in launching the EHEA, lists several challenges to higher education. Those having to do with its economic role are prominent. The report indicates "adapting to the jobs of the day after tomorrow and to a spirit of enterprise"[1] as one of the key missions of higher education and includes relations with companies (*entreprises* in French) and the way we "learn knowledge" as two of what it calls "four revolutions" (Attali 1998: 1). It further underlines that preparation for working life should become one of the major priorities for every higher education institution (4). This reflected a concern often heard from representatives of the business sector at the time that higher education did not provide graduates with the competences business needed. The report also maintains that the insertion of university graduates into working life was slow and uncertain (16). This concern was not least taken up by the European Commission, which, long after the Council of Europe had started making the other purposes of education explicit (Bergan 2005b; Council of Europe 2007), argued the primacy of the economy. In private conversation, this argument would often take the form of "yes, of course, democratic citizenship is important, but, for now, the economy is the most important thing." How long "now" would last was never stated. It was perhaps not until the terrorist attacks in Paris in January 2015, which accelerated the Council of Europe's work on Competences for Democratic Culture (see Chapter 3), that the EU gave due emphasis to the democratic mission of education. On March 17, 2015, the EU ministers of education adopted a declaration on promoting citizenship and the common values of freedom, tolerance, and nondiscrimination through education (European Union 2015) at an informal meeting in Paris.

The Council of Europe took a broader view of the purposes of education. The budding cooperation with the International Consortium for Higher Education, Civic Responsibility, and Democracy (International Consortium) on the democratic mission of higher education (see Chapter 5) as well as the broader project on Education as a Site of Citizenship, at the very end of the 1990s, pointed to the importance of education in developing democracy. The Council had not yet articulated the importance of a culture of democracy (see Chapter 3), and even if we maintained that preparation for employment could not be the only purpose of education, we had not yet spelled out what the other purposes may be.

The need to define the purposes of education more broadly than its role in contributing to the economy was further strengthened when higher education was brought into the GATS[2] negotiations under the auspices of the World Trade Organization in the early 2000s. Part of the background for this is that private higher education, including cross-border education, has been increasing rapidly, the consequences of which need to be considered carefully (Varghese 2007). Space does not allow a broader consideration of the role of education in GATS, but the vast majority of the academic community in Europe and most education policymakers felt quite strongly that the World Trade Organization should not determine higher education policy or set the terms of international cooperation in this area. As one author says, for-profit providers treat education just like any other commodity traded for profit (Varghese 2007: 9).

A Bologna seminar on the social dimension of higher education, in Athinai (Athens) in February 2003, provided us with a first opportunity to develop thoughts on the major purposes of higher education, which, at the time, we defined as three. A Council of Europe conference on the public responsibility for higher education held in Strasbourg, in September 2004, provided its Education Department with an opportunity to develop these thoughts further, so that the original three purposes became four:

- Preparation for the labor market
- Preparation for life as active citizens in democratic societies
- Personal development
- Development and maintenance of a broad and advanced knowledge base (Bergan 2005b)

The reactions to the Council of Europe's proposals in Athinai and Strasbourg were overwhelmingly positive, and the Council of Europe's Education Department channeled them into the discussions of both the BFUG and the Council of Europe's Higher Education Committee.[3] The latter approved a recommendation that was then submitted to the Committee of Ministers and adopted literally the day before the 2007 ministerial meeting of the EHEA (Council of Europe 2007). Starting with this ministerial meeting, the EHEA also took the official position that higher education has multiple purposes (Bologna Process 2007: 1.4). The clearest statement on the importance of the democratic dimension of higher education, perhaps, came through the communiqué that ministers adopted in Yerevan, in 2015, where they state that "by 2020 we are determined to achieve an EHEA . . . where higher education is contributing effectively to build inclusive societies, founded on democratic values and human rights; and where educational opportunities provide the competences and skills required for European citizenship, innovation and employment" (Bologna Process 2015d: 1–2). Ministers also said they would support higher education institutions in enhancing their efforts to promote intercultural understanding, critical thinking, political and religious tolerance, gender equality, and democratic and civic values, in order to strengthen European and global citizenship and lay the foundations for inclusive societies (Bologna Process 2015d: 2).

Even if the wording has varied somewhat between the different documents[4] adopted, all make it clear that the view of the major purposes of higher education as developed by the Council of Europe's Education Department between 2003 and 2005 were now the official position of both a pan-European intergovernmental organization—the Council of Europe—and the main framework for higher education reform in Europe: the EHEA.

The Multiple Purposes of Higher Education

If we accept the proposition that higher education has several purposes, it is worth exploring them in greater detail. Others may come up with different lists of purposes, but I hope that few decision-makers will now seriously argue that higher education has a single purpose, even if the argument that a higher education helps students "to get a good job," which we met in the Introduction, is frequently heard.

Preparation for the Labor Market

Saying that preparation for the labor market is not the only purpose of higher education does not, of course, mean that it is not a legitimate or important purpose. To most students—and their parents—labor market prospects are likely to weigh heavily in the choice of universities, study programs, majors, and specializations. How important this consideration is in their decision on whether to pursue higher education at all is less clear. Some vocational education programs may lead to relatively high-paying jobs. They may also be much less costly than a higher education program, certainly in countries with high tuition fees, like the United States,[5] but also in terms of delayed income, since vocational education is undertaken at a younger age than higher education and plumbers or carpenters enter working life earlier than teachers or engineers. Nevertheless, vocational education and training (VET) and the jobs for which it prepares tend to suffer from lack of esteem and social prestige. This may ultimately be rooted in a hierarchical view that assigns greater prestige to theory than to practice, which may find its origin in "the foundations of socioeconomic models and in prevailing hierarchical patterns of labour division in industrial and pre-industrial societies" (Tsakarissianos 2008: 34). This is again rooted in an elitist view of education and even in Platonic approaches to education designed to produce aristocratic, nondemocratic societies governed by philosopher kings. As Ira Harkavy and Lee Benson remind us: "Plato designed an educational system that would sort people into one of the three classes, with major attention and resources provided to those destined to become philosopher-kings. Fixed truths, rigid classes, and advanced education for the few are concepts that fit well with the antidemocratic, aristocratic form of society that Plato advocated to overcome the evils of Athenian democracy" (Harkavy and Benson 1998: 12; see also Benson et al. 2017).

The lack of esteem for VET may be a vicious circle. If it is predominantly students from less advantaged socioeconomic backgrounds who go into VET, if VET is seen as the default option for those who could not get into more prestigious theoretical education, and if VET graduates then end up in low-prestige—often, although not necessarily, also low-income—jobs, higher education is likely to remain attractive to many prospective students and their parents even if all higher education programs do not prepare for well-paying jobs or provide a high level of job security.[6] It is, therefore, an important responsibility for educational policymakers and practitioners—including those in higher education—to work to ensure equitable access to higher education as well as to improve the esteem for VET so that it is considered a real and equal alternative to higher education.

Higher education, then, does have an important responsibility in preparing its students for the labor market, but many study programs do not prepare their graduates for specific jobs. We may reasonably expect that most graduates in theology, law, and medicine will find employment directly related to their degree, but it is far more difficult to predict what jobs graduates in the humanities or social sciences will enter. Higher education is not for jobs alone but almost all study programs will need to consider students' employment prospects, identify competences that are relevant to the labor market, and present these in ways that future employers can relate to. Many higher education institutions in Europe provide career guidance to students, and public authorities are concerned with gathering information on how higher education graduates find their way through the labor market. The EU has made tracking graduate performance in the labor market a priority (European Union 2017) and has established a European Network of Graduate Tracking.[7]

Preparation for Life as Active Citizens in Democratic Societies

As we saw in the Introduction, national education laws often identify developing democratic citizenship as one of the key missions of education, and we exemplified this by a reference to the Norwegian Education Law, which says that Norwegian schools should further democracy, equality, and a scientific way of thinking (LOV-1998-07-17-6: para. 1.1). However, we also saw—in Chapter 3—that the Council of Europe identified a need to be explicit about the competences that European education systems should develop in their students both because these competences are essential and because describing them in such a way that they can be learned, taught, and assessed will help make preparation for life as active citizens in democratic societies a key purpose of education in practice and not only in rhetoric.[8] This realization led to the development of the Council of Europe's Reference Framework of Competences for Democratic Culture (RFCDC) (Council of Europe 2018b, 2018c, 2018d).

Perhaps the clearest statement I have heard on the essential role of higher education in building democracy was made by the then Colombian vice minister for higher education Javier Botero Álvarez at a conference organized by the World Bank, in the fall of 2005. I had been invited because the World Bank needed someone who could present the development of qualifications frameworks in Europe in Spanish to a Latin American audience, and I made the case that qualifications frameworks need to cater to all purposes of higher education. It was Vice Minister Botero, however, who made the strongest case for the democratic mission of higher education. At the time, Colombia was emerging from a long fight with drug cartels who destroyed the very fabric of Colombian society. The main local organizer of the conference, who hailed from Armenia, the Colombian city where the conference was held, told stories about how the cartels had ravaged the area and how locals knew which areas to keep away from because they were ruled by *narcos*. As I recall, Vice Minister Botero said outright that, based on the Colombian experience, if schools and universities did not prepare for democracy and social responsibility, whatever else education can do is of little importance.

Even if Colombia was in an extreme situation, Vice Minister Botero's arguments have broader validity. Higher education should develop a culture of democracy in their students as well as their staff, and, as we saw, the Council of Europe's RFCDC provides guidance aimed specifically at the higher education community (Council of Europe 2020d). This includes developing a commitment to public space, so that democracy becomes more than the act of voting and includes citizen participation and deliberation. It is part of the democratic mission of higher education to help develop a holistic view of democracy, so that students, graduates, and faculty are able and willing to weigh long-term and short-term concerns and priorities and also to assess what priorities are most important to them, so they can identify where compromises can be made and what principles need to be upheld at all costs. Single-issue politics may be gratifying, and sometimes even necessary, but societies cannot be governed merely by adding up positions on single issues.

Personal Development

From its very outset, education was probably mostly concerned with transmitting the skills that would ensure survival and at least modest material well-being. Contributing to personal development was nevertheless an early purpose of education. Humanities, as we recognize these disciplines and this approach to education today, emerged during the Italian Renaissance, roughly covering the fifteenth and sixteenth centuries, when humanists took the view that education should have a moral purpose, prepare students for leadership roles, and go beyond the utilitarian approach to education that had been prevalent in the previous centuries (Kallendorf 2008: vii).

The humanists, however, built on prestigious classic precedents. In *The Republic*,[9] Plato suggests that the objective of education is to teach us to love what is beautiful. It is doubtful whether this purpose would make it into policy documents in Europe today, but even many Europeans whose background in Classical Studies is minimal recognize our intellectual debt to ancient Greece. Personal development has not been very prominent in education debate in Europe over the past generation or so, but this purpose of education has nevertheless been reflected in laws and official statements. Thus, the Norwegian education laws of 1938 and 1959 both refer to the need for the education system to help students become "useful human beings intellectually and bodily," whereas the 1969 and 1998 versions emphasize students' intellectual and bodily development.[10] Personal development is recognized as an important purpose also in more satirical comments on education, such as that by Ambrose Bierce defining education as "that which discloses to the wise and hides from the foolish their lack of understanding" (Bierce [1911] 1967:105).

To further students' personal development, higher education programs must develop many of the transversal competences described by the Tuning project[11] and included in the RFCDC. These competences include analytical and critical thinking skills, presentation skills, knowledge and critical understand of the self, empathy, flexibility and adaptability, and skills of listening and observing. Especially, education at all levels needs to develop the ability and will to learn, described in the RFCDC as autonomous learning skills (see Figure 3.1 in Chapter 3 for the full list of competences).

Developing and Maintaining a Broad and Advanced Knowledge Base

Developing new knowledge and understanding is the main purpose of research, and providing students with the competences to understand and assess research is a key priority for higher education at all levels. At its most advanced levels, higher education should also provide students with the competences required for them to conduct research themselves, independently or under supervision. This is reflected in the Overarching Framework of Qualifications of the EHEA (Bologna Process 2005a, 2005b). At the bachelor's level,[12] students should know the main ideas and tendencies within their discipline. At the master's level, they should themselves be in a position to develop and apply new ideas within their field. At the doctorate level, they should demonstrate a systematic understanding of a field of study, master its methods of research, and themselves be in a position to conduct original research.

The point that the main mission of universities is to develop and disseminate advanced knowledge and understanding is not difficult to make. The point that this knowledge and understanding needs to encompass a broad range of academic disciplines as well as transdisciplinary research, learning, and teaching is also easy to make in theory but more difficult to translate into practical policy. Society's view of what kind of knowledge is needed has developed over time, from the medieval emphasis on theology, law, and medicine as well as the *artes liberales* (Zonta 2002) to today's very broad range of disciplines. It may be worth noting that the academic study of modern (as opposed to classic) languages is relatively recent. At Oxford University, the first professor of Modern Languages was appointed in 1848, and in 2005 the university held a series of events to celebrate "100 Years of Modern Languages at Oxford."[13] What is now the French Institut national des langues et civilisations orientales (INALCO—The National Institute for Oriental Languages and Civilizations) traces its roots to 1795.[14]

The main obstacle to developing a broad and advanced knowledge base is, therefore, not the intellectual acceptance of the need but rather financial resources and human capacity. To return to one of my favorite fields, languages and linguistics, it is obvious that Albanian universities have a particular responsibility for teaching and research in Albanian language and linguistics and, for that matter, history and literature. Even if there are Albanian communities outside of Albania, it is not as easy to make the case for why a German, Spanish, or Swedish university would offer study programs in Albanian language, literature, and history. At least in larger countries, study offers can be coordinated, so that a less widely spoken and studied language is offered in one university only. One could also imagine coordination at a European level, along the lines of the Nordic countries, where the Nordic Africa Institute is located in Uppsala,[15] the Nordic Asia Institute in København,[16] and the Nordic Institute of Latin American Studies in Stockholm.[17] Regrettably, the Nordic Council of Ministers decided to discontinue the Nordic Asia Institute as of January 2024.[18] But here we enter the realm of the public responsibility.

Public Responsibility for Higher Education

The view of the public responsibility for higher education is one of the more marked differences in approach between the United States and Europe. In Europe, the public responsibility is so important that ministers of the EHEA twice stated that higher education is a public good and a public responsibility (Bologna Process 2001, 2003). The ministers were, however, not stating the obvious. Rather, they were expressing concern that what had been a defining feature of higher education in Europe could no longer be taken for granted.

At least this was how the Council of Europe interpreted the fact that ministers underlined this responsibility at two successive ministerial conferences, two years apart. We quickly decided that while the extent to which higher education is a public good is an interesting intellectual discussion, the operational part of the statement was about public responsibility. The Council of Europe, therefore, set out to explore what the statement actually meant and what measures were required to secure that higher education would remain a public responsibility in Europe. The Council had already started exploring the issue in the presentation in Athinai in February 2003, referred to earlier, but most of the Council's work focused on a thematic conference in September 2004, which led to a publication (Weber and Bergan 2005; Bergan 2005b) and ultimately to a recommendation adopted by the Committee of Ministers (Council of Europe 2007).

By "public responsibility," we understood this to mean the responsibility of public authorities for higher education,[19] and this is where the views predominant in Europe part ways with those predominant in the United States. In spite of some nuances, there really is such a thing as a European view of the role of public authorities, and it is linked to the responsibility of public authorities for the national education system, of which higher education is a part. The Council of Europe took the view not only that this responsibility is crucial, as the ministers had indicated, but also that it needed to be nuanced. In the recommendation, we suggested—and member states accepted—that public authorities have:

- *Exclusive* responsibility for the framework within which higher education and research is conducted
- *Leading* responsibility for ensuring effective equal opportunities to higher education for all citizens as well as ensuring that basic research remains a public good
- *Substantial* responsibility for financing higher education and research, the provision of higher education and research, as well as for stimulating and facilitating financing and provision by other sources within the framework developed by public authorities (Council of Europe 2007: para. 7; the italics are mine)

The framework largely refers to the education system. Even if public authorities should consult and seek input from both the higher education community and relevant external stakeholders,[20] no body other than the duly elected legislative body can pass legislation, and only the competent public authority—meaning the public authority that has legal competence in the matter—can issue regulations that specify or complement this legislation. The public authorities decide which qualifications make up the national qualifications framework,[21] and they decide the regulations and framework for quality assurance. For members of the EHEA, this responsibility includes ensuring that national provision is compatible with the Overarching Framework of Qualifications of the EHEA (Bologna Process 2005a, 2005b) and the Standards and Guidelines for Quality Assurance in the EHEA (generally known as the ESG, for European Standards and Guidelines) (Bologna Process 2015c). This does not mean that public authorities carry out quality assurance themselves. To the contrary, the ESG stipulates that agencies should be independent and act autonomously and that they should have full responsibility for their operations and the outcomes of those operations without third-party influence (Standard 3.3). However, as specified in ESG Standard 3.2, quality assurance agencies operate on a mandate from the competent public authority. In most European countries, the competent public authority is national but in countries with a federal system, like Belgium, Bosnia and Herzegovina, or Germany, it can be located at the regional or, in some countries, even the local level, or the competence can be mixed depending on the topic.

The leading responsibility of public authorities for ensuring effective equal opportunities means that while it is ultimately the higher education institutions that ensure these opportunities, they do so within a framework established by public authorities. Institutions are subject to guidance and possibly sanctions by public authorities should they fail to uphold equal opportunities. To take a very obvious example, universities cannot establish discriminatory admissions practices, which would, in much of Europe, extend to any practice favoring children of alumni or donors.

Likewise, the substantial responsibility for financing and providing higher education implies that all funding, whether public or private, must be provided within the framework and regulations established by public authorities. It also means that private higher education institutions must operate within the framework that public authorities have established for the education system of which the institutions are or wish to be a part. Public authorities may allow institutions to operate from their territory without being part of their education system, as is the case with some foreign private institutions in some European countries, but they may also choose not to allow this. Greece, for example, which has a very restrictive view of private higher education as part of its system, does allow some foreign institutions to operate in Greece without belonging to the Greek system.[22]

In Europe, there is broad agreement both that public authorities are responsible for the education system and the framework within which higher education is provided and that public authorities have a strong responsibility for safeguarding the fundamental values of higher education, such as academic freedom, institutional autonomy, and student and staff participation in higher education governance.[23] This is a responsibility public authorities share with the higher education community of institutions, faculty, staff, and students, but public authorities can take measures to protect or, on the contrary, threaten these fundamental values that other actors cannot take. For example, the Hungarian authorities revised the higher education legislation, in 2018, in a way that targeted the CEU and in effect forced it to move from Hungary to Austria. In early 2016, the Turkish government targeted members of the academic community who criticized the government policies toward the country's Kurdish community, and it also targeted the academic community as part of its extensive measures against Turkish civil society following the failed coup in July 2016 (European Education and Culture Executive Agency, Eurydice 2018: 42; Matei 2020).

There is also broad agreement that public authorities have the responsibility for ensuring equal opportunity, including in higher education, and that higher education is subject to general laws and regulations; for example, concerning accounting and safety in laboratories. Again, these are responsibilities shared with the higher education community but for which public authorities have a specific role. Universities can, for example, adopt security measures that are stricter than those mandated by general public regulations, but they cannot invoke institutional autonomy to institute laxer security.

The issues on which there is ongoing debate, which I have elsewhere referred to as "twilight zones" (Bergan 2005b), are quite numerous and can only be touched on here. They have, however, been explored in greater detail elsewhere (Bergan 2005b; Bergan, Egron-Polak, and Noorda 2020). One issue may illustrate the kind of challenges we face. Higher education institutions are responsible for the information they provide to students, employers, and, particularly, prospective students. But is anyone other than the institution itself responsible for verifying that information or at least for intervening in cases of blatant abuse? Nobody has, to my knowledge, argued that there should be any kind of comprehensive control with the information provided by institutions, nor would it be possible to take such measures in democratic societies without infringing on institutional autonomy. At the same time, however, prospective students and their parents need reliable information on programs and institutions to help them make sound decisions about where they will invest significant time and financial resources over the next few years by choosing to enroll in study program A at institution Y rather than in program B at institution Z or any other program that looks tempting. At least in Europe, the choice has not been made easier by the advent of providers—I use this term rather than "institutions" for a reason—that operate outside of national education systems and that may largely or entirely offer online courses. Some may be good, but some are not, and they are unlikely to inform prospective students about their lack of quality.

To take an example close to home: when she finished secondary school, my youngest daughter was uncertain about what she wanted to do next, but she was interested in information and communication. She found a school that promised a qualification that was well recognized on the labor market. The school was not a bogus institution and offered in person courses at a physical location. Nevertheless, something did not sound right. It turned out that my suspicion was correct: the school was not recognized as part of the French education system, nor of any other system for that matter. It may well be that the program it offered was of acceptable quality and that the specific part of the labor market for which it prepared its students was eager to recruit its graduates. It may well be that my daughter would have earned a qualification that would be useful as long as she was happy to stay in this segment of the labor market. Had she wanted to pursue further studies or change her professional orientation, however, the fact that she would have had an unrecognized qualification could easily have meant that she would have needed to start from scratch. As it happened, I had the professional experience to read between the lines in the information the institution provided—which was probably technically correct but woefully inadequate—and the contacts to verify whether my suspicion was justified. Many prospective student and their parents do not, however, have this background. For the story, my daughter took a two-year degree in communication at a public university, decided this was not quite what she wanted to do, and, in the end, pursued a master's degree in administration and tourism. Today, she is very happy working as a sales manager at a hotel in Strasbourg.

My contacts were with the French ENIC. This is the French member of the European Network of National Information Centres on recognition and mobility (the ENIC Network),[24] which is coordinated by the Council of Europe and UNESCO. For institutional and legal reasons, the European Commission coordinates a network[25] that is formally separate but the two networks largely function as one.[26] Each national center provides information on the institutions and programs belonging to the higher education system of the country for which it is responsible (so, in the case of the French ENIC, on the institutions and programs making up the French system) as well as on how foreign qualifications are generally recognized in this country, even if in most countries the final decision is the competence of individual higher education institutions. The ENIC should be the first port of call for anyone with questions on the status of institutions and their programs and qualifications but awareness of the ENICs is relatively low outside of the world of higher education. Awareness of the kind of questions prospective students and parents—or for that matter prospective employers—would do well to ask and what reality may be hidden behind seemingly trustworthy formulations is probably even lower. I sometimes say that, in Europe, students spend less time and effort verifying an institution where they plan to enroll for at least three years than they would spend verifying the state of a used car if they planned to buy one. So, even if no public authority could or should verify all information published by an education provider, educating the broader public about the kind of questions that should be asked, providing reliable information about an education system and its components, and, ultimately, calling out offenders—those that provide false or incomplete information—are a public responsibility. In Europe, it is one that each ENIC fulfills.

Multiple Purposes, Public Responsibility, and the Local Democratic Mission of Higher Education

We explore several aspects of the local democratic mission of higher education in subsequent chapters, but it may nevertheless be useful to spell out some implications here. In their work with their local communities, higher education institutions should seek to cover all the major purposes of higher education (see earlier) to fulfill their responsibility toward the community, which cannot be limited to economic development alone. Thus, both higher education institutions and local communities should seek cooperation that encompasses a broad range of issues. Higher education institutions may be well placed to help strengthen the local economy, but the overall cooperation can and should have a broader scope. Where the cooperation focuses on the local economy, all partners should seek to ensure that this cooperation helps improve opportunities for local residents; for example, through projects that help improve their qualifications, offer both hope and opportunities to those in the local community that are the least included in the formal economy and have low qualifications, or increase the capacity of local residents to organize themselves in civil society associations and organizations.

Higher education institutions could establish counseling arrangements and offer critical services to those in the community who can ill afford to pay for these, such as medical services and legal counseling, as shown by the examples from Iceland and the Czech Republic in Chapter 7. They can encourage their students to participate under the supervision of duly qualified professionals, and both higher education institutions and local authorities can find these qualified professionals in the local community. The assistance higher education institutions may be able to provide should be adapted to the needs of the community and be provided as a supplement rather than as competition to the services offered by local professionals.

Higher education institutions and their members, not least student associations, could help improve social inclusion by working with local authorities and associations to keep demotivated children and youths in school, show people from disadvantaged backgrounds that higher education is not out of reach and also show how completing their secondary education and aiming for higher education can improve both individual lives and the prospects of the community, as the examples of DCU and Queen's in Chapter 7 show.

Chapter 7 describes several examples of how universities in Europe work with their local communities in a variety of ways that further democracy and inclusion. But the responsibility does not rest with higher education alone. Local authorities and community leaders need to see the higher education institutions in their city or region as potential partners in addressing the needs and challenges of the community and not only those of its economy.

Higher education institutions as well as local authorities and civic leaders need to identify the potential of higher education in strengthening democracy, participation, and inclusion. It is to the democratic mission of higher education that we now turn, first for a global consideration, and then for a look at how this democratic mission can be made local.

Lessons Learned

Among the lessons learned from this chapter are the following:

- Even if the role of education in furthering economic development and in preparing students for the labor market has tended to dominate public debate in Europe, a realization has emerged that education—including higher education—needs to serve several purposes. The Council of Europe has identified these as preparation for the labor market, preparation for life as active citizens in democratic societies, personal development, and the development and maintenance of a broad and advanced knowledge base.
- While the purpose of higher education is not only to prepare students for the labor market, almost all study programs will need to consider students' employment prospects, identify competences that are relevant to the labor market, and present these in ways that future employers can relate to.
- Educational policymakers and practitioners—including those in higher education—need to work both to ensure equitable access to higher education and to improve the esteem for VET.
- Education laws often identify developing democratic citizenship as one of the key missions of education. However, we need to be explicit about the competences that European education systems should develop in their students both because these competences are essential and because describing them in such a way that they can be learned, taught, and assessed will help make preparation for life as active citizens in democratic societies a key purpose of education in practice.
- Higher education must develop a commitment to public space, so that democracy becomes more than the act of voting and includes citizen participation and deliberation. It must also develop a holistic view of democracy, so that students, graduates, and faculty are able and willing to weigh the long-term and short-term concerns and priorities and also to assess what priorities are most important to them, identify where compromises can be made, and determine what principles need to be upheld at all costs.

- To further students' personal development, higher education programs must develop competences like analytical and critical thinking skills, presentation skills, knowledge and critical understand of the self, empathy, flexibility and adaptability, and skills of listening and observing, and not least the ability and will to learn.
- The main obstacle to developing a broad and advanced knowledge base is not the intellectual acceptance of the need to do so but rather financial resources and human capacity. Study programs and research capacities in disciplines for which the perceived need is less important—such as less widely spoken languages—could be coordinated at the national and even European level.
- The view of the public responsibility for higher education is one of the more marked differences in approach between the United States and Europe. By "public responsibility," Europe understands this as the responsibility of public authorities for higher education.
- The Council of Europe maintains that public authorities have the
  - *Exclusive* responsibility for the framework within which higher education and research is conducted
  - *Leading* responsibility for ensuring effective equal opportunities to higher education for all citizens as well as ensuring that basic research remains a public good
  - *Substantial* responsibility for financing higher education and research, the provision of higher education and research, as well as for stimulating and facilitating financing and provision by other sources within the framework developed by public authorities (Council of Europe 2007: para. 7)
- In their work with their local communities, higher education institutions should seek to cover all the major purposes of higher education to fulfill their responsibility toward the community, which cannot be limited to economic development alone.

5

The Development of a Global Cooperation for the Democratic Mission of Higher Education

Nineteen sixty-eight is an important year in recent European history, and it started with a student revolt. In part, it was connected to the broader revolt directed against the U.S. role in the Vietnam War, where some of the strongest protests were organized on campuses in the United States. It was, however, also a more generalized protest against the prevailing political and societal order. Often, this took the form of far-left politics, not least in Germany (BRD), where the student leader Rudi Dutschke became perhaps the most prominent face of this movement as a leader of the Socialist Student Union. His prominence, or at least the fact that his name is still remembered, may also be due to the fact that he was gunned down in March 1968.[1] A part of this student movement veered into terrorism through the Rote Armée-Fraktion (Red Army faction), better known as Baader-Meinhof. In France, there was a widespread movement in May that started as a student protest and then took on a much broader aspect and almost brought down the government of General de Gaulle.[2] What is broadly known as "May 68" still holds an important place in French collective memory, and some of the student leaders became prominent in French public debate, notably Daniel Cohn-Bendit. He was expelled to Germany because he had double citizenship and later became a prominent leader of the Green Party in the European Parliament. In Eastern Europe, the "spring of 68" had even more wide-reaching consequences, with liberalization in Czechoslovakia under the leadership of Aleksander Dubček, which was brutally stopped through the Warsaw Pact invasion on August 21, 1968.[3]

The consequences of the student revolt starting in 1968 were important, but they played out differently in the United States and in (western) Europe. In the United States, the students' protests were part of the civil rights movement as well as a broader protest against the Vietnam War, and this movement made students much more aware of their role as actors in broader society (Gitlin 1993). Arguably, universities had become more aware of their role as social actors toward the end of the Cold War (Benson et al. 2017: 72, 77). In the United States, an important development was that the higher education community became more politically and societally engaged outside of campus. In Europe, the student protests led to greater internal democracy at universities, notably with substantial participation by students, nontenured faculty, and technical and administrative staff in university governance bodies.

Toward Transatlantic Cooperation on the Democratic Mission of Higher Education

This different emphasis on the role of higher education as a democratic actor in broader society and on greater internal democracy formed an interesting and important backdrop when the idea of a transatlantic cooperation arose in the late 1990s. The historic political changes in Europe following the fall of the Berlin Wall were, however, more important, also because the Council of Europe's Higher Education Committee had a chair who had lived through these changes and who had established contacts with Penn already before the changes.

Krzysztof Ostrowski was a Polish political scientist who had worked with Penn, in particular, with Professor Henry Teune, in the 1980s. Even if he traveled to the United States frequently, Ostrowski remained committed to his home country. He also had extensive contacts with the Russian higher education community at a time when there seemed to be hope for a movement toward democracy in Russia, even if neither Ostrowski nor many others had any illusions about the difficult road to be traveled or the many obstacles on the way. These, of course, in the end proved to be fatal to democratic development in the country, especially after the arrival to power of Vladimir Putin. Ostrowski was acutely aware of Poland's role as an important member of the European family, regardless of political borders. I rarely saw him as upset as when he recounted an early experience in the passport control at Frankfurt Airport, long before Poland became a member of the EU and a party to the Schengen Agreement, which abolished border controls between the participating countries. The hapless immigration officer asked Ostrowski how long he intended to stay in Europe, and Ostrowski told the officer in no uncertain terms that he had been born in Europe, had lived there all his life, and intended to remain here until the end of his days.

The 1980s and 1990s, when Ostrowski had frequent contacts with Penn, were a crucial time at this university, when it became acutely conscious of the discrepancy between the academic excellence for which it strove and the poverty of its immediate neighborhood in West Philadelphia. This made the Penn leadership develop an institutional policy of community engagement (Benson, Puckett, and Harkavy 2007; Benson et al. 2017: 97–111). In 1992, the Netter Center for Community Partnerships[4] was established under the leadership of Ira Harkavy, to lead Penn's efforts in building mutually beneficial partnerships with its immediate neighborhood in West Philadelphia. This partnership would help revitalize the local community while advancing the university's academic mission. These developments at Penn certainly influenced Ostrowski's thinking about how local engagement was a significant aspect of the democratic mission of higher education.

Ostrowski's many activities included his role as the Polish governmental member[5] of the Council of Europe's Higher Education Committee. This committee, which had a variety of names throughout its existence, had one academic and one ministry representative from each state party to the European Cultural Convention,[6] and, as we saw previously, the Cultural Convention provides the framework for the Council's program on education and culture. Crucially, in the 1990s, the Cultural Convention was the first step for the countries of Central and Eastern Europe, and some other countries, toward joining the Council of Europe as members.[7] Ostrowski was the chair in 1999–2001 after having been vice chair in 1997–1999. That put him in a good position to encourage the Council of Europe to work on the democratic mission of higher education.

Ostrowski brought the Council of Europe's education sector into contact with Teune and Harkavy. By coincidence, the education sector had two officials with long-established contacts with the United States and an interest in transatlantic cooperation: its director Gabriele Mazza[8] and I. We had both been AFS exchange students to the United States, and Mazza had also undertaken part of his university studies there. Ostrowski as committee vice chair and then chair, Teune and Harkavy from Penn, and Mazza and I in the Council Secretariat formed a very useful alliance.

The timing of Ostrowski's initiative was fortunate also because the Council of Europe had started exploring the democratic mission of education more broadly. A legislative reform program for higher education had been launched already in 1992 to advise new member states in Central and Eastern Europe in their efforts to develop and adopt more democratic higher education laws.[9] The democratic mission of education got a further boost in 1997, when the

Second Summit of Heads of State and Government of the Council of Europe adopted a declaration that expressed their "desire to develop education for democratic citizenship based on the rights and responsibilities of citizens, and the participation of young people in civil society" (Council of Europe 1997: 4). They, therefore, decided to launch an initiative for EDC with a view to promoting citizens' awareness of their rights and responsibilities in a democratic society (Council of Europe 1997: 9).

Two years later, to mark the Council of Europe's Fiftieth Anniversary, the Committee of Ministers adopted the Budapest Declaration, in which the Council's member states vowed to combat racism, xenophobia, intolerance, and discrimination against minorities as well as to "build on the community of culture formed by a Europe enriched by its diversity, confident in its identity and open to the world," and "develop a new educational approach to democratic citizenship, based on the rights and responsibilities of citizens" (Council of Europe 1999).

The appendix to the declaration underlines that EDC provides citizens with a basis to play an active part in public life and thus to shape their own destiny and that of their society. Among the key issues identified in the appendix are the following:

- The evolving concept of democratic citizenship, in its political, legal, cultural, and social dimensions
- The core competences for democratic citizenship
- Learning democracy in school and university life, including participation in decision-making
- The links between the various approaches to Education for democratic citizenship based on citizens' rights and responsibilities such as human rights education, civic education, intercultural education, history teaching, democratic leadership training, conflict resolution and confidence building (Council of Europe 1999: appendix 3)

Several of the issues outlined were later reflected in the RFCDC (Council of Europe 2018b, 2018c, 2018d; see Chapter 3 for further details) as well as in the further development of the project on the democratic mission of higher education.

Out of the Declaration and Action Plan adopted by the Second Summit grew a project on EDC, which ultimately led to the adoption of a charter on EDC in 2010 (Council of Europe 2010, see Chapter 3). Before that, however, the Committee of Ministers adopted another recommendation that is, in my view, a much stronger statement than the vaguely worded charter, even if the 2002 Recommendation is less widely known. The 2002 Recommendation reiterates both that EDC is fundamental to the Council of Europe and that it should be at the heart of the reform and implementation of education policies (Council of Europe 2002). Crucially, the recommendation makes it clear that higher education is as important to EDC as any other part of the education system. The recommendation also outlines some competences that foreshadow the Council of Europe's RFCDC, such as:

- Settling conflicts in a non-violent manner
- Arguing in defense of one's viewpoint
- Listening to, understanding, and interpreting other people's arguments
- Recognizing and accepting differences; making choices, considering alternatives, and subjecting them to ethical analysis
- Developing a critical approach to information, thought patterns, and philosophical, religious, social, political, and cultural concepts (Council of Europe 2002 para. 2)

Complementary developments were occurring elsewhere. In the United States, forty-five academic leaders, including Harkavy, adopted the Wingspread Declaration, in December 1998, calling for a renewal of the civic mission of the American Research University (Boyte and Hollander 1999). The declaration voices some of the same concerns that were voiced in Europe and underlines not only that civic engagement is essential to a democratic society but that many Americans had withdrawn from participation in public affairs. It suggests not only that higher education could contribute to civic engagement but also that most research universities do not see this as their role. The Wingspread Declaration points out that U.S. universities have made considerable progress in increasing the diversity of their student bodies as well as their faculty, but the text is critical to the implementation of other key parts of their democratic mission. Among other things, the declaration expresses concern that leaders of research universities focus on the "efficiency of means" and neglect the continuing discussion about the civic purposes and democratic mission of higher education (Boyte and Hollander 1999: 8). The signers state that "a core element in the mission of the research university is to prepare students for engaged citizenship through multiple opportunities to do the work of citizenship" (9) and link this to the need for socially engaged scholarship as well as developing and maintaining ties to the local community.

Thanks to Harkavy and Teune, the Council of Europe knew about the Wingspread Declaration as well as the presidents' Fourth of July Declaration (Campus Compact 1999). Here, the signers challenge higher education to become engaged, through actions and teaching, with its communities and underline that institutions and their leaders have a fundamental task to "renew our role as agents of our democracy" (Campus Compact 1999: 1). The declaration underlines the importance of presidential leadership[10] but also that the civic mission must include all members of the academic community. Thanks to the contacts established and the budding cooperation, U.S. colleagues also knew about the Budapest Declaration and its emphasis on developing democracy both in and through education. Teune and Ostrowski were both key to establishing this transatlantic link.

Higher Education as a Site of Citizenship

The early phase of the EDC project focused on education as a site of citizenship. It was overseen by the Education Committee,[11] but the Higher Education and Research Committee decided to contribute a project on the University as a Site of Citizenship. The decision was, however, not uncontroversial in the committee. Some representatives felt that launching a project focusing on the role of higher education in furthering democracy strayed too far from what they felt to be the "real mission" of higher education and would make the committee too "political." Nevertheless, the proposal received strong support from many delegations, and, in the end, we were able to win acceptance for the project.

To my knowledge, the project on the University as a Site of Citizenship was the first Council of Europe project conducted jointly with partners in the United States. In one sense, it was unbalanced in that the European partner was an intergovernmental organization whereas the U.S. partner was a consortium of higher education organizations and institutions led by Harkavy of the Netter Center at Penn. In practice, however, the project functioned very well and led to a cooperation that has now entered its third decade. Fourteen U.S.[12] and twelve European universities[13] participated in the project, which was, in formal terms, two separate projects that were closely coordinated. The European project was conducted over two years, from March 1999 to March 2001. The European universities[14] represented a good spread in terms of both geography and type of institution, from relatively large classic universities to relatively new and more specialized institutions. From today's vantage point, it may be worth noting that both Russia and Ukraine were represented in the project, both with universities in cities or regions that play an important role in the Russian war on Ukraine. Samara is a region of considerable military importance, while Tavrichesky National University is located in several localities in Krym (Crimea), which has been under Russian occupation since 2014. It is also worth noting that one of the participating universities—Queen's—continues to play a crucial role in the further development of the project on the democratic mission of higher education.

Each university appointed a researcher to represent it in the project, which was overseen by a working group appointed by the Higher Education and Research Committee, in which U.S. representatives and the Council of Europe Secretariat also participated. Each researcher conducted surveys and other research at his or her own university and produced a project report for each institution. A grant of 25,000 US dollars from the National Science Foundation funded the U.S. research project, whereas the Council of Europe funded the European project.[15]

The research questions as well as the organization of the report had been agreed on among participants, so that each followed the same format. In reviewing the results of the project, it should be remembered that these reports are by now almost twenty-five years old. They give a good impression of views held and the state of affairs at the turn of the century/millennium but cannot be relied on to say much about current views. The brief presentation that follows relies on Frank Plantan's summary of the European project (Plantan 2004) as well as on my personal recollections.

One of the concerns that emerged quite clearly from the European project is the lack of student engagement with public space. In part, this translates into low participation in elections of student representatives in university governing bodies, which is even characterized as a *pervasive passivity* bordering on indifference" (Plantan 2004: 89, italics in the original). On the other hand, the reports for many of the universities made it clear that students had the feeling of not being heard. It is also interesting to see that the discussion we referred to in the project in the RFCDC (see Chapter 3) on whether schools and universities should seek to develop the practice of democracy or limit themselves to teaching its theory is also found in the project on the University as a Site of Citizenship. Institutions in countries that had a recent past under Communist regimes were largely negative to or even prohibited political parties on campus. Tavrichesky National University reported that it saw part of its education mission as "defending culture and education from political experiments" (Plantan 2004: 96). It is also worth noting that at the Lithuanian university in the project, student engagement had been strong in the period around independence but had diminished afterward. The Greek university reported a similar trend with a high degree of student engagement in the final period of the military dictatorship and the immediate aftermath of the restoration of democracy, in 1974, followed by diminished interest once democracy had been safely restored. This chimes with the observation reported by the French participant in the project that "it seems that the more democratic the society, the lower the participation rate" (Plantan 2004: 126).

For the purposes of this book, it is worth noting that even if there was considerable variation in the degree to which each university engaged in and with its local community, university-community cooperation was largely absent from the European responses. The University of Cergy-Pontoise was a marked exception, as it had been set up in a "new city"[16] on the periphery of Paris, and the university saw itself as having a mandate to "bring life to the town" (Plantan 2004: 110). This institution is also culturally and ethnically highly diverse even if its students are mainly recruited from its immediate environs. Queen's was another notable exception, as it had already embarked on the kind of community engagement that brought it to play a key role in later stages of the project, which is described in greater detail in Chapter 7.

The U.S. research project reported that an important distinction needed to be made between formal and actual practices of "shared governance" and also that, where faculty felt they had some say in decisions on resource allocation, they tended to be more positive toward democratic participation (Teune and Plantan 2001: 9). This project echoed the Fourth of July Declaration (Campus Compact 1999) in concluding that presidential leadership is crucial in determining to what extent a university is committed to civic education and to promoting democratic processes and decision-making on campus (Teune and Plantan 2001: 13). In the participating U.S. institutions, students played an active role, through formal representation, in deciding issues related to student life, and at one institution—San Francisco State University—students were also represented on the budget committee with voting rights (Teune and Plantan 2001: 14). Student representation on university governing bodies was nevertheless weaker in the United States than in Europe. On the other hand, the U.S. report brings out the importance of service learning in fostering civic engagement (17–18) and underlines the importance of community engagement (25–28). Both are areas where European higher education could learn from the United States.

Toward a Lasting Transatlantic Cooperation on the Democratic Mission

For several reasons, it took some time for the next phase of the cooperation to take off. The discussion within the committee that had preceded the project continued to an extent, even if the success of the project made the circle of critical voices smaller and less outspoken. The most active phase of the project coincided with the launch of the Bologna Process, which set out to create the EHEA[17] (see Chapter 1). The Bologna Process quickly took center stage in both the European higher education debate and the Council's higher education program, which also needed to devote quite some time and energy to developing good recognition practices following the entry into force[18] of the Lisbon Recognition Convention[19] in February 1999 following the fifth ratification by a state party and to developing the first subsidiary texts to the convention.

Within the Council, we were facing questions of whether it was appropriate that we cooperated with partners outside of Europe. These concerns, which were found in the Committee of Ministers as well as within the Secretariat, were twofold. On the one hand, there was a fear that cooperating with partners in the United States would take a toll on budgets that were already under pressure, even if the worst cost cutting periods were still to come. On the other hand, there was concern—especially in the Committee of Ministers—about "mission creep," at least in a geographic sense of the term. Several influential member states felt that the Council should focus on geographic Europe, and some Permanent Representations were even seemingly unaware of the fact that the European Cultural Convention included countries that were not Council of Europe members. The rapid expansion of Council membership in the 1990s (see Chapter 1) may be part of the background for these attitudes, but the argument that cooperation between Europe and other parts of the world should be undertaken in the framework of the UN was also used with some frequency. Linked to both sets of arguments was the fact that the Education program had not yet developed its position as a key element of the Council's work to further democracy, human rights, and the rule of law. This would be established within the next ten years, in no small part because of the work on EDC and the democratic mission of higher education.

The Council of Europe and the International Consortium (see later) also took the time to assess what form a more sustained transatlantic cooperation could take. The project on the University as a Site of Citizenship had been successful, but both partners were convinced that a sustained cooperation needed more than a new research project. That is why we decided to explore the policy implications of the democratic mission of higher education through a series of regular conferences that we came to label Global Fora. At the outset, that may have been a pretentious name for conferences where the vast majority of participants came from either Europe or the United States. However, there were also a few participants from other parts of the world, and, as we see later, the idea of organizing Global Fora gave us a broader goal to work toward. By then, much of the criticism of "out of area" cooperation in the Council of Europe had fallen silent, at least as long as the Global Fora could be held in Europe.

From the European side, the cooperation was driven by the Council of Europe, and within the Council by a tandem made up of the Higher Education and Research Committee and the Secretariat. It was important that this cooperation had strong support from successive chairs of the committee as well as from key people in the Secretariat, above all Mazza. From the U.S. side, Harkavy, Teune, and Penn, through the Netter Center, were the most important leaders, and they managed to involve broad parts of the U.S. higher education community through the International Consortium.[20] The International Consortium had been established in 1999 and was largely made up of U.S. members, but South African and Australian members had joined in 2002 and 2003, respectively, and there were contacts to South Korea.[21] The International Consortium was largely driven by its U.S. Steering Committee, chaired since the outset by Harkavy and originally made up of representatives of the American Association of Colleges and Universities, the American Association for Higher Education,[22] the American Council on Education, and Campus Compact. The International Consortium was later expanded to include the American Association of State Colleges and Universities, the AITF, Democracy Commitment, and Student Affairs Professionals in Higher Education. Through her long involvement with the International Consortium, Caryn McTighe Musil of the American Association of Colleges and Universities has been a particularly strong support for the cooperation. Even if it was largely made up of representatives of higher education NGOs, the International Consortium could not have developed as it did without the dedication of Harkavy and the Netter Center. Joann Weeks, the associate director of the Netter Center, played an important role as the day-to-day coordinator of the International Consortium. When Weeks retired in 2020, this role was taken over by Rita A. Hodges, who had already been involved in the cooperation for several years.

It is indicative of the importance of our transatlantic cooperation that the International Consortium was actually established in Strasbourg, when many U.S. partners were there for a meeting within the project on the University as a Site of Citizenship. The International Consortium played an important role in this project, but its role grew as the transatlantic cooperation developed into new forms. While the Global Fora would be the cornerstone of this cooperation, we did not want to limit it to a series of conferences with little follow-up in between and no durable trace in the academic literature. We, therefore, instituted regular meetings between the Council of Europe and the International Consortium. In the early days, these were held once or twice a year, normally in Strasbourg, connected to other activities, but occasionally also in Philadelphia, where Council of Europe representatives would contribute to conferences organized by the International Consortium. I remember, in particular, the impression caused by Josef Jařab. At the time, he was a Czech senator and a member of the Parliamentary Assembly of the Council of Europe, where he was the sponsor of and driving force behind a recommendation on academic freedom and university autonomy (Council of Europe 2006b). But Jařab was also a former rector of the University of Olomouc, a professor of English and American literature, and not least a long-time dissident under the former Communist regime. His low-key account of his experience as an engaged academic under difficult circumstances made a deep impression both at the first Global Forum and at a conference in Philadelphia.

At the time we reassessed the cooperation, the Council of Europe had just launched its Higher Education Series,[23] which was intended as a book series covering the most important topics in the European higher education debate. The first volume was published in December 2004 (Bergan 2004) and included Frank Plantan's article on the University as a Site of Citizenship (Plantan 2004), while the second volume (Weber and Bergan 2005) was dedicated to an exploration of the public responsibility for higher education (see Chapter 4). We, therefore, decided that we would publish a book on the basis of every forum. By now, the series includes twenty-six volumes, the latest of which was published in December 2023.[24]

The Responsibility of Higher Education for Democratic Culture

We had a chance to test the format of the renewed cooperation in June 2006, when we held the first Global Forum.[25] Together, the Council of Europe and the International Consortium prepared the forum carefully, but we did not need much time to decide on the venue. On both sides of the Atlantic, we felt that the Council of Europe Headquarters in Strasbourg would be the most appropriate venue. It would mark the importance of higher education to democracy and would also signal the importance of the cooperation to decision-makers in the Council of Europe, which is why we invited the Secretary-General of the Council of Europe Terry Davis[26] to speak. For U.S. participants, the Council was an attractive venue both because of its role in developing democracy, in particular, after the fall of the Berlin Wall, and its role as the seat of the European Court of Human Rights.

In choosing the theme of the forum, we wanted to underline both the role and the responsibility of higher education toward society and the fact that democracy will not be achieved through institutions and laws alone. The 2005 Summit of Council of Europe Heads of State and Government had accepted the idea of a democratic culture that enables institutions, laws, and elections to be democratic in practice (Council of Europe 2005b), and we wanted to demonstrate that higher education is essential to developing democratic culture. We, therefore, chose 'The Responsibility of Higher Education for a Democratic Culture" as the theme of the first Global Forum.

This forum set a precedent for later conferences by ensuring a good mix of presentations from both Europe and the United States. In addition to Jařab, speakers included Frank Rhodes, President Emeritus of Cornell University; Aziz Pollozhani, minister of education of North Macedonia;[27] and Thomas Hammarberg, the Council of Europe Commissioner for Human Rights and a former Secretary General of Amnesty International. Tatsiana Khoma, who represented the European Students Union, had a particular story to tell, as she had been expelled from her university in Belarus because of her work in the student movement. After this, several European universities vied to offer her a place of study, and she ended up studying economics in Wien. The sessions focused on developing a culture of democracy and underlined that this culture must be made sustainable. The fact that speakers came from different backgrounds was important for bringing out a good variety of perspectives.

As this was the first of what was intended to be a series of Global Fora, we put forward a draft declaration to clarify what the basis for our work on the democratic mission of higher education was and how this work could develop (Council of Europe/International Consortium 2006). The draft had been developed jointly by the Council of Europe and the International Consortium, and it was discussed thoroughly at the conference. The declaration has no formal status other than as an expression of the views of those who participated in the conference, but the Council's Higher Education and Research Committee later took note of it and accepted it as the basis for its further work on the democratic mission of higher education.

The declaration juxtaposes what it sees as the global spread of democratic ideas and societies and a persisting crisis of confidence. Had the declaration been written today, almost two decades later, it would probably have emphasized the crisis of confidence more strongly and been less optimistic about the spread of democracy. It makes the case for education and schooling as key forces in the development of societies and underlines that "democracy can only flourish with strong supportive institutions and laws and a pervasive democratic culture, which encompasses democratic values, ways of knowing and acting, ethical judgments, analytical competencies, and skills of engagement" (Council of Europe/International Consortium 2006: 2). The words are different, but many of the ideas they express later found their way into the RFCDC. These thoughts are reflected in the first book in the Council of Europe's Higher Education Series, which is based exclusively on the outcomes of the transatlantic cooperation (Huber and Harkavy 2007). To underline the importance of the cooperation, this book, as with every subsequent book on the basis of a Global Forum, except one, had coeditors from both Europe and the United States.

Converging Competences

The declaration laid the philosophical and ideological foundation for a cooperation that was intended to last. That intention could, however, become a reality only if the first Global Forum was followed up by further conferences and publications. As Musil says in the title of her article from the first Global Forum, we needed to be "knee-deep in democracy" (Musil 2007).

The next Global Forum was held a little over two years later, in October 2008, and once again the venue was the Council of Europe Headquarters in Strasbourg.[28] The theme for this forum was "Converging Competences: Diversity, Higher Education, and Sustainable Democracy." The forum followed up the emphasis on sustainable democratic culture that had been prominent at the first Global Forum and added a focus on competences, which is to say the outcomes of education. Again, the lineup of speakers was impressive, with the keynote delivered by Derek Bok, former president of Harvard University. The U.S. speakers also included two who continue to play an important role in the cooperation even today: Musil, of the American Association of Colleges and Universities, and Nancy Cantor, who was then chancellor of Syracuse University and later of Rutgers University–Newark. Students were also well represented, as Manja Klemenčič, a Slovenian now on the faculty of Harvard, was a former Secretary General of the European Students Union[29] and Ligia Deca was its president when she spoke at the conference. Deca has remained involved with the cooperation and was appointed minister of education of Romania in October 2022 after having been the education and science adviser to the president for several years.

In addition to the topic of converging competences, the presentations and discussions focused on the role of higher education in and for modern societies and for democracy and dialogue (Bergan and Damian 2010). In a set of recommendations and conclusion (Council of Europe/International Consortium 2008), which, again, had no formal status but proved very useful both for the further development of the cooperation and for the work of the Higher Education and Research Committee, participants reaffirmed several of the positions taken by the 2006 Global Forum, including a strong emphasis on democratic culture. They also recognized that the increasing diversity of both the U.S. and European societies is inadequately reflected in the higher education community, and they reaffirmed their commitment to fulfilling the full range of purposes of higher education as they had been officially defined by the Council of Europe the previous year (Bergan 2005b; Council of Europe 2007; see Chapter 4). Some of the recommendations made again foreshadow parts of the RFCDC, not least the need to develop a whole school/whole institution approach (Council of Europe 2018d: 89–100; 2020b: 37–43).

Reimagining Democratic Societies

Almost three years passed before the Council of Europe and the International Consortium could convene the Third Global Forum, and this time we moved out of Strasbourg. Thanks to the European Wergeland Centre[30] and its director Ana Perona Fjeldstad, we were able to hold this forum at the University of Oslo, my alma mater. A highlight was when the rector of the University, Ole Petter Ottersen, spontaneously took participants to the newly restored University Aula, which has mural paintings by Edvard Munch and where the Nobel Peace Prize ceremony was held until the Nobel Committee awarded the Peace Prize to Mikhail Gorbachev in December 1990, a month before he sent Soviet troops to quash the independence movement in Lithuania and Latvia. For security reasons, the ceremony was then moved to Oslo City Hall, where it has been held since.

The theme of the 2011 Oslo Global Forum[31] was "Reimagining Democratic Societies: A New Era of Personal and Social Responsibility" (Bergan, Harkavy, and van't Land 2013a). The speakers included Jan Egeland, who was, at the time, the director of the Norwegian Institute of International Affairs[32] and who was UN Undersecretary-General for Humanitarian Affairs and Emergency Relief Coordinator from 2003 to 2006, as well as Eduardo Padrón, the longtime President of Miami-Dade Community College and later a recipient of the Presidential Medal of Freedom.

The emphasis on "reimagining" reflected the fact that, even if at the time it was felt that democracy worked reasonably well in Europe and North America, there was some unease about how our democracies would develop, especially in the aftermath of the 2008 financial crisis. In Europe, Belarus was an obvious example of a society moving far away from democracy. Also in Europe, public protests against education policy—typically against the EHEA—had connotations of broader political protest, including against globalization. In the United States, the notion of locality was gaining importance, as shown by the emphasis on anchor institutions. That same year, a Council of Europe Group of Eminent Persons chaired by former German foreign minister Joschka Fischer had explored how diversity and freedom could be combined and identified eight major risks to democracy:

- Rising intolerance
- Rising support for xenophobic and populist parties
- Discrimination
- The presence of a population virtually without rights
- Parallel societies
- Islamic extremism
- Loss of democratic freedoms
- A possible clash between religious freedom and the freedom of expression (Council of Europe 2011a)

The reference to "democratic societies" rather than "democracy" continued the reflection on the importance of democratic culture, which had already been at the heart of the first two Global Fora (Bergan, Harkavy, and van't Land 2013b). The injunction to reimagine democratic societies was given added urgency one month after the conference, when, on July 22, 2011, Norway suffered its worst terrorist attacks since World War II. In two separate attacks, first on government buildings in Oslo and then against the summer camp of the Labor Party youth organization at Utøya, a single homegrown terrorist with an extreme-right agenda killed seventy-seven people, most of them young and politically active. As horrible as the killings were, the reaction of both civil society and Norway and of political leaders of all affiliations gave hope, since there was a strong call for more democracy rather than repression (Bergan 2013: 45–46).[33]

Higher Education for Democratic Innovation

The need to rethink democracy was also at the heart of the 2014 Global Forum[34] (Bergan, Gallagher, and Harkavy 2015), which was held at Queen's, thanks to Professor Tony Gallagher, who had been involved in the cooperation for many years. Belfast was a powerful setting for a conference on democratic innovation because of Northern Ireland's experience with community strife during the period known as the Troubles[35] and because of Queen's role as an engaged university taking measures to make both major communities, Catholic and Protestant, feel at home on campus (see Chapter 7). The presentations focused on the university and the city, innovation and inclusion, and new technologies.

The speakers this time included Ahmed Bawa of Universities South Africa and Walid Moussa, who was at the time a Maronite priest and president of Notre Dame University in Lebanon, and also three representatives of the Sandy Row community center with which Queen's works (McDonald et al. 2015; Gallagher and Harrison 2015). The Belfast Forum innovated by drawing on the local engagement of Queen's to offer participants a preconference day of community visits. These included visits to a science shop, after-school homework clubs, and the Sandy Row community center. I participated in the latter and found it particularly impressive, as is described in Chapter 7.

The role of universities in mediating and mitigating conflict (Bjeliš 2015; Hall 2015) and public engagement (Manners 2015) were key topics. For the purpose of this book, it is particularly important to note that this was the first Global Forum at which the importance of local community engagement and university-community cooperation was highlighted (Gallagher and Harrison 2015; Harkavy 2015; Bergan 2015). It was, therefore, a first step on the road that led the Council of Europe to initiate European cooperation on the local democratic mission of higher education, which we explore in Chapter 6.

A Democratic Imperative

The fact that many Europeans and, certainly, the Council of Europe as well as many in the United States felt that democracy was increasingly under pressure is reflected in the title of the fourth Global Forum:[36] Higher Education for Diversity, Social Inclusion, and Community: A Democratic Imperative (Bergan and Harkavy 2018). This time, we moved to southern Europe, to LUMSA University in Roma,[37] in June 2017. Again, three years had passed since the previous forum. Reverting to a schedule of a Global Forum every two years was one of the recommendations by participants at the Rome Forum.

The 2017 Global Forum was held under the impact of what Europeans tend to refer to as "the refugee crisis" (i.e., the rapid increase in the number of refugees from the Middle East—in particular, Syria—from the summer of 2015), which challenged European societies in many ways and, among other things, led to the Council of Europe and partners developing the EQPR, which is described in Chapter 8. It would be an exaggeration to claim that "the refugee crisis" caused xenophobia in Europe, because xenophobia existed already, but it strengthened hostility toward foreigners and others felt to be "different from us" in ways that are still felt in European politics. For both U.S. and European participants, the election of Donald Trump to the U.S. presidency was also of great concern, even if the worst consequences of his presidency had not yet been borne out, which comprised concern for how foreigners were treated, including the notion that undesirable foreigners could be kept out of the country by building a wall on the border with Mexico and that there were no moral or legal obstacles to separating immigrant children from their parents. The broader background to the 2017 Global Forum was an increasingly polarized political and societal debate and the diminished ability and even will of political actors to seek a common ground and find solutions across political divides. The notion that facts may be irrelevant and that there can be such a thing as "post-truth" politics or a "post-truth" era (Bergan 2018; Pasquarella 2018) were also on participants' minds.

Both a conference session on inclusion and diversity in higher education and a specific session on how higher education can cater to refugees and migrants were complemented by a session on "Universities and Their Communities—Role as Anchor Institutions," with presentations based on the experience of South Africa (Bawa 2018), Southeast Europe (Bjeliš 2018), and the United States (Cantor and Englot 2018; Taylor, Luter, and Buggs 2018) as well as a reflection on possible European policy perspectives on universities and their communities (Smith 2018). The forum was preceded by a small-scale conference on the local mission of higher education, held at the premises of the Congregation for Catholic Education, which was another important step toward the Council's project on the local democratic mission (Chapter 6).

Academic Freedom, Institutional Autonomy, and the Future of Democracy

In 2019, the Global Forum returned to where it had started: the Council of Europe Headquarters in Strasbourg (Bergan, Gallagher, and Harkavy 2020).[38] It took place with the background not only of increasing concerns about a backlash of democracy in both Europe and the United States but also of the higher education community coming under strong pressure in several countries of the EHEA (European Education and Culture Executive Agency, Eurydice 2018: 42; see Chapter 4 for a more detailed discussion) and, in particular, the Hungarian government's attack on the Central European University through the amendments to the higher education law in 2017 (Chapters 1 and 4). We, therefore, felt it was urgent to consider academic freedom and institutional autonomy and relate both to the future of democracy. It was important to make the case that neither is a question of privilege but rather of the democratic nature of our society. One cannot imagine that academic freedom or institutional autonomy could be fully implemented except in a society imbued with democratic culture, just as one cannot imagine a fully democratic society that would not practice academic freedom and institutional autonomy.

Even though the 2019 Global Forum was also preceded by a smaller conference on the local mission of higher education, less attention was devoted to university-community cooperation than at the previous two Global Fora. On the other hand, we had more presentations with a perspective from outside of Europe and the United States than at previous fora: East Asia (Dang and Kamibeppu 2020), Australia (Nyland and Davies 2020), and the Mediterranean with an emphasis on North Africa (Scalisi and Marchionne 2020). The OAS, which had joined the cooperation in 2018, contributed a presentation, and IAU remained strongly involved as a co-organizer of the forum, as did the Magna Charta Observatory.

The forum was held at a time when work was underway to revise or add to the Magna Charta Universitatum (Magna Charta Observatory 1988), which in the end resulted in a supplementary text (Magna Charta Observatory 2020). While the preceding Global Fora had not adopted statements or declarations, we now felt it was important that this transatlantic cooperation, which was already expanding its geographic scope, speak out, and that it was particularly important to do so at a Global Forum organized at Council of Europe Headquarters. The Global Forum participants, therefore, adopted a declaration (Bergan, Gallagher, and Harkavy 2020: 251–255).[39] The declaration makes the case for close links between these fundamental values of higher education and democracy itself and suggests that the future of democracy is at risk without academic freedom and institutional autonomy. It also underlines the importance of democratic debate on campus and suggests that "any limits on freedom of expression must be based on protection of the specific rights of others (e.g., to protect against discrimination or defamation) rather than on expediency or to advance a single political ideology" (Bergan, Gallagher, and Harkavy 2020: 252). It also makes the case that colleges and universities have an institutional responsibility to work in democratic partnership with their community: "demonstrate[ing] openness, transparency, responsiveness and accountability as well as the will and ability to work with and contribute to the communities in which colleges and universities reside." Participants could not know that, less than a year later, COVID-19 would fundamentally change the way higher education worked and that holding major international gatherings face-to-face would not be possible for some time to come.

The Impact of COVID-19

The COVID-19 pandemic appeared, in at least China, in the fall of 2019, even if the world was largely unaware of the pandemic and its potential impact. In early 2020, some people started wearing face masks in European airports, and, in late January, I for the first time saw immigration officials wearing masks, in the passport control in Bucureşti. When I asked my local pharmacy whether wearing a face mask when traveling was advisable, they answered that it probably could not hurt. The COVID-19 pandemic struck Europe, North America, and other parts of the world with full force as of February to March 2020. Higher education institutions quickly had to move their teaching and learning online, as did primary and secondary schools, where students and their parents were probably even less well prepared for this rapid shift. Four of the leaders of the cooperation published an opinion piece in University World News in April 2020 arguing that universities must shape the post-COVID-19 world (Harkavy et al. 2020), and we quickly decided we needed to follow up this brief article with a more substantial book on the higher education response to COVID-19 (Bergan et al. 2021).

It is indicative of the state of our understanding of COVID-19 in the spring of 2020 that we felt we needed to act fast to ensure that the book would still be topical when it was published. All of our invited authors rose to the challenge. We got the last submissions by the end of August 2020, and the book was published six months later. This was the first book we edited together that was not based on a Global Forum, but, once it was published, we organized several webinars to discuss its contents. In addition to the main webinar launching the book, organized by the IAU and Hilligje van't Land, we held one in Spanish aimed at a Latin American audience, one aimed at an Irish audience—both facilitated by Ronaldo Munck and DCU—as well as a podcast aimed at a U.S. audience and produced by Marisol Morales, at the time of Campus Compact.

We wanted to provide a broad overview of issues and experiences both geographically and thematically. The book, therefore, provides an overview of challenges and responses as seen by higher education leaders and representatives of public authorities as well as reflections on the challenges faced in specific policy areas like academic freedom and institutional autonomy, recognition of qualifications, quality assurance, and financing higher education. We included articles presenting the perspectives of students and higher education staff. In addition to contributions from Europe and the United States, we had articles based on the experience of Africa (in particular, Uganda), Japan, and Latin America (in particular, Ecuador).

The work on this book also stimulated reflection within the Council of Europe on the broader education response to COVID-19. The Education Committee had been the first Council of Europe steering committee to meet online, on April 24, 2020,[40] and a second meeting in June approved a proposal to develop an action plan and to prepare an extraordinary ministerial conference. Luckily, in April, we had agreed that if our committee chair, Maria Fassari, lost connection, I would step in until she could log back on. She did lose connection, and I had to chair the meeting for quite some time before the chair's connection was restored. After the April meeting, we were all drained, but, by June, a large online meeting already felt like routine. The Education Department quickly set up a dedicated web page,[41] and the extraordinary ministerial conference was held online in October 2020, under the Greek presidency of the Committee of Ministers.[42] The conference adopted a declaration on the education response to COVID-19 (Council of Europe 2020b) and endorsed the Roadmap for Action that the Education Department had developed (Council of Europe 2020c).

The Need for Higher Education Leadership

One of the minor consequences of the COVID-19 pandemic was that the seventh edition of the Global Forum could not be held as foreseen in 2021. It would have been challenging for most European participants and almost impossible for participants from the United States and other parts of the world to travel at that time. An online event would not have offered the possibilities for personal interaction between participants that has proved to be such an important part of the forum. For an event that is global in scope, juggling the time zones of the world would also be an almost impossible task, as we have seen even with our regular meetings of cooperation partners. We started regular online meetings well before COVID-19 hit, and while these meetings are at comfortable times for those of us based in Europe or on the U.S. East Coast, our colleague in California has to log in for a very early morning coffee and our Australian colleague has to stay up late at night. We, therefore, decided to postpone the Global Forum for one year and were in the end able to gather at DCU in June 2022, thanks to the hospitality of Professor Munck, who has been involved in the cooperation for several years on behalf of Campus Engage Ireland,[43] and the DCU president, Professor Daire Keogh.

By this time, what had started as a transatlantic cooperation had gone global. The OAS had already joined the cooperation in 2018 and contributed a presentation to the 2019 Global Forum. The IAU had contributed to our cooperation for several years, starting with then IAU president Goolam Mohamedbai's presentation to the first Global Forum in 2006. Van't Land had contributed to several Global Fora and also been involved in the planning and running of the cooperation from her previous position in the IAU Secretariat. After she was appointed Secretary General, she proposed to the IAU Administrative Board that the IAU formally join the cooperation, which it did in 2019. Two years later, we translated the broadened scope of our project by renaming it the Global Cooperation for the Democratic Mission of Higher Education.

In planning the 2022 Global Forum, we felt we needed to underline that higher education must lead and not only adjust to societal development. What we had seen in both Europe and the United States but also elsewhere in the world since the previous forum three years earlier underlined that the values on which higher education is based, as well as the knowledge and understanding that higher education provides, are crucial to developing the kind of societies in which we would wish our children and grandchildren to live. In many ways, the Global Cooperation has been guided by what the Chilean sociologist Eugenio Tironi said about education: if you want to answer the question "what kind of education do we need?" you first have to answer another question: "what kind of society do we want?" (paraphrased from Tironi 2005).

We, therefore, decided to focus the forum on the need for higher education to take a leading role in developing the kind of society we want and chose the title, "Higher Education Leadership for Democracy, Sustainability, and Social Justice"[44] (Bergan, Harkavy, and Munck 2023). The program reflected the broad scope of our ambitions through sessions focusing on how universities and colleges can work together to respond to populist attacks on democracy itself, how a commitment to the UN Agenda 2030 and related Sustainable Development Goals contributes to the democratic mission, how academia can engage in social and racial justice work within and beyond its campus, how institutional practices can help sustain and engage the most at-risk students, and how universities can build relationships with local communities, especially those most devastated by the pandemic and its aftermath, to address inequalities.

The program also reflected the fact that the forum was incorporated as part of the program of the Irish presidency of the Council of Europe's Committee of Ministers. The Irish minister for further and higher education, research, innovation, and science, Simon Harris, spoke at the opening, and his colleague Thomas Byrne, the minister of state for European affairs, offered closing remarks. This was the first time we had had two current ministers speaking at the same forum. We also had a more global group of speakers than at previous fora, with Argentina, Australia, Brazil, Mexico, Peru, and South Africa represented. Speakers from the United States and Europe were also more diverse in both personal background and geographic representation than previously.

From Transatlantic to Global and Local Cooperation

What started as a transatlantic cooperation and even met with some resistance from Council of Europe member states who felt the Council's Education program should not look beyond Europe, has now developed into a global cooperation. The global dimension was somewhat present from the first Global Forum, mostly through the IAU. Before that, the European and U.S. research on the University as a Site of Citizenship project had been followed up by studies in Australia and South Korea, and both Australia and South Africa had joined the International Consortium. Nevertheless, it was with the formal adhesion of the OAS and the IAU and the transformation of the undertaking into the Global Cooperation for the Democratic Mission of Higher Education that our cooperation took a decisive step beyond Europe and North America. Consolidating this global scope is one of the main challenges the partners will face over the next few years. The obstacles are financial as well as practical, and they touch on the governance of the Global Cooperation as well as exploring the possibility of holding future Global Fora outside of Europe.

In parallel to developing the global scope of our cooperation, the local dimension of the democratic mission of higher education took on increasing importance. This was largely thanks to the participation of the AITF in the International Consortium. Both presentations at the 2011 and 2014 Global Fora and continuing discussions among partners convinced the Council of Europe of the need to explore how a European platform could strengthen the contribution of higher education to furthering local democracy in Europe. It is to the development of this mission that we turn in Chapter 6.

Lessons Learned

The main lessons learned in this chapter include:

- In both Europe and the United States, 1968 marks a growing awareness of the importance of higher education to developing democratic citizenship. In Europe, the developments often summarized as the "fall of the Berlin Wall" (1989) further improved awareness of the importance of democracy.
- A transatlantic cooperation driven by colleagues affiliated with Penn's Netter Center and the Council of Europe developed from the late 1990s. It built on important initiatives on both sides of the Atlantic, such as the Wingspread Declaration and the presidents' Fourth of July Declaration in the United States and the Second Summit of Council of Europe Heads of State and Government as well as the Council's Budapest Declaration.
- A project on the University as a Site of Citizenship in 1999–2001 was the first step in this transatlantic cooperation. It was followed by regular Global Fora from 2006 onward. The seventh Global Forum was held in 2022.
- In the Council of Europe, those advocating transatlantic cooperation on the democratic mission of higher education had to overcome arguments maintaining, on the one hand, that the Council of Europe should not cooperate with non-European partners and, on the other hand, that the Council's higher education program should focus on structural reform and the recognition of qualifications.
- The transatlantic cooperation developed into a truly Global Cooperation for the Democratic Mission of Higher Education through the adhesion of the OAS in 2018 and the IAU in 2019. Consolidating the global scope of the cooperation is one of the main challenges the partners will face over the next few years.
- The seven Global Fora held since 2006 have all focused on key aspects of democracy: the responsibility of higher education for democratic culture (2006); the importance of competences and diversity (2008); reimagining democratic societies, with an emphasis on personal and social responsibility (2011); democratic innovation, including the role of universities in mediating and mitigating conflict (2014); diversity, social inclusion, and community as a democratic imperative (2017); academic freedom, institutional autonomy, and the future of democracy (2019); and the need for higher education to lead and not only adjust to societal development, with

an emphasis on leadership for democracy, sustainability, and social justice (2022).

- The Global Cooperation was quick to address the impact of COVID-19 on higher education, and, in particular, on its democratic mission through a book and series of webinars and a podcast.
- Much of the early work on the democratic mission of higher education foreshadowed the Council of Europe's RFCDC.
- The transatlantic and later global cooperation has proved to be an invaluable exercise in multiperspectivity.
- At least from the 2011 Global Forum, a perception of increased threats to democracy, societal polarization, and disregard for academic knowledge and understanding were an important part of the backdrop for the work. The Council of Europe came to refer to these developments as a backlash of democracy.
- The local democratic mission of higher education was discussed as one of several topics at the Global Fora in 2011 and 2014 but only developed as a topic in its own right at the first of three invitational seminars as of 2017.

6

Toward a European Platform for the Local Democratic Mission of Higher Education

Especially in the smaller European countries, the university was and often still remains national in scope. As we see in Chapter 7, the Universities of Iceland, Malta, and San Marino all conduct significant outreach activities and work with broader society in a variety of ways, but it is not always easy to distinguish between their national roles and what they do in and with their local communities. My alma mater, the University of Oslo, was established in 1811 as the Royal Frederik University—named for the Danish king at the time, since Norway was part of Denmark, if only for another three years. Its mission was seen as national and even as one of nation building. That view of its mission was not shared by the Danish authorities.[1] Even though some research and academic teaching were located elsewhere, it was only in 1946 that Norway gained its second university, in Bergen, with roots in the Bergen Museum going back to 1825.[2] In Denmark, the University of København was established in 1479,[3] whereas the second-oldest university in the country, Aarhus, was established only in 1928.[4]

Whether they saw their mission as national or not, many European universities have long had good contacts with their immediate environments. However, they have less often seen cooperation with their local community as part of their core mission, and much of the contact has been with local economic actors. This is, of course, consistent with the commonly held view that the main mission of higher education is to prepare students for the labor market (Chapter 4). This chapter explores how the global cooperation has also led to a focus on the local democratic mission of higher education and how such a platform could be developed further as part of European cooperation.

The Example of U.S. Anchor Institutions

As noted in Chapter 5, Europe has strong traditions involving students, faculty, and staff in higher education governance, whereas the United States has a stronger tradition of higher education institutions engaging as actors in broader society. The latter includes engagement with the local community. It was important to what is now the Global Cooperation for the Democratic Mission of Higher Education that the AITF[5] became a partner in the International Consortium. It was also significant that the International Consortium chair, Ira Harkavy, was both the founding chair of the AITF and the founding director of Penn's Netter Center for Community Partnerships.[6]

As we saw in the previous chapter, the local dimension of the democratic mission was present in the project on the University as a Site of Citizenship (Plantan 2004) as well as in the early Global Fora, the first of which included a representative of the Congress of Local and Regional Authorities in Europe, which is a body within the Council of Europe.[7] It was, however, at the Global Forum held at Queen's in June 2014 that university-community cooperation was highlighted more broadly. Participants in this Global Forum had an opportunity to participate in site visits during a preconference day. These site visits highlighted the role of Queen's in working with its local community to improve social inclusion and education opportunities. This important role was further highlighted at the conference and in the publication that followed through two powerful contributions, one of which outlined the role of Queen's as an engaged university in a divided society (Gallagher and Harrison 2015), while the other illustrated how this civic engagement could be carried out in practice through work with a community center and local youths in a disadvantaged neighborhood (McDonald et al. 2015).

Also at the 2014 Global Forum, presentations on how Widener University had managed to turn its relationship with its local community in Chester, Pennsylvania, from one of conflict to one of collaboration (Harris and Pickron-Davis 2015), on higher education institutions as pillars of their communities (Guarasci and Maurrasse 2015), and on a historical overview of U.S. higher education, community engagement, and democratic innovation (Harkavy 2015) provided what was likely the first major presentations of the AITF to a European audience. These presentations placed the development of the AITF, which was founded in 2009, into the broader context of how the civic and democratic mission of higher education has developed in the United States. It may be interesting to note that, at the time, AITF had around six hundred members, whereas the number is now close to one thousand.[8]

Harkavy presented a strong argument for local community engagement in terms that resonated with higher education leaders: "When institutions of higher education give very high priority to actively solving real-world problems in their communities, a much greater likelihood exists that they will significantly advance learning, research, teaching and service and thereby simultaneously reduce barriers to the development of mutually beneficial, higher education–community partnerships. More specifically, by focusing on solving universal problems that are manifested in their local communities (such as poverty, poor schooling, inadequate healthcare), institutions of higher education can generate knowledge that is both nationally and globally significant and be better able to realise what I view as their primary mission of contributing to a healthy, democratic society" (Harkavy 2015: 276). He elaborated on John Dewey's famous proposition that democracy must begin at home by adding that the home of democracy is the engaged neighborly university and its local community partners (Harkavy 2015: 280), which Harkavy illustrated through the example of Penn and its strong cooperation with its local community since 1985. This included, for example, revising an undergraduate seminar at Penn in medical anthropology to focus on community health and nutrition in West Philadelphia.

For my part, I explored the potential of higher education as community actors in Europe (Bergan 2015). I linked this potential to the need for institutions to fulfill the four major purposes of education as defined by the Council of Europe (see Chapter 4) and to see these as complementary rather than contradictory. As an example, many of the qualities and competences that make graduates attractive on the labor market also make them well suited to engage as active citizens in democratic societies and help their personal development. I outlined some major challenges facing European societies at the time and tried to identify possible higher education responses.

One of the issues was the marginalization of many young people from disadvantaged backgrounds, and the opportunity for universities to both motivate young people for higher education and help them not only access a university but also complete their study programs. The Roma population is in a particularly precarious situation in many European countries, for reasons that have to do with the lifestyle and culture of the community as well as with attitudes to Roma in broader society, including among local community leaders. Universities could be inspired by the experiences of Widener, Queen's, and others to develop policies and practices that seek to bring the Roma community into a relationship of cooperation and improved opportunities with both local communities and the local university. Relations to the Muslim communities in countries or regions where it is a significant but relatively recent and marginalized minority is another area where universities can be of assistance.[9] They can not only work with the Muslim community to improve access to higher education but also help improve the knowledge and understanding of the Muslim community and of Islam in the broader society, of course, without any idea of proselytization. The point is to improve the knowledge of Islam as a cultural community and also develop an understanding in largely secularized societies of why religion plays an important role for many people, not least among those belonging to cultural and religious minorities. An example from my home country shows this was possible with a different minority, in that the Catholic Church—which was and still is a small minority in Norway—has gone from being marginalized and faced with hostility to being an accepted and integrated part of Norwegian society (Gran, Gunnes, and Langslet 1993). Many Catholics in Norway are immigrants, but many are also native-born first-generation Catholics—in other words, converts—as am I. Just as this small minority was integrated and became respected through an institutional framework (as well as hard work), so higher education can and should provide an institutional framework through which present-day minorities can improve their opportunities and standing in society. In the case of Catholics in Norway, part of the key to success was engaging with broader society rather than remaining in a relatively closed circle of like-minded people. That is also an important lesson for higher education.

I also underlined the importance of universities fostering civic engagement and emphasized that democratic societies will remain democratic only if citizens engage in public space. I argued that while Europe probably trains more highly qualified specialists than ever before, it is more questionable whether we educate those specialists, meaning that we provide them with the transversal competences they need to put their specialist competences into a broader societal context, enabling them not only to ask critical questions about their role and that of their discipline in broader society but also to find the answers to the critical questions (Bergan 2015: 296). The article also looks at what different groups within the higher education community as well as local community partners could do to develop institutional strategies for community engagement, and it argues the need for a European movement of anchor institutions.

The Local Mission of Higher Education in a European Setting

The considerable space given to exploring the local role of universities at the 2014 Global Forum was followed by discussions between Harkavy, David Maurrasse (founding chair and director of AITF, respectively), and me on how we could best explore and raise awareness of what we still called the local mission of higher education at a European level. We decided we needed to organize specific meetings on the local mission rather than continue to deal with it as one of several topics at the next Global Forum, and we decided to start modestly with a small invitational seminar. This was scheduled to take place in Paris in June 2016, but a combination of floods due to heavy rain[10] and transportation strikes[11] made us reschedule.

In the end, we held the seminar on the eve of the 2017 Global Forum. Thanks to Father Friedrich Bechina, FSO,[12] we were able to hold it at the Congregation for Catholic Education, of which he was the undersecretary. Both participants and organizers found the seminar stimulating, and we organized two further similar gatherings over the next two years. The third was also held back-to-back with but separately from a Global Forum, in Strasbourg in June 2019, whereas the second meeting was held as a stand-alone event at DCU in October 2018, thanks to the invitation of Professor Ronaldo Munck. On this occasion, we took the opportunity to organize a public debate on the role of higher education in furthering democracy in downtown Dublin, in cooperation with the Irish University Association. The meeting organized at and by DCU also gave rise to a book (Bergan, Harkavy, and Munck 2019a).

Each of the three seminars included some twenty-five to thirty participants, and they were invitation-only events. At all three seminars, we sought balance both geographically and in terms of the size and profile of the institutions presented and also some participation from public authorities. While organized by the Council of Europe, the AITF played a crucial role in preparing each seminar. Harkavy contributed to all three events, while Maurrasse contributed to two. In addition, at each seminar we included presentations on the work of a number of European institutions to ground our discussions of how we could best further the work on the local mission of higher education at the European level based on the diversified experience of European universities. Presentations included the experiences of the Universities of the Aegean, Iceland, and Kraków as well as Queen's, DCU, and several Czech universities. They also included the CEU (Matei 2019) as well as the Universities of Andorra and Cagliari. Some of these presentations provide the basis for the more detailed consideration in Chapter 7 of how European universities cooperate with their local communities. We included presentations on the experience of the United States (Weeks 2019) and South Africa (Bawa 2019) as well as of the AITF (Maurrasse 2019).

In my view, the local mission of higher education is linked to the debate on education quality, or maybe the absence of debate, at least on some key aspects of the concept. Quality assurance had become a key ingredient of the EHEA (see Chapter 1) and had given rise to the ESG, first adopted in 2005 and revised in 2015 (Bologna Process 2015c). No European minister or rector could admit to striving for anything but the highest quality. However, the European debate on education quality was largely on how to achieve it, and much less on what quality may be and why it is important. Quality was largely taken for granted, and the unfortunate prominence of rankings did not help. Rankings present an easy to grasp but utterly inadequate view of higher education quality. They give the illusion that by measuring the quality and quantity of research mostly in natural sciences, one can say something meaningful about the overall quality of a university, including the quality of its teaching and learning environment (Bergan 2011; Rauhvargers 2011, 2013). There is also an argument, made by Christine Musselin, that university leaders' strong focus on rankings may have led them to neglect one of their most important roles: educating citizens (referred to by Douglass 2021: 39).

The Council of Europe had, therefore, decided to explore not only the how but above all the what and the why of education quality. The starting point for this work was that it makes little sense to attempt to measure or assess quality if we do not know what we are trying to measure. To take an analogy from sports, we cannot assess the quality of marathon runners by assessing their results in the long jump or shot put. This project resulted in a recommendation (Council of Europe 2012) by which member states agreed to take a nuanced view of education quality.

This debate was crucial also to the local mission of higher education. By saying that the quality of higher education needs to take account of a range of factors, and not only the quality of research in certain academic disciplines, as most rankings do, it is easier to argue that how well universities implement the local mission, as well as their overall democratic mission, should be considered in the assessment of their overall quality. How the quality of an institution is assessed should depend on the missions it defines for itself. Public authorities and others, including all who fund an institution, may have views on the missions of a specific institution, but they cannot reasonably argue that an institution whose primary purpose is to provide good quality teaching at the bachelor's level for students from a specific region should be assessed according to the same criteria as a university aiming to be a world-class teaching and research institution. To put the argument in U.S. terms: you cannot assess a community college according to the criteria used to assess a research university. The link to the institution's mission is important. Increasingly, European universities are expected to formulate mission statements, and there is little reason why, for most of them, serving their local community should not be part of their mission.

There was agreement that the local mission is part of the overall work of higher education in favor of democracy. Or, as we summed up after the second seminar, at DCU:

- Higher education institutions need to be anchored or embedded in their local communities.
- Knowledge transfer is a two-way process between the higher education institution and the community.
- Engaging with the local is not incompatible with global engagement.
- Dialogue needs to be conducted within and between communities, hence also in local frameworks.
- Higher education needs to support all forms of democracy including the democratization of knowledge, education, and understanding of the world around us.
- We need to respect the diversity of higher education and cannot put forward a "one size fits all" democratic engagement mission.
- As science, knowledge, and even facts are brought into question, we need to reaffirm the European values of the Enlightenment as the best way to keep the democratic mission on track. (Bergan, Harkavy, and Munck 2019b: 137)

Participants in the three seminars agreed that the local mission is important. Even if there were encouraging signs in Europe of a greater openness to the democratic mission of higher education, and even if there was widespread cooperation between universities and local actors in the economic area, awareness of the broader local role of universities was insufficiently developed. The agreement extended to the need to explore and further the local mission of higher education as a European concern, but there was some divergence of views on how this could best be done. The AITF was an example and a model, but, in spite of the call made by the Council of Europe's Director General for Democracy, Snežana Samardžić-Marković, at the 2014 Global Forum for the creation of a network of anchor institutions in Europe (Benson et al. 2017: 118), most of us believed it could not be duplicated for European purposes. A couple of participants argued that Europe was saturated with higher education networks and similar structures and that there was little scope for yet another one. They argued that we should rather work to include the local mission in the agenda of existing organizations and networks. To a clear majority of participants, however, this was not a valid option, especially because the existing organizations had shown little readiness to put the local mission on their agendas thus far. We, therefore, believed that a more established European cooperation specifically focused on the local mission was required, and we suggested to the Council of Europe's committee responsible for education[13] that it approve a project within the overall work on the democratic mission of higher education.

Toward a Council of Europe Project on the Local Mission of Higher Education

The Council's Education Committee accepted our suggestion and appointed a working group to put forward a proposal. This is, of course, a classic modus operandi of intergovernmental organizations and one that is open to challenge. There is a saying in Norwegian that when the Devil wanted nothing to happen, he appointed the first committee.[14] Nevertheless, a good working group can clarify proposals that a larger committee would find it difficult to develop but on which the committee can then act. This is what happened in our case.

Even if it were important that the group not be too big, it was equally important to include a variety of backgrounds and experiences, including those of the United States and AITF more specifically. Harkavy and Maurrasse were, therefore, appointed to the working group, which was chaired by Maija Innola, at the time the vice chair of the Council's Education Committee and later its chair. Other members included Hilligje van't Land of the IAU, John Smith of the EUA, and two longtime partners in the work on the democratic mission: Tony Gallagher of Queen's and Ronaldo Munck of DCU. In the final stages, Cécilia Brassier-Rodrigues from the University of Clermont-Auvergne also participated in the work. She had contributed to other Council projects, notably one supporting the integration of refugees in the academic environment.[15]

One important addition to the group was Ninoslav Šćukanec Schmidt, who represented Croatia in the BFUG and was cochair of the working group that developed the principles and guidelines for the social dimension of higher education (Bologna Process 2020a). More important for our purposes, Šćukanec Schmidt is the executive director of the Institute for the Development of Education in Zagreb.[15] The institute has run two successive projects on community engagement in higher education in the EU: TEFCE (Towards a European Framework for Community Engagement of Higher Education) followed by SHEFCE (Steering Higher Education for Community Engagement).[17] The first project developed a tool for institutional reflection for community engagement—the TEFCE Toolbox (Farnell et al. 2020)—as well as recommendations on embedding community engagement in higher education policy. The follow-up project, SHECFE, ran through 2023 and produced university action planning for community engagement, policy recommendations for system-level support, a European online platform, and a prototype for an online tool enabling users to search a limited database of institutions and access information on their community engagement performance and practices. In June 2023, this project gave rise to an EU online platform on community engagement.[18] This platform, however, seems to be conceived of mainly as an online resource center supporting institutions and other projects in their community engagement, whereas the platform proposed in the Council of Europe context would be a project bringing together partners working on joint or similar activities.

As a first step, the Council of Europe commissioned the Institute for the Development of Education to develop an overview of existing projects and initiatives (Farnell, Skledar Matijević, and Šćukanec Schmidt 2020). The study provides a good overview of actors in community engagement in higher education; public engagement with science; higher education, innovation, and local/regional development; and university initiatives to support the UN Sustainable Development Goals. Most of the initiatives covered are transnational, and most are linked to the EU. For reasons of space, one example from each category will have to suffice.

Within the European Universities Initiative,[19] which is an EU flagship project, CIVICA—the European University of Social Sciences—is a network of ten European higher education institutions, which, according to its website, aims to "develop the European university of the future: grounded in excellent teaching and learning, offering seamless mobility, contributing innovative solutions to societal challenges, and creating a path for other universities to follow."[20] The member universities aim to find solutions to complex societal challenges and to combine teaching, research, and innovation to mobilize and share knowledge as a public good and to facilitate civic responsibility in Europe (Farnell, Skledar Matijević, and Šćukanec Schmidt 2020: 7).

The European Science Engagement Association was established in 2011 and has evolved from a meeting place for science festival organizers to a collaborative international community for public engagement practitioners. It encourages and supports innovative formats of science-society dialogues across Europe.[21] In addition to organizing an annual conference, it participates in EU-funded projects. Two of them led to the establishment of its European Science Engagement Platform,[22] which promotes networking, tool kits, and resources for science engagement and communicating science to various audiences (Farnell, Skledar Matijević, and Šćukanec Schmidt 2020: 15).

"Smart specialization" is one of the European Commission's many initiatives with an economic development agenda. It is defined as "a place-based approach characterised by the identification of strategic areas for intervention based both on the analysis of the strengths and potential of the local and/ or regional economy and on an Entrepreneurial Discovery Process (EDP) with wide stakeholder involvement" (Farnell, Skledar Matijević, and Šćukanec Schmidt 2020: 19). A main aim is to help each region define and develop its competitive advantages. Universities contribute to the Smart Specialisation

Agenda by helping design and implement Research and Innovation Strategies for Smart Specialisation (RIS3)[23] and identify priorities for their regions, in cooperation with regional authorities.

The Copernicus Alliance was established in 1993 and is a European network of universities and colleges committed to sustainable development. It aims to enable European higher education institutions and their partners to identify challenges in higher education for sustainable development and to develop processes, tools, and knowledge to address these challenges from a whole-institution perspective. The alliance provides a platform and organizes events to enable its current and future members to share resources and codevelop innovative education for sustainable development initiatives.[24] Its slightly less than thirty members[25] are mostly universities but also include a Rectors' Conference, a quality assurance agency, and a ministry responsible for the environment.

One of the partners in both the Global Cooperation for the Democratic Mission of Higher Education and the project on the local democratic mission, the IAU, is also strongly engaged in education for sustainable development. In 2018, it launched the IAU Global Cluster on Higher Education on Sustainable Development to promote the role of higher education institutions in building more sustainable societies. The cluster encourages a holistic approach to the UN Sustainable Development Goals and promotes a whole institution approach, where institutions aim to embed sustainable development in their strategic planning and academic and organizational work.[26]

The Institute for the Development of Education's study reasonably concludes that there are very many different European initiatives that support the increased engagement of universities with society, ranging from EU-level funding schemes in higher education and research to networks and organizations active at the European and national level (Farnell, Skledar Matijević, and Šćukanec Schmidt 2020: 28). The study also puts forward recommendations as to the elements that should guide the Council of Europe's work and suggests some "final reflections and recommendations." These include:

- Addressing the resource gap between universities' engagement with local communities relating to innovation, entrepreneurship, and employment and their engagement with communities with fewer resources, relating to social, cultural, civic and environmental questions.
- Using the term community engagement—rather than the local mission—as an "umbrella term" to cover the range of ways in which universities cooperate with different communities to address different societal needs.

- Work to include the development of community engagement in higher education among the policy goals of the EHEA. (Farnell, Skledar Matijević, and Šćukanec Schmidt 2020: 29)

The Proposal: A European Platform on the Local Democratic Mission of Higher Education

The working group made good use of the study, even if it did not follow all its recommendations. In particular, the group disagreed with the suggestion that we use the more generic term "community engagement." The group, in fact, suggested the project be renamed, but in a different direction. It considered that the terms "local" and "mission" are both essential to what it suggested the Council of Europe undertake, but it further suggested that the project be not only on the local mission but on the local *democratic* mission of higher education. This sharpened focus underlines what the working group sees as the essential component of any Council of Europe project in this area.

The project submitted to and approved by the Council's Education Committee,[27] in March 2022, emphasizes the need for a coherent approach to the local democratic mission by underlining that the platform on the local democratic mission of higher education is an opportunity to create a pan-European framework connecting the different aspects of higher education's societal engagement and thus support universities in institutionalizing their cooperation with local communities (Council of Europe 2022a: 3–4). The project description places the platform in the broader context of the Council of Europe's contribution to the EHEA, where the Council has been a strong voice for upholding the fundamental values of higher education as well as the RFCDC and the Council's work on inclusive education. The Education Committee decided to renew the mandate of the ad hoc working group on the local democratic mission of higher education, with setting up the platform as its main task. The ad hoc group includes the chair of the Council's Education Committee, the chair of the EHEA working group on the Social Dimension in Higher Education, four policymakers representing the academic community, four representatives of the AITF, and observers representing the IAU and the EUA (Council of Europe 2022a: 13).

A first key element in the platform's understanding of the local democratic mission is an emphasis on *place*, on the reasoning that you cannot be local unless you have a link to place. In most cases, what the ad hoc group refers to as "the institution's proximate geographic community" (Council of Europe 2022c: 3) will be the city in which the university is located. In some cases, however, it can also be a part of a city, such as Penn's work in West Philadelphia or that of DCU in the Dublin neighborhood of Ballymun. It can also be a region. Queen's, for example, works with neighborhoods within Belfast as well as in all of Northern Ireland more broadly (for both DCU and Queen's, see Chapter 7). In the smallest European countries, such as Andorra, Liechtenstein, and San Marino, it may even be difficult to distinguish the local from the national (for San Marino, see Chapter 7).

The second element is that universities need to work not only *in* but *with* communities. The link to place is important, but it should not be misunderstood to mean that as long as an initiative is local, cooperation and contact with the local community—the people who live and work there—do not matter. To the contrary, these are essential. As the working group puts it: "The institution should engage in a sustained way with one or more stakeholders in the local community, such as public authorities, schools, hospitals, civil society, cultural organizations, or businesses. It should see itself as an actor in, of, and for the local community and preferably have an adopted or accepted institutional policy for how it engages with the local community" (Council of Europe 2022c: 4).

The third element is that the project must be values based. It should be a project on *democracy*, not on just any kind of local involvement. This is, of course, fitting for an organization devoted to democracy, human rights, and the rule of law, and it should also give this Council of Europe initiative a specific profile. As the working group suggests: "While it may be possible for a higher education institution to be an actor in its local community without having an explicit values basis—as in at least some kinds of business engagement—it would be difficult to conceive of a Council of Europe initiative that did not build on a commitment to democracy, human rights, and the rule of law. This is therefore the basis for the Platform, which will also draw on AITF's values of collaboration and partnership; equity and social justice; democracy and democratic practice; and commitment to place and community" (Council of Europe 2022c: 4).

The ad hoc group considered that there was a need for a European initiative in the true sense of the term that would encompass all fifty States Parties to the European Cultural Convention.[28] The platform should aim to support the role of higher education in furthering democracy through working with the local community. It should address universal issues and examine how these can be dealt with in a local context, such as contemporary concerns of furthering knowledge creation, informed citizenship, and civil society. The platform should also consider the need to build higher education—and society more broadly—on a solid ethical basis. In this, it could link to the Council's ETINED Platform on ethics, transparency, and integrity in education.[29] Social inclusion through education is another key issue that should be included in the work of a platform aiming to further the local democratic mission of higher education, and it is worth noting that the Council of Europe's Education program for 2022–2025 includes an emphasis on education for inclusion and sustainability.

In view of the modest resources that can be invested in the platform, setting priorities will be particularly important, and these need to take account of the Council's possibilities and limitations as an intergovernmental organization. The ad hoc group suggests four priority activities:

- Advocacy
- Policy development
- Identifying examples of promising practices[30]
- Undertaking studies or other work on specific issues

Advocacy and policy development are linked, and both come naturally to an intergovernmental organization. In particular, a policy recommendation can draw political attention to the local democratic mission of higher education and provide valuable support to institutions and others who wish to develop initiatives in their own countries and settings. By experience, this is an important function of recommendations adopted by the Committee of Ministers, which are not legally binding but nevertheless carry considerable weight.

By providing overviews of activities of relevance to the local democratic mission carried out in various contexts and identifying examples of promising practices, ideally from as large a part of Europe as possible and also from other parts of the world, the platform can provide a "bank" of ideas that universities can draw on for their own initiatives. It is important that the overviews be analytical rather than merely narrative, and this is often the most challenging aspect of describing examples of practice. It will be important to identify what worked in which contexts and why, and equally important to identify what worked less well. Even if there is national and institutional prestige attached to practices and initiatives, many European countries are relatively open about both their less successful and their successful experiences. Claiming you are always successful will not strengthen your credibility. The extent to which examples are transferable to other contexts should be an important selection criterion. The examples provided by participants and others should be supplemented by specifically designed studies.

Higher education leaders as well as their counterparts in local communities are obvious target groups for carrying out the activities under the platform. However, leaders are not a uniform group. In the world of higher education, they not only include presidents, rectors, and those with similar job titles but also deans and heads of department as well as student leaders and leaders of faculty and staff organizations. In local communities, they include not only elected public officials but also those in key positions in the city administration as well as leaders of associations and NGOs of all kinds, from theater to sports, faith communities, and people who may be widely listened to in the community without having a formal leadership position. While leaders are important, so are community members who do not have leadership positions, whether in the academic or the local community. Students, faculty, staff, and members of the local community are all important, even if all are not easy to reach.

The scarcity of resources also dictates that the platform be modest in scope. Ideally, the platform will ultimately gather representatives of universities as well as of local communities, but it will be launched on the basis of developing partnerships with organizations and networks with an interest in and/ or experience of working on the local democratic mission of higher education and through these reach out to involve individual institutions. Representative higher education organizations like the IAU, EUA, and EURASHE[31] already expressed an interest in the proposed platform at an early stage and should be invited to be part of the launch. The European Students' Union and Education International should also be invited to join as early as possible. It will not be possible to involve a high number of universities from the very beginning, and representatives of the higher education organizations also suggested these organizations may be well placed to propose universities that could be invited as it becomes possible to extend membership. Nevertheless, a few universities that have been involved in the work on the democratic mission of higher education for some time, such as Queen's and DCU and some others, could be invited to participate in the launch.

Identifying partners in local communities will be equally challenging, but the Council of Europe has two bodies that could be of particular importance. The Congress of Local and Regional Authorities in Europe[32] is the representative body of local public authorities, while the Intercultural Cities Network[33] gathers cities and regions interested in managing diversity as an advantage for all of society. The latter currently gathers some 160 cities and regions, mostly from Europe but also from other parts of the world. We invited a representative of the Intercultural Cities Network to speak at the third invitational seminar, in Strasbourg. She underlined that when the Secretariat of the network visits participating cities, they try to see as many different partners in the local community as possible. Discouragingly, higher education institutions are often the most difficult to reach, which is an indication of the need for both the network and the proposed platform on the local democratic mission of higher education.

Prospects and Challenges

As we saw, the third and final invitational seminar was held in June 2019. Shortly after the Education Committee had approved the proposal to explore the idea of a platform, COVID-19 struck Europe, and the working group had to do most of its work online. The first meeting was, in fact, held at the end of the first week of confinement in France. I have recollections of participating in the meeting stretched out on my bed, as my back was paying the price of a very intensive transition to running the whole Education program online and spending twelve to fourteen hours per day in front of the computer, almost without a break. The transition to online work inevitably slowed down the project, and we also clearly felt that working online was less efficient than holding at least some meetings face-to-face. Then, by the time the working group could submit its proposal and have the committee approve it, the Education Department faced a challenging transition period. I retired in February 2022, and my successor needed some time to take stock of the situation. This period also coincided with the drafting of an Education Strategy, which was adopted in September 2023 and covers the period 2024–2030 (Council of Europe 2023c; see Chapter 3). Regrettably, the strategy makes little explicit reference to the democratic mission of higher education and no direct reference to its *local* democratic mission.

All of this means that while we had intended for the platform to be launched in the fall of 2022, the work has been delayed. At the time of writing, I am not aware of a firm timetable to launch the platform, but both the committee and the Secretariat have confirmed their commitment. It will nevertheless be important to avoid too long a delay to ensure the continued interest of potential members of the platform, all of whom are also pressed for time and resources. An encouraging sign was, however, given in mid-February 2024, when the Council's Sub-Group on Higher Education Policy wholeheartedly supported the inclusion of the local dimension of higher education in the Council of Europe's Education program for 2024–2027.[34]

Even if the obstacles should not be underestimated, the potential benefits of the platform are very real, to higher education as well as to local communities and to society. In many quarters, higher education suffers from its image as an ivory tower. I do not believe this has ever been an accurate image of universities, otherwise they would not have survived for close to a millennium. Nevertheless, at a time when the value of research and academic knowledge is increasingly questioned and many members of society fall for the simplistic arguments of populists left and—above all—right, universities cannot afford to forgo any opportunity to demonstrate their value to broader society. We should not forget that those who fall for simplistic rhetoric are voters not only in national elections; they are also members of local communities, and they vote in local elections.

Working with their local communities provides universities with an important opportunity to demonstrate their worth, including to those whose encounters with school were unhappy ones. Universities are in a position to help with local health provision and with furthering social inclusion, as illustrated by the University of Iceland as well as by the Czech examples that will be described in Chapter 7. They can support local schools and motivate children and young people to stay in them, as shown by the example of Queen's in Chapter 7. They can assist local businesses, not only by providing the competences the businesses need but by helping create a thriving and secure local environment (Harris and Pickron-Davis 2015). Universities can also help local communities discover and, in many cases, face their own history. Academic knowledge and understanding may encourage divided communities to heal their wound, as the example of the Council of Europe's history education project in Cyprus shows (see Chapter 3). Practicing multiperspectivity belongs to the future as much as to the past. Developing a commitment to one's local community and the public space it offers should be an important task for all levels of education, including higher education. In this respect, cooperation between universities and local communities provides an excellent opportunity to put the Council of Europe's RFCDC into practice, in schools and in the community at large.

All of these are demanding tasks. Both universities and local communities would fulfill them better if they could learn from others who have grappled with similar issues, even if in different circumstances. A Council of Europe platform on the local democratic mission of higher education can help them do precisely that. It will also help the Council of Europe fulfill its mission of fostering democracy, human rights, and the rule of law. In the same way that other parts of the Education program have been recognized as essential to the Council of Europe's overall mission and the future of our continent, I am convinced that the platform will soon be seen as an integral and important part of that mission, even if this will take longer than I had originally hoped. The platform will both inspire and be inspired by the cooperation many European universities have already established with their local communities. It is to an exploration of the many facets of these existing cooperation initiatives and schemes that we now turn in Chapter 7.

Lessons Learned

Among the lessons learned in this chapter, I would highlight the following:

- The U.S. experience, in particular that of the Netter Center at Penn and of the AITF, has been essential to developing a vision of the local democratic mission of higher education within the Council of Europe. However, the U.S. experience cannot be duplicated in Europe, which needs to develop its own approach.

- The presentations of both the U.S. experience and that of Queen's at the 2014 Global Forum provided an important impetus. Among other things, the presentations demonstrated that there is no contradiction between local civic engagement and high-quality scholarship.
- Many of the qualities and competences that make graduates attractive on the labor market also make them well suited to engage as active citizens in democratic societies and help their personal development.
- Europe probably trains more highly qualified specialists than ever before, but it is more questionable whether we *educate* those specialists, providing them with the transversal competences they need to put their specialist competences into a broader societal context, enabling them not only to ask critical questions about their role and that of their discipline in broader society but also to find the answers to the critical questions.
- Rankings present an easy to grasp but utterly inadequate view of higher education quality. We need to define quality in terms of the objectives we want higher education to achieve, and so far we have not done so to the extent required.
- How the quality of an institution is assessed should depend on the missions it defines for itself. By saying that the quality of higher education needs to take account of a range of factors, it is easier to argue that how universities implement the local mission, as well as their overall democratic mission, should be considered in the assessment of their overall quality.
- We need to respect the diversity of higher education and cannot put forward a "one size fits all" democratic engagement mission.
- In Europe, the local democratic mission of higher education can best be furthered through European-wide cooperation. This cooperation needs to focus on the specific local *democratic* mission of higher education (and not just its local mission more broadly), must emphasize institutions' link to place ("the institution's proximate geographic community"), must require that universities work not only *in* but *with* communities, and must be values based.
- In March 2022, the Council of Europe's Education Committee approved a proposal to establish a platform to connect the different aspects of higher education's societal engagement and thus support universities in institutionalizing their cooperation with local communities.

- A Council of Europe platform should focus on advocacy, policy development, identifying examples of promising practices, and undertaking studies or other work on specific issues. The platform should not only be a forum for exchange of experience and mutual learning but also seek to develop policy recommendations.
- The platform should involve representatives of both higher education and local and regional communities.

7

European Universities Working with Their Local Communities

This chapter explores some of the ways in which European universities work in and with their local communities. Needless to say, the examples will be just that—examples. No overview of this topic could possibly be complete. However, the selection is not random. It aims to show at least some of the variety found in Europe. The examples are taken from various parts of Europe as well as from different kinds of universities. Some are universities with traditions of several centuries while others are relatively recent. Some are classic universities with a broad range of academic disciplines and strong fundamental research while at least one of them specializes in just a few academic areas and some are oriented toward applied education and research.

Categories and Examples of Cooperation

One of the aims of this chapter is to provide an analytical overview of the different ways in which European universities fulfill their local democratic mission, which to some of them is relatively new. Therefore, the examples are organized thematically rather than geographically. The brief overview of categories and examples that follow are examined in greater detail in the rest of the chapter.

Higher Education Helping Develop the Local Economy

Economic cooperation and development may not be the prime focus of this book, but the economic role of higher education remains important, as illustrated by one of Europe's large traditional universities, the Jagiellonian University of Kraków. It can also help promote democracy.

A Broader Societal Mission

The broader societal mission of higher education is illustrated by examples from three quite different countries: Iceland, the Czech Republic, and San Marino. Each illustrates a different aspect of this mission: societal outreach, student engagement, and a comprehensive organization of university-community cooperation. The University of Iceland exemplifies the education mission beyond campus that many universities undertake. As the main university in a small and relatively homogeneous society, the University of Iceland also illustrates a broader societal mission. The examples from universities in the Czech Republic, in particular, demonstrate the importance of student engagement and outreach and illustrate a range of different activities in various parts of the country. In San Marino, the university has developed a comprehensive model for cooperation with the broader society through what is known as a territorial pact. Even if the Sammarinese Territorial Pact is national, this model for organizing contacts and cooperation between the university and a broad range of stakeholders could serve as a model for local communities in much larger countries, as it provides a comprehensive structural framework for this cooperation involving all stakeholders.

One Institution, Several Local Communities:
The Multicampus University

Moving to southern Europe, the University of the Aegean challenges our concept of what a local community is. Rather than operating in a compact geographic setting, the University of the Aegean serves a far-flung community, with campuses on six Greek islands.

The Engaged University

Some Europeans live in precarious contexts with little hope of entering higher education and also with little motivation to do so. Access to higher education, and measures to help students complete their degrees once they have been admitted, is one important aspect of engagement. As the National Coordinating Centre for Public Engagement in the United Kingdom underlines, the concept of an engaged university is broader than access and completion. This kind of university embeds public engagement into its work. It includes engagement specifically in its institutional mission and strategy and champions this commitment at all levels. It involves faculty, staff, students, and representatives of the public in shaping the engagement strategy and its delivery.

The engaged university sees exercising social responsibility as an integral part of its mission and seeks to maximize the benefits the institution can create for the public.[1] DCU is a highly engaged university that focuses on helping overcome social and economic divides. Given its location in a disadvantaged part of northern Dublin, it sees community engagement not as an option but as part of its institutional DNA, and it presents a good number of ways in which higher education's local democratic mission can be put into practice.

An Engaged University in a Pluricultural Setting

Queen's works to alleviate the deep social divisions that are found both between and within each of Northern Ireland's two major communities. One example is Queen's work to motivate young people from a nearby Protestant working-class area, where few people looked at Queen's as a realistic option to help prepare their future. In this sense Queen's is a classic engaged university. Its engagement goes beyond this classic role, however, because of the particular situation of Northern Ireland. In spite of its eminently Establishment roots, Queen's has worked to diversify its academic community to make both Catholics and Protestants feel at home on campus.

Higher Education Serving Ethnic and Linguistic Minorities

Europe is home to numerous minorities, whether ethnic, linguistic, or religious or of long-standing or recent origin. In Europe, the term "minority" has less of a racial connotation than in the United States, and Europeans are reluctant to use the term "race." This is not to say racism does not exist in Europe—it clearly does—but migration, language, and religion tend to be seen as more salient categories. It is also important to keep in mind that because of Europe's experience with Nazism, the term "race" carries particularly negative connotations.

The Sámi have solid roots in the far north of Europe and have been a minority for much of their history. Their minority status has long been an indication of societal marginalization, but, over the past generation or so, the Sámi as well as the broader Nordic society have made considerable efforts to preserve and develop Sámi language and culture. A small higher education institution—Samisk høgskole/Sámi allaskuvla—where teaching and research is entirely in Sámi is part of this effort.

Swedish speakers, on the other hand, are a minority of little more than 5 percent in Finland, but they are in a very different position from the Sámi. Not only are their numbers greater but also Swedish speakers are the former political and social elite of Finland, they are part of a broader Swedish-speaking community with Sweden as its focus, and they are served by Åbo Akademi University. The university may be relatively small, but it is well established, active in international cooperation, and located in the part of Finland that still has the largest Swedish-speaking population.

*Preserving and Developing a National Language
and Culture in a Bilingual Environment*

Maltese are not a minority in their own country, but Malta is a de facto bilingual or even plurilingual country with a strong English-language heritage in addition to Maltese, and Italian is still widely used. Even if most of its teaching is in English, the University of Malta plays a key role in developing Maltese language and culture as well as in the broader development of a small island society with a strong international orientation.

I now look at these examples in greater detail before attempting to identify some trends and draw some conclusions.

Higher Education Helping Develop the Local Economy

If we discuss university-community cooperation in Europe, most readers will probably first think of the role universities play in the economic development of their local community and regions. We start with this form of cooperation not because it is more important or more democratic. It may even be less interesting for our purposes than the other kinds of cooperation we discuss in this chapter, although economic cooperation can also further democracy. The logic is rather to start with what may be more familiar to many readers and then venture into areas that may be less well known.

Economic cooperation has several aspects, not all of which are related to the democratic mission of higher education. Nevertheless, providing improved economic opportunities for the local community and its residents does help inclusion and participation. Democracy does not work particularly well on empty stomachs, and improving the business opportunities and employment conditions of people in the local community increases their well-being and puts them in a better position to engage more broadly as citizens. So does the increased competence that can and should come with this kind of university-community cooperation. Providing local residents with the competences they need to obtain employment locally has positive impacts on their motivation and capacity to contribute to their local community. Improved employment also means improved opportunities for local companies. In particular, by buying locally, universities can directly help local businesses.

Economic cooperation between universities and the local community will also be easier to bring about and sustain in democratic societies, and this is one of the reasons I now focus on the Jagiellonian University in Kraków. This university—often referred to as just the Jagiellonian—is one of Europe's traditional and prestigious universities. Today, it is a member of the EUA, the Guild of European Research-Intensive Universities,[2] and several European networks.[3]

The Jagiellonian was established in 1364, and at least from the fifteenth century onward, it attracted students from several parts of Europe.[4] Throughout its institutional life, the Jagiellonian has covered almost every academic field. In its early days, it covered the classic areas of all medieval European universities: what we would today call the professional study programs of theology, law, and medicine as well as the *artes liberales* (Zonta 2002). In addition to Poles, the university's faculty and students included Ruthenians, Lithuanians, Hungarians, Germans, Czechs, Swiss, English, Dutch, French, Spanish, Italians, and Tatars. As elsewhere in Europe, the language of teaching, learning, and publication was Latin, whereas the language of the community surrounding the university was the local vernacular. Some foreign members of the academic community probably learned Polish, but this was not an academic requirement. There was interaction between members of the academic community and the local population, but how much of it was viewed positively and marked by mutual respect is difficult to know.

As academic fields developed, so did the Jagiellonian, albeit it not without exceptions. One of these is my second reason for choosing the Jagiellonian as an example. With the advent first of World War II after Poland was attacked by Nazi Germany in September 1939 and then of Communist rule in Poland from 1945, the Jagiellonian was able to continue its work, except during parts of World War II, but under severe restrictions. Some scholars were unable to continue even if the institution survived. Areas of social sciences and the humanities like philosophy, theology, history, political science, and economics were particularly exposed, and applied research was not well developed. Repression and restrictions were not uniform throughout the Communist period, and there was some scope for civil society action. The toughest time was that of the Stalinist period, roughly from 1948 to 1953.[5]

With the fall of the Communist regime in 1990, the Jagiellonian could again play a more active role in society. Since then, it has developed stronger cooperation with its local community as well as with the whole Małopolska ("Little Poland") region, the part of southeastern Poland in which Kraków is located. Much of this cooperation focuses on economic development (Kistryn 2019).

As its name suggests, the Center for Technology Transfer (CITTRU) helps broader society benefit from the technologies developed at the university, and it stimulates local start-ups, many of which originate from the university or at least from among its academics and graduates. CITTRU has access to what it calls a portfolio of more than 150 "new market products and services" covering a range of natural and life sciences, including chemistry, biomedicine, and medical technology. It also helps business and other stakeholders establish contact with researchers in these fields as well as in pharmacy, mathematics, computer science, environmental science, and material science and also the humanities and social science. A program called "Collaboration of Scholars with the Economic Environment" stimulates and coordinates cooperation between academics and business. It covers various stages of the cooperation process, which includes identifying research projects that have a potential for business applications and analysis of market potential, legal protection issues, marketing, and assistance with establishing commercial contracts. CITTRU can also help with the legal and administrative coordination of commissioned studies, and it coordinates the efforts of the Jagiellonian University in obtaining patent protection for research results with business potential.[6]

The Jagiellonian university does not limit its cooperation with the local community to technology and natural sciences, however. It has a Center for the Evaluation and Analysis of Public Policies, which cooperates closely with local public authorities, as does the Center and Department of Regional Geography. Other areas in which the Jagiellonian University has a regional impact include the life sciences and biology (Kistryn 2019). Importantly, the Jagiellonian University is part of the attraction of Kraków as one of Poland's main tourist and cultural destinations. Its university museum, located in the beautiful Collegium Maius building, presents visitors with an overview of the history of the university and its role in the life of both the city and the country. I had a chance to explore this museum when the Council of Europe ran a project on the heritage of European universities as part of the 1999 campaign "Europe, Our Common Heritage." The then director of the museum, Professor Stanisław Waltoś, was a member of the project group for a Council of Europe project on the heritage of European universities, and we held one of the project meetings at the museum (Sanz and Bergan 2002).

In 2021, the university adopted a new strategy, which presents a vision of the Jagiellonian as a renowned research university and a leading research center in Central and Eastern Europe as well as an institution with "high standards of student education integrated with science and the environment" (Jagiellonian University 2021: 4). The strategy sees no contradiction between global ambitions and local engagement:

> The University articulates global aspirations and engages in the development of its local environment—the city of Kraków and the Małopolska region as a whole. It substantially contributes to the improvement of public health, disease prevention, protection and improvement in the quality of life and health, natural environment conservation and solves social and economic problems, many of which

are related to digital transformation and climate change. It is committed to culture development and the protection, documentation and dissemination of material and spiritual heritage. It takes a stand on matters vital for Poland, those which are evidence-based, rationally justified and in agreement with the University's values. (Jagiellonian University 2021: 5)

In addition to the university's commitment to its city and region, it is worth noting the strategy's emphasis on contributing to solving the problems of broader society, such as public health and sustainable development, as well as its promise to speak out on issues of importance to society and to do so in agreement with the university's values. The strategy explicitly commits the Jagiellonian to "collaborat[ing] with the local-authorities of Kraków and the Małopolska region in the development of the city and region, provide research and expert support to contribute in solving local problems" (Jagiellonian University 2021: 9).

The Jagiellonian, then, is a prestigious traditional university that has survived extensive societal changes and also contributed to some of them. It has European and global ambitions but is also committed to and engaged with its local and regional community. This engagement is above all directed toward scientific innovation and economic development. It emphasizes start-ups, technology, and natural and life sciences but it also encompasses social sciences and the humanities. Given its prominent place in both the history and the contemporary life of Poland, the Jagiellonian does not always find it easy to distinguish between its national and its regional and local roles, but its commitment to Kraków and the Małopolska region is confirmed by its current strategic plan, adopted in mid-2021. In the political climate in Poland, which until December 2023 had a populist right government that was often criticized for both its nationalist positions and reducing individual liberties (Applebaum 2018), and which is still a strongly polarized society, it is worth noting that in spite of its strong emphasis on economic development, the Jagiellonian's strategy includes an explicit commitment to speaking up on current issues on the basis of its academic values. This commitment was and is likely to bring the Jagiellonian into conflict with at least national but possibly also regional and local political authorities as well as important segments of society on some issues.

A Broader Societal Mission

As we saw in the introduction to this chapter, the societal mission of higher education is broad, and I have chosen to focus on three universities that illustrate different aspects of this mission.

Societal Outreach

If the Jagiellonian sometimes finds it difficult to distinguish its role at the local level from the role it plays nationally, this is even more true for the University of Iceland, which serves both a national community of some 375,000 people and the roughly one-third of the Icelandic population that lives in its capital, Reykjavík, and environs. Reykjavík is the seat of the University of Iceland and the center of much of Iceland's public life.

Iceland has the northernmost capital in Europe, and Reykjavík is located at approximately the same latitude as Fairbanks, Alaska. The country is relatively isolated geographically, even if it is now reasonably well connected by air. Iceland is a highly literate society in which reading, writing, and storytelling hold an important place in popular culture. Language is a key part of Iceland's cultural identity, and Icelanders are fiercely protective of it. They are, for example, reluctant to accept foreign loanwords and prefer to coin new words from Icelandic roots to describe new realities, so a theater becomes a "playhouse" (*leikhús*). Where many other European languages have adopted variations of the word "university," Icelandic uses the term *háskóla*—a Germanic root meaning "high school"—so that the university is known as Háskóli Íslands. From modest beginnings, in 1911, and an early history as an institution whose main aim was to educate future public officials, the University of Iceland developed into a full-fledged university with teaching and research in a broad range of academic disciplines.[7] For a long time, the University of Iceland was the only higher education institution in the country, which may explain the particular status and place it still has in Icelandic society today. The university is essential to upholding Icelandic culture and language.

History, geography, size, and the relative lack of higher education institutions in other parts of the country, therefore, converge to make the University of Iceland a national institution. Of the seven institutions listed on the Study in Iceland website,[8] three are in the Reykjavík area, two in Borgarnes, a good hour's drive away, and two in the northern part of the country. None even come close to the University of Iceland in size and national importance. By way of example, in February 2022, the University of Iceland had 9982 students, the University of Reykjavík 2779, the University of Akureyri 1680, Bifrost University 599, the University of the Arts 513, the Agricultural University of Iceland 436, and Hólar University a mere 219 students.[9] As we have seen, a substantial part of the population also lives in the greater Reykjavík area. Akureyri, in the north, has some seventeen thousand to eighteen thousand inhabitants. It is Iceland's fourth-largest city and the largest one outside of the greater Reykjavík area.

Whether local or national, the University of Iceland sees itself as having a societal mission. Its societal engagement includes measures to increase public interest in and understanding of research and academic work as well as cooperation and communication with primary and secondary schools (Gésts-dóttir 2019). Measures to widen access to higher education and to reach groups that may otherwise not consider higher education an option include developing professional education programs in some areas, a vocational diploma program, and the use of digital technologies for distance learning. The university's public engagement activities span widely[10] and include:

- "University in Society," a lecture series aimed at the general public, situated squarely within a Nordic tradition of enhancing the cultural horizons of the broader public[11] and spanning a broad field. Nevertheless, most lectures address issues of society, and many aim to provide advice to parents who may be concerned about how their children could best face social and societal problems, such as anxiety. The practical focus of the lecture series also demonstrates to the general public that a university is not necessarily an institution removed from society or lodged in the proverbial ivory tower. The website presenting the lecture series[12] makes it clear that it is in line with the University of Iceland's strategy, which states that "the University of Iceland stands for a vibrant discourse with the general public and professionals on pressing societal issues." Another lecture series, called "Science—Plain and Simple,"[13] also aims at a broad public but focuses on natural science and the use of science in people's daily lives.
- Outreach activities aimed at children and youths. The Children's Culture Festival[14] aims at a young public and is held every year in April in Reykjavík, in cooperation with the local authorities. It introduces children up to the age of sixteen to a broad spectrum of arts. It emphasizes participation, so that each child can develop his or her own artistic abilities. The University of Youth[15] allows twelve-to sixteen-year-olds to spend a week in the summer at the university and be introduced to a range of academic disciplines they are unlikely to encounter in school but that they may wish to study later. The Web of Science is, as its name indicates, a website[16] where people can find answers to countless questions and also ask questions themselves. It covers most areas of academic research conducted by the university.
- A program aiming to improve social inclusion by providing opportunities and support for young people from immigrant backgrounds whose families have little or no history of higher education. The program, called Sprettur,[17] offers both financial and social and educational support, assistance from a mentor, and help for

furthering participants' personal development. They enroll for four years and meet three times a month. Rather than focus on academic achievements within a specific study program, Sprettur offers a supportive environment for people whose study goals vary but who come from backgrounds that would make it difficult for many of them to succeed academically without this extra support. The program is cross-disciplinary rather than subject specific, and it aims to help participants succeed in their studies regardless of their discipline.

- Active use of television, which has long been used for educational purposes in the Nordic countries and may be particularly important in sparsely populated areas. I have memories of watching educational TV programs at school in Norway in the late 1960s and early 1970s. Even if there is a shift to the internet, also in the Nordic countries, television remains important, at least to the older parts of the population. Up until the 1980s, public television had a near monopoly and hence an important role in setting national agendas. With a vastly enlarged array of both public and private TV channels, satellite reception, and the internet, this is no longer the case, but public television still has a national cultural and educational mission to which the University of Iceland contributes. One example was the *Treasures of the Future* program series, shown on Icelandic TV to mark the university's centennial in 2011, that aimed to introduce people to the diverse work of University of Iceland faculty.[18]

The University of Iceland hence sees itself as an active participant in the life of the broader Icelandic society. It aims to play a cultural rather than a political role, and it seeks to educate the broader public about the importance of higher education and research to a modern society. The university does so, in part, by providing courses and activities aimed at a broader public that will help members of the public address issues of importance to their daily lives. It also caters to the desire of many members of the general public to broaden their cultural horizons. This may be a particularly important task in Iceland, which has a long and solid tradition of both written and oral expression, and where people are generally both interested in and well aware of the history of their society.[19]

Student Engagement

In several programs at the University of Iceland, students do volunteer work, under supervision of faculty when required, to help the broader public (Géstsdóttir 2019), and many focus on the Reykjavík area. Many of these activities have a double purpose: they offer valuable help to the public, but they are also part of the training program for the students themselves. Activities include offering free or reduced rate legal services as well as dental,[20] public health, and mental health services. Nursing students work with primary schools to educate children about self-image and its importance. The Teddy Hospital is a particularly innovative program that invites young children to take their "injured" teddy bears to the hospital, so they can see how a hospital functions. Should the children need to be hospitalized themselves, they will have some idea of where they will go and what will happen there, which will hopefully help the children overcome any fear they may have.

The Czech Republic provides a good selection of student outreach activities from several universities. The Palacký University in Olomouc traces its history back to 1573.[21] Here, students and staff provide open lectures throughout the region to demonstrate the importance of research and fact-based decision-making. Some of the topics chosen are controversial current affairs issues like the EU or migration, and these topics are particularly important to the democratic mission of the university in view of the current wave of nationalism and right-wing populism seen in many parts of Europe. The Czech Republic is no exception even if the outcome of the presidential election in January 2023 was encouraging.[22] In 2016, the Palacký University established a special Volunteering Center, which was the first at a Czech university. The center sees volunteering as "an opportunity for self-development, to support civic engagement, and to fulfil the 'third mission' of the university—i.e. community outreach. It's all about extending the relationship of the university into its surroundings and focussing on society-wide themes."[23]

The center both stimulates and coordinates volunteering activities, and its list of partners is impressive. The website lists twenty-five community partners in addition to the university itself, and these range from film and theater through social work to providing training in information technology. Student volunteers may help provide psychosocial support to oncology patients and their families, support and counsel victims of crimes, or help families with children who have been diagnosed with autism spectrum disorders and communication deficiency. They can also engage in social services through the Catholic relief organization Caritas, a hospice, or a Center for Social Prevention, or they can help provide school meals for children from disadvantaged backgrounds or tutor children from families who receive social and humanitarian assistance. The full portfolio of partners and volunteering activities testifies to a university engaging with the needs of the local community, in particular, to further social inclusion and integration.

Social inclusion is also an important topic in Brno, the country's second-largest city, where social workers, municipal authorities, and the Masaryk

University cooperate in a project aimed at facilitating the transition into broader society for young people who have been raised in orphanages and need to leave the institution at an age when they are not quite ready for life as independent adults. In 2022, the university quickly established an assistance program for students who had to flee Ukraine because of the war.[24] In Hradec Králové, a city of slightly less than one hundred thousand inhabitants due east of Praha (Prague), the "Night Outdoors" program has a double aim: to help homeless people and at the same time develop empathy and commitment in students, who share the conditions of homeless people for a night (Wildová, Fliegel, and Vokšická 2019: 106–107). As in several other countries, outreach activities in law and medicine at several universities combine practical training for students and offering services free of charge to people who may otherwise not be able to afford, or would not think of seeking, professional help. Some activities are also aimed specifically at either children or senior citizens (Wildová, Fliegel, and Vokšická 2019: 106–107).

As we can see from these examples, student engagement and volunteering cover a broad field of activities. Some help vulnerable groups in the local community and at the same time contribute to developing the professional skills of the student volunteers. Typically, such programs concern regulated professions like law, medicine, dentistry, or psychology.[25] Activities often aim to assist persons who are particularly vulnerable, and some focus on specific age groups. These are often children or young people, but some also aim to help older people. The "Night Outdoors" program in Hradec Králové is perhaps unusual in that, in addition to providing help to a vulnerable group, it also seeks to develop empathy and hence commitment among students.

A Comprehensive Organization of University-Community Cooperation

San Marino is one of the smallest countries in Europe in both territory and population. It is entirely surrounded by Italy, with the road to Rimini as the main route in and out of the country and Bologna Airport as the closest major air connection. Cooperation and interaction between the two countries are strong. Many Italians reside in San Marino, and many Sammarinese reside abroad, in particular, in Italy, which most Sammarinese do not really consider a foreign country.

The University of San Marino[26] was established in 1985. Today it has upward of one thousand students, a majority of whom are Italian. Conversely, many Sammarinese study abroad, in part, because the university has a limited offering of academic programs. It has three departments—Economics, Science, and Law; Humanities; and a renowned Institute of Historical Studies. There are currently no other higher education institutions in the country, but its parliament recently adopted a framework law on higher education that takes account of the possibility of establishing other public or—perhaps more likely—private institutions in the future.[27]

Given the size of San Marino, the distinction between what is national and what is local is very difficult to draw. Thus, the territorial pact (*patto territoriale*) encompasses the whole country, but it could be of considerable interest also to others if it were taken as a model for organizing the cooperation between a university and its broader local community in a given city or region. Territorial pacts are found also in regions of Italy, but the Sammarinese Territorial Pact was established through the current Delegated Decree on Universities, dating from 2023 (Repubblica di San Marino 2023), rather than through laws or regulations on local government. Article 27 of the decree stipulates that the territorial pact constitutes the meeting point between the university and the "territory," that the rector of the university is also the president of the pact, and that the pact is composed of representatives of the university as well as public institutions, cultural, economic, and professional associations, and labor unions and civil society.

The legislation stipulates that the pact has four functions. It can make proposals as concerns the development of the university, it is consulted and gives opinions on the strategic plan and development of the university, it provides information to the groups represented in the pact, and it can raise funds for specific projects for a specified period of time. Hence, the pact can initiate proposals, and it also has the right to be heard on proposals initiated by others, notably by the university itself. In sum, the pact is a consultative body in which the university and its main stakeholders in broader society consider issues of joint concern. Much of the cooperation focuses on socioeconomic issues. The territorial pact is also rooted in the university's current strategic plan, which underlines that the "third mission" (i.e., outreach activities, service to society) is part of the university's activities, including its contribution to sustainable development (Università degli Studi di San Marino 2019: 36–37). Above all, the strategic plan underlines that the university has always paid attention to the demands of the particular situation of San Marino (what it terms "the Sammarinese reality") and that the examples are too numerous to draw up a complete list.

Some examples can nevertheless be mentioned here. Under the Department of Economics, Science, and Law, there are research projects on the cultural heritage of San Marino as well as on reimagining the structure of public transportation (Università degli Studi di San Marino 2019: 11). The Department of Humanities works closely with Sammarinese schools and carries out activities on dyslexia (15) and learning disorders. The university also uses the territorial pact to engage community partners in projects to improve social inclusion in and through higher education.[28] Recently, an agreement was signed with the association Titancoop and Fondazione XXV Marzo for co-operation to safeguard and support the social, cultural, and economic development of the San Marino community.[29]

A particularly interesting example of interaction between the university and its local and national community is the Permanent Observatory on the Condition of Youth in San Marino.[30] It was set up in 2009 and is run by the Department of Humanities in cooperation with the public authorities responsible for public health, sociosanitary, and socioeducational services along with the Mental Health Unit of the Social Security Institute. As can be surmised from its name, the aim of the observatory is to help and counsel young people. Currently, it focuses on youth participation, which is, of course, important to developing a culture of democracy as well as on preventing violence against women, for which a development of attitudes is required for longer-term prevention. The observatory maintains and continues to develop a database that provides a basis for policy decisions, it studies and assesses preventive measures, and it works to involve the broader public in it projects through public events and days of study.

One Institution, Several Local Communities: The Multicampus University

We may think of a local community as a relatively compact entity: a city, a metropolitan area, or at least a coherent area where distances are not too great. In the smallest European countries, such as Andorra, Liechtenstein, or San Marino, it may be difficult to distinguish between the university's local and its national role, but, in these cases, we are also talking about a compact territory and a small population.

The University of the Aegean[31] is different. It is an island university in a country that is rich in islands and spans an area from almost 42 degrees to just under 35 degrees north and from approximately 19 to 29 degrees east. Exactly how many islands Greece has is subject to discussion, partly because of the lack of agreement on a definition but estimates seem to vary from around twelve hundred to about six thousand. Most are uninhabited and much of the population lives on the mainland. Many Greeks nevertheless live their whole lives on an island, and previous generations would have left their island rarely and only by ship. Today, Greece boasts an extensive network of ferries and domestic flights, but travel and communication between different parts of the country are, nevertheless, far from straightforward.

The University of the Aegean has campuses on six islands[32] in the southeastern part of Greece, with its headquarters in Mytilene on the island of Lesvos. In this sense, the University of the Aegean is both local and regional in an area that is important to Greece's tourist industry. The university's catchment area is also a tense border region that is the first or the second port of call for many refugees from the Middle East, who often pass through Turkey, and the university has made it one of its missions to assist them. Over the almost forty years since it was set up as a public institution in 1984, the university has become part of the identity of the region, and there is local pride in the fact that the University of the Aegean is generally considered to be a high-quality university. Its local mission is based on a solid academic performance (Spyropoulos 2019).

The university is located in a region that is important to tourism, which is one of the main sources of income for Greece. In 2019, the last full year before the COVID-19 pandemic hit, tourism contributed approximately 20 percent of the Greek gross national product.[33] While the sea and the sun are undoubtedly an important part of the attraction of Greece, so is its cultural heritage. The University of the Aegean organizes or contributes to events that highlight this heritage as well as events that emphasize the conditions for free expression, on which an important part of the Greek classic heritage rests. Thus, the university helps the region develop an important part of its economy, while, at the same time, contributing to developing and valorizing its cultural and historical heritage. The university receives support from both national and local public authorities for its archaeological research and excavations, which, again, are important to both tourism and the university's broader cultural mission.

The university also runs more classic outreach activities, such as an open lectures series, in which the faculty from the Department of Humanities present their areas of expertise to a broader local public, and faculty contribute to TV productions on Greek culture. It also helps the local community address social problems. For example, the incidence of drunk driving is higher in this region than elsewhere in Greece, and the university is involved in prevention measures.[34] The university also encourages students and staff to donate blood and organizes occasional blood bank drives.[35]

The University of the Aegean is not only located in a strategically important part of Greece; it is also an area that sees a high number of refugees arriving by boats and makeshift embarkations. Many of the refugees come from the Middle East, especially Syria and Iraq, and they are part of the vastly increased flow of refugees to Europe since the summer of 2015, which is covered in greater detail in Chapter 8. The University of the Aegean made an early decision to cater to refugees. Measures include not only reserving some places of study for qualified refugees but also public events that seek to give refugees a voice and to explain their situation to the local population. Thus, the university works both to improve the conditions of a particularly vulnerable population and to increase awareness of their situation and potential among voters who could easily be tempted to vote for xenophobic populist parties if they were to feel threatened by the number of refugees in their area.

The Engaged University

As we saw in the introduction to this chapter, an engaged university embeds public engagement into its institutional mission and strategy. I illustrate this with two examples that are located a little more than 160 kilometers (100 miles) apart on the island of Ireland but are under the jurisdiction of two different countries: the Republic of Ireland and the United Kingdom.

The Archetype of an Engaged University

In the Republic of Ireland, DCU is an archetypical engaged university. It was formally established in 1989 but its roots go back to a National Institute of Higher Education set up in 1975 and an agricultural college dating back to the mid-nineteenth century. The DCU Glasnevin campus is located in Ballymun, a disadvantaged area in northern Dublin. DCU made an early decision to serve its immediate local community and was one of the first Irish universities to develop a community engagement policy (Ozarowska 2019). Its commitment and engagement is an important part of DCU institutional policies and identity, as indicated by its prominent place on the institutional website. DCU is a key actor in the development of the Ballymun community (Montague 2023), not only by providing courses and learning programs tailored to the needs of local residents but also by opening up its campuses to include the community for cultural events.

DCU's community engagement is organized through a specific entity called DCU in the Community.[36] In 2022, its summer school, which is open to anyone interested, included sessions on topics like mental health, psychology, mediation (as an alternative to litigation), and climate change. The topics were of immediate concern to the local community and brought the knowledge, understanding, and experience of the academic home to local residents. A Bridge to Education course[37] helps people who have been away from formal education for some time prepare to enroll in higher education. It furthers communications, research, and study skills as well as personal and professional development. The course includes learning styles and strategies, helps students set learning goals and map their own experience, and also helps develop computer and IT skills that are now indispensable for success in higher education studies, but that may not be part and parcel of the experience of learners returning to education after many years away. A course at the bachelor's level focuses on community organization management and includes topics like community development theory; analysis of the community, the voluntary sector, and policy context; leadership and management theories; leadership in the community; organizational theory, structures, and processes; and financial management.[38]

As part of an overall Irish effort, DCU also offers students an opportunity to volunteer in their community. A specialized website[39] helps connect students and organizations looking for volunteers, and it has separate sections for those who look for volunteering opportunities and for those who look for volunteers. Like the Manifesto on Public Engagement by the U.K. National Co-ordinating Centre for Public Engagement (2019), the Irish student volunteer initiative emphasizes the mutual benefit to students and the organizations in which they volunteer. In many parts of Europe, having a traineeship or experience as a volunteer on one's résumé is a significant advantage when applying for one's first jobs. In addition, the work as a volunteer is often a very rewarding experience for students in its own right. A random glance at the student volunteer part of the website identifies opportunities for helping out at the Limerick Christmas market, volunteering as a social media page manager or fundraising coordinator, working with children suffering from autism, working with primary school students in "homework clubs," or combining international and local experiences by volunteering in communities in Mozambique or India. DCU has also identified an official Charity Partner, Barretstown,[40] which offers free and medically endorsed therapeutic recreation camps and programs for seriously ill children and their families. Student and staff volunteering is an important part of DCU's work with Barretstown.

The DCU Centre for Engaged Research[41] was until very recently headed by Professor Ronaldo Munck, who—like Professor Tony Gallagher of Queen's— is one of the leaders of the broader Global Corporation for the Democratic Mission of Higher Education, run by the Council of Europe, the International Consortium,[42] the IAU and the OAS, as described in Chapter 5. The DCU Centre aims to promote and facilitate more meaningful and impactful research through engagement with society, for example, with community organizations or vulnerable and/or marginalized groups. As pointed out by both the DCU Centre on its website and by Ira Harkavy in a recent article (Harkavy 2023), engaged research has the potential to develop knowledge that is indispensable to communities and, in turn, plays a key role in addressing social issues and developing policy. Involving the public in the research process empowers the community to influence change positively. Engaged research places the community at the heart of the research project and includes the community throughout the various research stages. The community is not a mere research object but a research actor. Current projects, among other things, aim to improve employment opportunities for young people with disabilities, develop a social justice game to promote gender equality and tackle gender-based and sexual abuse and harassment, and improve understanding of COVID-19 and the ways in which this pandemic may be addressed, notably through improved participation in vaccination schemes. An intergenerational music research project looked at how adolescents (aged fourteen to seventeen) and older adults (aged sixty-five to seventy-four) use music to manage change during distinct transitional periods of their lives.

An Engaged University in a Pluricultural Setting

Queen's is Northern Ireland's oldest university, and it is historically very much a part of the provincial establishment. In many ways, it sees its local mission as linked to all of Northern Ireland, so it defines a regional as much as a local role for itself.[43] Given the particular context of Northern Ireland, measures such as opening the traditionally Protestant university to a larger number of Catholic students and faculty, from the 1960s onward, as well as the participation of students from Queen's in the early days of the civil rights movement had local as well as regional impact.[44] In view of Queen's rich history and the particular context of Northern Ireland, the discussion of Queen's will be relatively extensive.

During the period known as the Troubles, which was a period of political violence between 1968 and 1995 on the background of a centuries-old bitter conflict between the Catholic and Protestant communities, Queen's eventually became an engaged university. This decision was, however, not made without difficult internal discussions in which many of its faculty maintained that engaging with a divided society would break with the university's obligation of distance and neutral detachment (Gallagher 2019). Queen's has now adopted a Social Charter,[45] and it is party to the U.K.-wide Manifesto for Public Engagement referred to earlier (National Co-ordinating Centre for Public Engagement 2019). Queen's encourages its faculty and students to undertake research with local and regional relevance, and it provides advanced medical services to the local community. Especially, it works with various parts of the local community in Belfast to motivate young people to aim for higher education as well as to provide them with the competences required to do so. Science Shops[46] and work with community centers and their local leaders are important parts of this engagement to improve social inclusion (McDonald et al. 2015). Queen's work in its immediate neighborhood also has regional impact.

For this author, it was a particularly impressive experience to visit the Sandy Row community center in a working-class loyalist (i.e., Protestant) area that is Queen's immediate neighbor. Local leaders told us that people from the community walked past Queen's every day but never dreamed of setting foot on campus. Two of the community leaders had served time in jail (sixteen years for one and ten years for the other) for crimes committed during the Troubles, and, on their release, they were shocked by how their community had developed. Traditionally, working-class Protestants had access to well-paying but low-skill jobs; however, the economic development had eliminated many of those jobs. The result was apathy in the local community, especially among youths, who saw no obvious future for themselves. There was also a rise in crime, which the community leaders found difficult to contain, given that they had themselves been convicted of violent crimes. This, on the other hand, gave them a strong sense of urgency, and the cooperation developed with Queen's focused not only on helping local secondary school students academically but also on motivating them to aim for higher education.

Rather than engaging professors, who would have been seen as distant and only marginally relevant role models, Queen's enlisted university students to work with local youths at the community center. The university students were just a few years older, and some came from similar backgrounds to those of the Sandy Row youths. Therefore, they understood the problems of local youths in a way few if any Queen's professors would have. Not least, Queen's students served as credible role models. They convinced many local youths that, if they had succeeded at university, youths from Sandy Row could, too. Professor Gallagher was key to making the cooperation a success.

On the basis of its Social Charter, Queen's launched a new initiative in 2021 called Communities and Place.[47] The guiding idea of this initiative is to develop partnerships between the academic community, the local community, and policymakers. The initiative emphasizes tackling disadvantage and improving opportunities for children, young people, and communities. Queen's underlines that this is a place-based project aiming to identify solutions to persistent social issues and effect long-term change through cocreation. At the same time, Queen's international contacts and partnerships will help identify possible solutions, not least by pointing to measures that have worked well elsewhere. The initiative draws on experience from several institutions outside of Northern Ireland through an international advisory board that, in addition to Gallagher, includes three other key actors in the project on the Democratic Mission of Higher Education (Chapter 5): Munck of DCU, Harkavy of Penn's Netter Center, and me. It does not aim to duplicate other experiences but rather to see what measures have worked in what circumstances and why and whether similar measures could work in the Northern Irish context.

Queen's key local partner in this project is the Market Development Association.[48] Contrary to what its name may lead one to believe, this is not a business or marketing association but rather a community group based in the Market area of South Belfast. In the fall of 2022, this initiative included an education program over ten weeks. The program was opened by Northern Ireland's then minister for communities Deirdre Hargey, and each week focuses on a specific topic. These include the importance of grassroots community activism as a vehicle for positive change, the origins and history of the Market area, human rights, how local residents can challenge systemic inequalities and improve their health and well-being, overdevelopment, work, health, and education. The university's goal with this program is to work with local residents to help identify solutions to local concerns and for local residents to take ownership of these efforts.

Queen's community engagement is carried out in the spirit defined in the manifesto referred to earlier: "Public engagement describes the myriad of ways in which the activity and benefits of higher education and research can be shared with the public. Engagement is by definition a two-way process, involving interaction and listening, with the goal of generating mutual benefit" (National Co-ordinating Centre for Public Engagement 2019: 4). In this context, public engagement is defined broadly and encompasses the varied ways in which the academic community of students and staff can engage with others outside the university. Thus, community engagement, community-based learning, and cultural engagement are all examples of engagement, and the list of examples is not exhaustive. The different forms of engagement do have one common denominator: mutual benefit. Local communities benefit from engagement, but so do universities and individual members of the academic community.

The role of Queen's in seeking to forge unity in a divided community may be contrasted with the experiences of Cyprus and Bosnia and Herzegovina. In both countries, divisions also run deep, and the higher education landscape does little to overcome these decisions. Since the Turkish invasion of Cyprus in July 1974, the country is de facto divided, and, even if there were a will to cater to both Greek and Turkish speakers within a single institution, the practical obstacles to doing so would be almost insurmountable. As described in Chapter 3, the Association for Historical Dialogue and Research (an NGO) undertakes very important cross-community work in its specific domain.[49] In Bosnia and Herzegovina, the civil war of the 1990s has resulted less in linguistic divides, even if subtle differences[50] can take on great importance in given situations, than in communities segregated into strongly divided local communities, within a state with very weak federal structures, and with two of the three main communities looking beyond the borders of the state, to Serbia and Croatia, respectively.

Higher Education Serving Ethnic and Linguistic Minorities

Both DCU and Queen's combine good academic reputations with a strong and multifaceted community engagement aimed at helping marginalized groups improve their lives. Marginalized groups may also be ethnic, linguistic, or religious minorities. Many countries of Europe are home to indigenous minorities as well as minority communities of more recent dates, and a specific group may combine several minority characteristics. Not all minorities are marginalized, however, and, in the following sections, we examine an institution serving a minority that was historically marginalized—and to a considerable extent still is—as well as one that was historically a power and cultural elite but is now less central to its national community.

A Marginalized Minority: The Sámi

The Sámi[51] are an indigenous population living, for the most part, north of the Arctic Circle in Norway, Finland, and Sweden, with a small group living also in Russia. Smaller groups live further south in Norway and Sweden, and, through internal migration, there are Sámi communities also in some of the larger cities in the southern parts of both countries, notably in Oslo. It is difficult to estimate the total Sámi population, as criteria vary between self-identification, fluency in Sámi and use of the language in daily life, and ancestry. Most estimates are in the seventy thousand to eighty thousand range for the total population, with the largest groups being in Norway. In 2017, just under seventeen thousand voters had registered to vote in the elections for the Norwegian Sámi Parliament, whereas some eight hundred students in Norwegian primary schools receive their full education in Sámi (Kommunal- og distriktsdepartementet 2019: 8), even if they also develop fluency in Norwegian.

Traditionally, Sámi were reindeer herders and, therefore, had a nomadic lifestyle that made access to education even more difficult.[52] Sámi children were largely educated at boarding schools, and relatively few had more than the minimum mandatory education. During a large part of the twentieth century, the Norwegian government pursued a policy of "Norwegianization" (fornorsking), an important part of which was promoting fluency in Norwegian and, as far as possible, eradicating the use of Sámi. This was not a specifically Norwegian phenomenon but part of a broader trend in Europe in the 1930s and 1950s to promote national languages and cultures at the expense of regional and minority ones. In Alsace, the slogan "It is chic to speak French" (c'est chic de parler français) was given added emphasis in the wake of World War II by the fact that Alsatian, besides not being recognized as a language in its own right,[53] was seen as a dialect of German and, hence, the language of the enemy.

In both postwar France and Norway, the education system was a very efficient tool for "unlearning" the regional language and promoting the national one. In Alsace today, being bilingual in French and Alsatian is to some extent a sign of lower educational and socioeconomic status, as Alsatian is mainly used in private contexts, rural environments, and among groups with lower socioeconomic status. Norway developed differently, for several reasons. One important reason is that linguistic variety—dialects and accents—has fairly high status in Norway and it is perfectly acceptable to use one's native dialect in official contexts, including radio and television. Norwegian is rich in dialects, but most of them are relatively easy to understand for other speakers of Norwegian. If language diversity was accepted within Norwegian, was there any valid reason not to accept the use of Sámi?

In the case of Sámi, there was also a broader political reason. From 1968 onward, plans were laid to use the Alta River in Finnmark, Norway's northernmost province, to produce electricity. Building the dam required to produce electricity would entail major changes—in the view of many, damage—to the river and to areas that were traditional Sámi grounds.[54] People sharing environmental concerns as well as concerns about the effect of the dam on Sámi culture and ways of life combined to organize civil resistance and disobedience in 1978–1979. This made what became known as "the Alta case" a highly controversial issue, where divides were partly environmental concerns versus economic interests and partly diverging views of the importance to be given to a minority population. Norway was increasingly criticized internationally for its treatment of the Sámi. Norwegian courts were also critical of the way the authorities had proceeded but nevertheless found that the proceedings were legal. Construction resumed in 1981–1982, the dam was completed, and the demonstrations against it ceased.

What was a short-term defeat for the majority of the Sámi population did, however, lead to a major review of the way Norway treats this minority. The government appointed a commission to review the Sámi's legal protection. The commission was headed by Professor Carsten Smith, who at the time was a high-profile law professor at the University of Oslo and later became chief justice of the Norwegian Supreme Court. A specific Sámi legislation was adopted in 1987, a clause on Sámi language, culture, and society was added to the Norwegian Constitution in 1988, and the Sámi Parliament was established, with an advisory role, in 1989.

Higher education provision in and for Sámi must be seen in this light. The University of Oslo, as the country's first, and for a long time only, university, established a chair in Sámi in 1874. The chair was discontinued in 2000 when the University of Tromsø—the major city in northern Norway, with a population of close to eighty thousand—became the only university in the country to offer Sámi studies (Butenschøn et al. 2012: 51). Today, while three Norwegian higher education institutions provide higher education in Sámi, only one of these—Samisk høgskole/Sámi allaskuvla[55]—conducts teaching and research entirely in Sámi (Kommunal- og distriktsdepartementet

2019: 20). This institution was established in 1989, in the aftermath of the Alta case, and now has somewhere between 150 and 200 students. The academic programs focus on areas of immediate concern to the Sámi community, such as Sámi language and culture, teacher education, and social sciences focusing on Sámi conditions.

Even if these study programs are of considerable importance to the Sámi community, and to preserving Sámi language and culture, the institution appears somewhat isolated from the broader higher education community. The case of higher education provision in Sámi in Norway shows not only some ambiguity and reticence in the way broader society treats an ethnic and linguistic minority but also the very real challenges in combining integration and maintaining the cultural specificity for a minority group that is small in numbers and has historically been marginalized to the point where it is difficult to say exactly who belongs to it. Not all those who self-identify as Sámi speak the language, and they are, therefore, unable to benefit from the relatively limited higher education programs that are now offered in Sámi.

A Formerly Dominant Minority: Swedish Speakers in Finland

The Swedish-speaking minority in Finland presents a very different picture.[56] While the Sámi have never held political power outside of their core areas and have suffered discrimination from the Norwegian, Swedish, and Finnish majorities even there, the Swedish-speaking population constituted the political elite in Finland until sometime after Finnish independence in 1917.[57] Swedish speakers have resided in Finland at least since the fourteenth century, possibly even since the twelfth century. Around 1809, when the Grand Duchy of Finland was erected as part of the Russian Empire, Swedish speakers made up about 15 percent of its population, whereas today they make up about 5 percent of the total Finnish population.[58] Swedish is still spoken in certain areas, notably along the western coast and in Helsinki, the capital (known as Helsingfors in Swedish), but is no longer a majority language in any region other than the Åland archipelago, which is entirely Swedish speaking, and certain rural areas in the western parts of mainland Finland. Swedish remains an official language in Finland, alongside Finnish, but a non-Finnish-speaking foreigner with a good knowledge of Swedish will for the most part nevertheless find it easier to get along in English than in Swedish. I can testify to this from my own experience.

For centuries, Finland was part of the Swedish realm, until 1809, when it became part of the Russian Empire. The Finnish elite, however, remained largely Swedish speaking, often with limited knowledge of Finnish. Marshall Carl Gustaf Mannerheim, who played a leading role in early to mid-twentieth-century Finnish history, is a case in point. Pehr Evind Svinhufvud, who was Finland's third president (1931–1937), was also a Swedish speaker. The original language issue in higher education in Finland was, therefore, less about promoting Swedish than about promoting Finnish. As part of the national romantic movement in Europe in the nineteenth century, Finns became increasingly conscious of their own language and culture, albeit with the added complication of Finland being under Russian suzerainty. The Fennoman movement, which promoted Finnish language, literature, and culture, was in part led by native Swedish speakers like the philosopher Johan Vilhelm Snellman and the poet and medical doctor Elias Lönnrot, who wrote the Finnish national epos *Kalevala*. There was also a Svecoman movement, which fought to keep Swedish as the only official language. In 1863, Tsar Alexander II issued a decree announcing that Finnish was to be co-official with Swedish within twenty years, but it was only in 1902 that the promise became reality. Finnish independence came fifteen years later, followed by a bitter civil war.

Åbo Akademi University,[59] therefore, presents a very different picture from Samisk høgskole/Sámi allaskuvla. With its main campus located in the city called Turku in Finnish and Åbo in Swedish, in southwestern Finland, Åbo Akademi University is a full-fledged university catering to the Swedish-speaking minority in Finland. Åbo Akademi University has a good academic reputation and is an active participant in European and international academic exchange. Åbo Akademi University is a classic, if relatively small, university with approximately 5,700 students, 650 faculty, and some 550 other staff.[60] The university has a clear international orientation as well as strong ambitions for quality learning, teaching, and research. In this sense, it is not significantly different from other major Finnish or Nordic universities.

At the same time, Åbo Akademi University plays an essential role in maintaining and developing Swedish-speaking culture in Finland. Most of its teaching is in Swedish, even if some courses are provided in English for the benefit of international students and the institution also offers Finnish as part of its program in languages and linguistics. As the website states, the university offers courses and programs in the native languages Swedish and Finnish and the foreign languages English, French, German, and Russian.[61] For most of its study programs, the university does require proven competence in Swedish.

As we saw earlier, the proportion of native Swedish speakers in the overall population of Finland is steadily decreasing but ties with the broader Swedish-speaking cultural community remain strong. Swedish as spoken in Finland, however, has distinctive traits including a readily identifiable accent influenced by Finnish stress patterns, and Swedish-speaking culture in

Finland is not merely a reduced version of overall Swedish culture. Sending Swedish-speaking Finnish students to Swedish universities would not be an adequate measure to preserve and develop Swedish as a minority yet official language in Finland. Åbo Akademi University, therefore, plays an important role not only as a liaison between Sweden and Swedish speakers in Finland but even more so as a cornerstone in developing and protecting the language and culture of the Swedish-speaking minority. One indication of this is the emphasis it places on teacher education, ranging from preparing preschool through primary and secondary school teachers to programs in special education and in educational leadership. While the main campus is in Åbo/Turku, the university also has a smaller campus in Vasa (Vaasa in Finnish), further north on the Baltic coast and traditionally a Swedish-speaking area. Even if the city itself is today majority Finnish speaking with a Swedish-speaking minority, parts of its surrounding area are still majority Swedish speaking. The campus in Vasa is, therefore, a strong signal to the local Swedish-speaking community.

Like many other universities, Åbo Akademi University runs outreach activities. The Academy Forum is a series of lectures open to the public, and it is significant that the series is held in Vasa. With YLE Åboland, the local Swedish-language branch of Finnish state television, Åbo Akademi University contributes to a series called *What Does Science Say?* which focuses on the humanities, psychology, and theology.[62] The series was launched as part of the centennial celebrations of the institution in 2018, and topics that have been covered include discussions of whether immigrants to Finland should be integrated in Swedish (by implication, not just in Finnish), measures against obesity, whether Swedish- and Finnish-speaking Finns have different approaches to music, and language, environment, and emotions. One program asks whether the proverbial—and, in my experience, wrongly stereotypical—Finnish lack of loquaciousness is a serious handicap in doing business with Germany.

In contrasting our two examples, we see that Samisk høgskole/Sámi allaskuvla caters to a small minority group, not all of whose members are fluent in Sámi, and focuses on a narrow range of study programs in fields where the needs of the Sámi community cannot be satisfied through other means (e.g., through study programs at other universities in Norway). Åbo Akademi University serves a much larger linguistic minority with strong ties to its broader language community in Sweden but most of whose members are also highly proficient in Finnish. It does so by offering a strong program of teaching and research in a wide range of academic disciplines. This ensures that the Swedish-speaking community in Finland has access to higher education and research in its native language and with due regard to Finnish conditions.

Preserving and Developing a National Language and Culture in a Bilingual Environment

Maltese language and culture are not those of a minority, and throughout its history Malta has been a crossroads influenced by several cultures and languages. Maltese is a Semitic language strongly influenced by Italian. Most Maltese are fluent in both Maltese and English, the latter spoken with a distinctive accent, and many are also proficient in Italian, which was the language of cultured communication for centuries (Brincat 2021). A saying has it that the Maltese use English when they want to open up to the world and Maltese when they want their conversations to remain confidential.

The University of Malta, therefore, does not have a role in preserving and developing a minority culture but rather in ensuring that a distinctive national language and culture will continue to develop and coexist with English. The university recognizes this double cultural and linguistic heritage, just as it recognizes that the specifically Maltese part of its heritage is in greater need of protection than the globalized English part. This is reflected in the university's current strategic plan, in which one of the strategic themes is national impact, and under this theme a goal is to "protect and preserve the Maltese language while simultaneously continue to cherish the English language" (L'Università ta' Malta 2019: 7).

In the more detailed part of the strategic plan, two subgoals are particularly relevant. Under "Championing Cultural Heritage and Identity," the plan states that "as the only public comprehensive University in Malta, the University of Malta has a crucial role in preserving and developing national culture, safeguarding cultural heritage and defending national identity. We will strive to instil in our students an awareness and appreciation of the Maltese identity and culture by building a sense of community rooted in strong democratic ideals and embracing values of tolerance, fairness and non-discrimination in today's multicultural society" (L'Università ta' Malta 2019: 37). Under "Honouring the Maltese Language," the plan underlines that "the rebranding of the University in 2018, with an emphasis on its official name as L-Università ta' Malta, clearly points towards the importance that the University accords to the protection and development of the Maltese language. Protecting and preserving the Maltese language must be achieved while simultaneously continuing to cherish the English language, and also promoting students' proficiency in at least one other foreign language. We will promote initiatives to encourage students to write both humanistic and scientific scholarly publications in the Maltese language, to continue enriching their linguistic repertoire. . . . We will aim to develop a language policy and offer international students and staff the opportunity to study Maltese. We will continue to promote language skills in Maltese in specific settings such as

the caring professions" (L'Università ta' Malta 2019: 37). While clearly emphasizing the need to protect and develop Maltese, this will not be achieved
at the expense of the de facto other national language, English, nor will it be
done at the expense of an international openness that the university considered crucial to a relatively small university in a small island country. English
remains the main language of instruction.[63]

The small size of the country makes it difficult to distinguish between the
local, the regional, and the national. Nevertheless, the university has established one unit—the Cottonera Resource Centre[64]—to act as a bridge between
some of the communities in the inner harbor area and the University of Malta and to "act as a hub that co-ordinates links between these communities
and the University, facilitating resource-transfer and capacity building" (quote
from the website). The Cottonera Resource Centre, then, serves the area known
as both Cottonera and the Three Harbours and made up of the municipalities of Vittoriosa, Senglea, and Cospicua. Cottonera is a socially deprived area
that is going through a transition period as regeneration and revitalization
projects are being undertaken. For centuries, the area, on the south side of
the Grand Harbour, was considered as the scion of industrialization and
trade unionism in Malta, but it saw drastic economic and social deteriora-
tion after World War II (Cutajar and Vella 2018: 1).

The Cottonera Resource Centre aims both to promote and provide higher
education to residents of these communities and to promote the area's economic and heritage potential. Activities include:

- Organizing conferences, seminars, and public lectures related to
  the Cottonera area
- Cooperating with local public authorities and civil society on projects, initiatives, and events that seek to promote the area
- Conducting or facilitating research on issues or topics related to the
  area as well as making existing research results more accessible to
  the community
- Managing community-based education initiatives, both formal and
  nonformal
- Building networks with entities active in the community, especially education institutions, agencies looking after the interests of
  groups that face social disadvantage, and entities that help in career guidance and in the promotion of employment[65]

The Cottonera Resource Centre has adopted what it calls a community center approach and underlines that the community's own view of priorities for
development will guide its activities.

In 2017–2018,[66] activities and projects for children and youths were a main focus, with classes helping prepare local children for an important school exam, with an element of individual tutoring, as well as robotics and drama classes designed to stimulate creativity and problem-solving. The Cottonera Resource Centre also organized a six-week summer school for children from the area. Activities and projects for adults focus on lifelong learning courses and the University of the Third Age (see later). In 2017–2018, courses included Maltese archival heritage, Malta during the nineteenth century, Maltese Bobbin Lace Making, and Maltese as a foreign language (for immigrant residents). These offerings were in English, but two courses were also provided in Maltese. Community outreach projects included a legal clinic offering free legal advice, free counseling sessions to individuals experiencing emotional and/or psychological difficulties, play therapy for children, and basic English and Maltese classes for adults needing to improve their literacy (L'Università ta' Malta/Cottonera Resource Centre 2019).

The University of the Third Age (U3A) linked to the Cottonera Resource Centre is part of a broader University of Malta effort to stimulate learning among older residents, dating back to 1993. As the website says: "The Maltese U3A trusts that as long as one lives, one feels a natural yearning to know more, to explore and to understand. The University of the Third Age is making this possible for everyone. The U3A encourages creativity and will propose several projects for this purpose. The U3A also supports the organisation of special interest groups for pursuing hobbies or other interests."[67] Today, the University of the Third Age operates in six locations on the main island and one in Gozo, the smaller of the inhabited Maltese islands. It promotes knowledge and learning as an end in itself rather than as a means to improving one's academic credentials, has no admissions requirements, and is open to everyone above the age of sixty, irrespective of any prior educational or academic qualifications.

Malta is strongly oriented toward economic growth. In addition to the university's cultural mission, many of its projects with broader society have a business or economic development objective. Enterprise and industry impact constitute a separate chapter in the strategic plan, including engaging industry in curriculum development, embedding industry knowledge in the learning experience, enhancing learning through enterprise projects, and expanding executive education (L'Università ta' Malta 2019: 30–34).

This economic focus, however, coexists with a broader focus on the university's societal mission and impact, the overall goal of which is to create an inclusive university for an inclusive society. Measures and objectives include supporting persons with disabilities, providing assistance for underrepresented and first-generation students, and promoting diversity. The university makes an explicit commitment to advancing gender and LGBTQ rights, which is not trivial in a relatively conservative and traditional society. The strategic plan also commits the university to engaging the campus community and to promoting public outreach. As part of this commitment, the university wants to support recognized student societies, ensure that evening courses cater to the needs and interests of part-time students and consider providing full-time day programs on a flexible part-time basis when required by the learner, consider expanding specific outreach services, and improve collaboration with nonstate actors, in particular, civil society and industry. Interestingly, the Cottonera Resource Centre is seen as a model for similar outreach programs in other parts of Malta, including on Gozo (L'Università ta' Malta 2019: 25–29).

The University of Malta, then, engages with broader society to further both cultural and economic development. It takes account of the particular double cultural and linguistic heritage of Malta and, without downplaying the English part of that heritage, which is key to its efforts to be a university of European and global reach, it gives special emphasis to Maltese language and culture. Rather than a situation with a majority and a minority culture, Malta has a "double majority" heritage, one part of which is nevertheless in particular need of support and development. If the University of Malta would not take up this responsibility, it is, indeed, difficult to see where academic competence and outreach in Maltese language and culture would be undertaken. Although the Gozitan identity seems to remain strong—at least this is what Maltese friends and contacts tell me—the small size of the country makes it difficult to distinguish between what is local and what is national. Nevertheless, some of the university's outreach activities target local communities with severe socioeconomic challenges. The efforts undertaken in this sense in the Three Harbours (Cottonera) area now seem to serve as a model for the development of similar initiatives elsewhere in the country.

A somewhat similar link between higher education and language also exists in Belgium and Switzerland. Both are plurilingual states but the relationship between the different language communities is more conflictive in Belgium, where both the Catholic University of Leuven/Louvain and the Free University of Bruxelles/Brussel were split along language lines in the late 1960s. In each case, the conflict ended up with two distinct institutions, one Flemish and the other French speaking. In Switzerland, universities teach in German or French according to their location, with an Italian-speaking university established in the south of the country as recently as 1996 and the University of Fribourg/Freiburg[68] as the country's only bilingual university (French/German). No institution has the fourth official Swiss language, Rhaeto-Romance,[69] as its main language, but Rhaeto-Romance can be studied at the Universities of Fribourg/Freiburg and Zürich.

General Findings

From a relatively extensive list of concrete examples, let us now turn to a more analytical summary of what the examples tell us about cooperation between universities and local communities in Europe, again without any pretense of presenting the complete picture. The summary will try to make sense of the diversity presented in the examples by answering five questions. At the end, I try to distill a few conclusions and lessons learned.

Institutional Policy or Passionate Individuals?

The local democratic mission of higher education could not become a living reality without the commitment of individuals, who do the everyday work. These committed individuals must come from all cooperation partners. A small group of committed members of the academic community will not suffice if they have no counterpart in the local civil society, public authorities, or the business community. The reverse is, of course, also true. A local community cannot cooperate with a university if the university is indifferent. As the saying goes, it takes two to tango.

Passionate individuals can do wonders, but they will find it difficult to establish lasting cooperation. That requires institutional commitment. What we have seen in our examples is that most of them are rooted in institutional decisions, such as the strategic plans, or even in legislation. The Territorial Pact in San Marino is an example of the latter, while universities as diverse as Kraków and Queen's and those of Iceland and Malta have included community outreach among their institutional priorities in their strategic plans. Working with and in the local and regional community is, therefore, not just something individual academics may choose to do; it is something the university does as a matter of institutional policy. This has positive consequences for funding, institutional support, and the way peers in the academic community see community engagement projects as legitimate or not.

The same is true for partners in the local community. Local authorities, civil society organizations, and/or local businesses need to commit institutionally, and members of the local community must see the cooperation as beneficial. As the Council of Europe Platform on the Local Democratic Mission of Higher Education (Chapter 6) underlines, universities must work *with* and not just *in* their local communities. The CITTRU at the Jagiellonian University clearly has great legitimacy in the local business community as well as with local authorities and a strong standing in the local and regional community. The work DCU and Queen's undertake with their local communities has the support of local authorities and leaders in the local civil society as well as in the community more broadly, and they also illustrate the importance and benefit of working closely with community organizations and members. The University of Malta's work in and through the Cottonera Resource Centre likewise enjoys broad local support from the three local councils as well as from local residents.

Institutional commitment cannot be taken for granted. It needs to be developed and then maintained, as the experience of Penn shows in the United States, where an institutional commitment to its local community undertaken in the 1980s translated into the establishment of the Netter Center for Community Partnership in 1992. The Netter Center is again key to maintaining the university's commitment to its neighborhood. In Europe, the decision to make Queen's an engaged university, made in the 1980s during the Troubles, did not go unchallenged, but it has now ensured that Queen's plays a key role in both the economic and the broader societal development of Northern Ireland. The commitment was maintained and developed further after the end of the Troubles, and it could prove crucial should intercommunity tensions flare up in the wake of Brexit, where one particularly challenging issue is whether there will again be a "hard" border between Northern Ireland and the Republic of Ireland.

It is difficult to establish an overview of the extent to which an institutional commitment to community engagement across Europe has increased significantly over the past couple of decades, but anecdotal evidence suggests that it has. Two elements underpin this assertion. First, public debate no longer emphasizes the economic role of higher education as the predominant purpose of higher education to the extent it tended to do when the Bologna Process was launched in 1999. The notion that higher education has several purposes, including a broader societal and democratic purpose, was developed by the Council of Europe (Bergan 2005b; Council of Europe 2007) and is now solidly anchored in the communiqués adopted by the ministers responsible for higher education in the framework of the EHEA, starting with the 2007 London Communiqué (Bologna Process 2007). Second, as described in Chapter 5, the Council of Europe and the International Consortium have been organizing Global Fora on the Democratic Mission of Higher Education every two or three years since 2006, lately also with the IAU and the OAS. While U.S. participants have largely been institutional leaders—presidents, deans, and similar positions—there has been an evolution in the composition of European participants. The Global Fora have always had representatives of public authorities, which play a more important role in setting higher education policy in Europe than they do in the United States. Among those representing universities, however, there has been a clear development from a high proportion of committed individuals without institutional responsibilities toward a much stronger representation of institutional leaders. This would indicate that institutional leaders, whose job title in Europe is typically rector, are now more strongly committed to the democratic mission of higher education than their predecessors were some two decades ago.

On What Do We Cooperate?

The list of areas for university-community cooperation is almost as diverse as the universities and local communities themselves. Furthering local and regional economic development with the help of the knowledge, understanding, and research results developed by universities is an important element. This is a predominant part of the outreach activities at the Jagiellonian, and it is present at most universities. The list of areas for cooperation is, however, very broad and goes well beyond the economy.

The broader development of local and regional communities has a societal as well as an economic aspect. As the examples of both DCU and Queen's show, social/societal and economic development can go together. People from disadvantaged backgrounds with low formal competences and limited skills will not easily find employment without undertaking further education. This is particularly true in our increasingly complex societies and economies, where jobs for the unskilled are few and far between. People with low qualifications often find it difficult to cope with modern societies, from dealing with public authorities to influencing decisions that concern their communities. In these conditions, life as active citizens in democratic societies— which the Council of Europe defines as one of the major purposes of education (Council of Europe 2007)—is exceedingly difficult to achieve. Projects aiming to develop competences in the local community and motivating local residents—in particular youths—to aim for higher education, help improve residents' self-esteem and life skills as well as employment skills. In addition to DCU and Queen's, the University of Malta's work through the Cottonera Resource Centre is an example.

The University of Iceland demonstrates the broader cultural mission of the university through its outreach activities aiming either at an interested general public or at specific groups like children or young people. Other universities covered by this chapter, like Åbo Akademi University, also emphasize this broader cultural mission.

The range of examples from the Czech Republic shows the importance and variety of student volunteering. Many of these projects aim at helping vulnerable members of the local community, and some—like the "Night Outdoors" program in Hradec Králové—go further and aim to develop a longer-lasting commitment and compassion in students. Activities directed at children cover many areas, ranging from the University of Iceland's Teddy Hospital to the project at Masaryk University aimed at facilitating the transition into broader society for young people who have been raised in orphanages.

The cultural mission of the university takes on a particular dimension when it comes to protecting and developing minority cultures and languages. This may concern a marginalized minority culture with few members, many of whom may not be proficient in the minority language. In this chapter, this is exemplified by Samisk høgskole/Sámi allaskuvla. Åbo Akademi University, a Swedish-speaking Finnish university, is a very different example, namely that of a full-fledged university that serves a minority population with a past as a cultural and power elite but whose proportion of the population is now declining markedly. It is also a university that has strong contacts to a broader Swedish-speaking community based across the Baltic Sea in Sweden as well as well-developed international cooperation, in addition to broad contacts with other Finnish universities. The University of Malta exemplifies a third case: that of an institution furthering a national language, Maltese, specific to the country, that coexists with a global language, English, which is de facto also a national language in Malta. The University of Malta must develop Maltese without downplaying the importance of English, which is, incidentally, the language of instruction for most of its study programs.

Where Is Our Local Community?

Local communities are often relatively compact but the example of the University of the Aegean shows that the community may be spread out, and that it may be difficult—or at least time consuming and expensive—to move from one part of the community to another. In the case of Queen's, it sees itself as having both a local mission, exemplified by its work with the Sandy Row community in its immediate neighborhood, and a regional role directed at all of Northern Ireland. It also has a double identity as both an Irish and a U.K. university, and different parts of its academic community identify more strongly with one of these identities than the other.

The cases of Malta and San Marino, but also those of the Jagiellonian, show that it may be difficult to distinguish the local mission of a university from its broader national and international role. In the case of the Jagiellonian, this is not due to the size of the university or of the country in which it works but rather to its long history of academic prominence, which has given it a strong national role, although it is not located in the capital (even if Kraków was once the capital of Poland, a fact of which its residents are acutely conscious). Malta and San Marino are small in both extension and population, and San Marino has only a single university, at least so far. The University of Malta does work with specific local communities but many of its outreach activities—not least those aiming to further economic development—are national in scope. The Territorial Pact in San Marino, which has the university at its center—is national in scope but could serve as an interesting model for universities and local communities in larger countries.

What Makes the Local Mission Democratic?

Our examples in this chapter range broadly. They all illustrate how universities can work in and with their local and regional communities. Do they also illustrate how the local mission of higher education can strengthen democracy?

As is well known, "democracy" comes from the Ancient Greek δῆμος (dimos, mostly Romanized as dēmos), meaning people, and κράτος (kratos), meaning rule. Democracy, then, is rule by the people—or as President Abraham Lincoln famously said, "Of the people, by the people, for the people."[70] This is a good start, but as the Council of Europe's Youth Department points out, "There are so many different models of democratic government around the world that it is sometimes easier to understand the idea of democracy in terms of what it definitely is not. Democracy, then, is not autocracy or dictatorship, where one person rules; and it is not oligarchy, where a small segment of society rules. Properly understood, democracy should not even be 'rule of the majority,' if that means that minorities' interests are ignored completely. A democracy, at least in theory, is government on behalf of all the people, according to their 'will.'"[71]

As we have seen several times in this book, a more traditional view of democracy, emphasizing laws, institutions, and elections, needs to be updated with an emphasis on democratic culture. This updated and enhanced understanding is important for assessing whether any given initiative furthers democracy. Democracy requires that citizens be active, that they not only vote but also participate and deliberate. To do so, they need competences and resources. From this point of view, university-community cooperation that develops competences, that furthers social inclusion, and that empowers people furthers democracy. The Council of Europe defines four major purposes of education, including preparing for life as active citizens in democratic societies (Bergan 2005b; Council of Europe 2007), but also underlines that these purposes are complementary not contradictory.

This modern vision of democracy is shared by European ministers responsible for higher education, who in 2015 stated that "by 2020 we are determined to achieve an EHEA where . . . higher education is contributing effectively to build inclusive societies, founded on democratic values and human rights; and where educational opportunities provide the competences and skills required for European citizenship, innovation and employment" (Bologna Process 2015a: 1–2).

Nine years earlier, the participants in the first Global Forum that focused on the democratic mission of higher education, organized by the Council of Europe and the International Consortium, expressed similar views. The participants stated that "democracy can only flourish with strong supportive institutions and laws, and a pervasive democratic culture, which encompasses democratic values, ways of knowing and acting, ethical judgments, analytical competences, and skills of engagement" (Council of Europe 2006a: 1). They reaffirmed their belief that higher education is essential to furthering democratic culture and to fostering citizen commitment to sustainable public policies and actions that go beyond considerations of individual benefits. Not least, they reaffirmed their conviction "that complex environmental, economic, and societal issues can only be solved at local, national, and global levels if citizens can combine basic democratic values with a knowledge and understanding of the relationship of these challenges" (Council of Europe 2006a: 2).

Seen in this light, universities cooperating with their local communities to improve economic opportunity and provide people in the local community with a deeper knowledge and understanding of societal issues on the basis of academic learning and research—and encourage their students to engage in this societal mission—which includes community engagement in their institutional mission and strategy and work to strengthen cultural and linguistic diversity, can all further democracy. The examples in this chapter show several ways in which universities, by working with their local communities, can strengthen democracy locally and beyond. These examples are not exhaustive, and they should be adapted rather than duplicated.

Only Local, or Also National and International?

This author is highly skeptical of rankings (Bergan 2011: 159–174), but, in an age where rankings are regrettably and unjustifiably seen as giving an indication of the overall quality of a university rather than just of its research in natural sciences, few universities will limit their ambitions to the local. Samisk høgskole/Sámi allaskuvla may be an exception, as it is a highly specialized institution serving a small cultural community in a language spoken almost exclusively by members of that community or by ethnic Norwegians who have moved to the Sámi core areas (and not all of whom speak Sámi).

The other universities examined in this chapter, as well as most other European universities, have ambitions beyond their local community. In some cases, their ambitions may be national, but, more often than not, universities also aim at achieving and maintaining international standing, expressed through international cooperation, research being cited internationally, and—well—inclusion in the international rankings that many university leaders criticize but few ignore.

One clear conclusion from the examples in this chapter is that universities do not have to choose between having local, national, and international roles. Åbo Akademi University serves a minority language and cultural community residing in specific parts of Finland, but, in addition to this specific role, it also has national and international ambitions. It is active in international academic cooperation and exchange, and the university does not wish to see this limited to its cultural and linguistic cousins in Sweden.

The high-quality education and research that comes with international cooperation, exchange, and ambitions can and should be used to the advantage also of the local community. Community outreach is not, and should not be, something universities do only if they are not "good enough" to do anything else. It should be part and parcel of what universities do, and, as the examples in this chapter show, it is. Universities that were to limit their horizon to the local would easily stagnate. The academic world is international, and few, if any, disciplines are developed in a single institution only. This applies even to the most seemingly local or national disciplines, such as less widely spoken languages and the cultures they carry. But, likewise, experience and competence developed through international cooperation can and should be applied in concrete contexts, and those contexts are often local. Research results obtained by others may need to be adapted, but research, learning, and teaching that are not put into practice locally will easily propagate the myth of the ivory tower. Had the myth been true—in other words, had it not been a myth—universities would not have survived for centuries, as one of the world's oldest organizational models. At a time when the term "alternative facts" is no longer seen as a contradiction or even necessarily written in quotation marks, the university must demonstrate its importance to the broader society of which it is a part. It can do so at the national level, but it can and should also do so by working with its local community.

Main Conclusions

The examples in this chapter as well as the earlier summary enable us to draw a few main conclusions. In cooperating with their local communities, European universities rely on a combination of committed leadership and enthusiastic volunteers. This is true within the academic community but also within the broader local community. Leaders must make cooperation possible, and enthusiastic individuals within both the academic and the local community are needed to move university-community cooperation from a policy goal to a practical reality.

This cooperation can concern almost any topic and interest of both the university and the local community. Nevertheless, initiatives that stimulate participation, broaden and deepen knowledge and understanding, improve economic and societal opportunities for local residents, and consider the local community as a true partner rather than just an object of study or recipient of assistance are those that will merit continuing support by public authorities and institutions alike. Making such initiatives sustainable should be a political priority.

In most cases, the local community is a city or a metropolitan area. It is neither too large nor too small. However, in some cases, the local community can be a neighborhood within a city, and, in some cases, it can be a larger area, such as a region. This can be the case even where communication and travel are difficult. Europe also has the particularity of having a few countries that are among the smallest in the world, where trying to distinguish the local and regional from the national has little practical importance when it comes to higher education.

To be democratic, university-community cooperation cannot be content with creating structures and regulations. It must encourage participation and develop what the Council of Europe has come to label a culture of democracy. It must help develop the competences students, faculty, and staff as well as local residents need to be active citizens in democratic societies. This includes not only the ability but also the will and commitment to engage in public space.

Fulfilling their local democratic mission is not something universities need to choose to do at the expense of other missions. They can fulfill this mission both in addition to and as part of other missions. They can be local, national, and international all at the same time. To fulfill the local democratic mission of higher education, we need European cooperation to develop joint policies and inspirational practices that can be transferred between and adapted to quite different contexts.

In particular, community engagement is not something universities do only if they are not good enough in fulfilling their missions of research, learning, and teaching. On the contrary, engaging democratically with their local communities can strengthen all aspects of their mission. The mission of higher education is a coherent whole and more than the sum of its individual components, and engaging democratically with their local communities can strengthen all aspects of their mission.

Lessons Learned

The key lessons learned from this extensive chapter include:

- It is important that members of the academic community be aware of and attentive to the role the university can play in its local community and that their perception of this role be both nuanced and broad. The role must be seen as going beyond cooperation with local economic actors and consider what potential allies they can find in their local communities to further (local) democracy through education but also identify which groups are in particular need of engagement.

- Although engaged individuals in the higher education community are essential, institutional engagement requires commitment by the leadership. University leaders must see the local democratic mission as part of what the university should do. For example, at both the Jagiellonian University Kraków and the University of Malta the university strategies define the role of the university in its local and regional community.
- Leadership is equally important in the local community. Universities need the cooperation of community leaders to develop partnerships. Ideally, this will include the elected political leaders of the community, as shown by DCU's cooperation with its immediate neighborhood. Local civic leaders are, however, also essential, as demonstrated by the work Queen's is conducting in and with community centers. In this case, civic leaders wielded a moral authority in the local community without which the cooperation would very likely not have come about.
- Cooperation between universities and their local community leaders needs to be just that—cooperation, which is a two-way process. Universities can, of course, make offers, but for cooperation to be successful, the university response to local community needs is best defined jointly by the university and the local community. The Territorial Pact encompassing the University of San Marino and its local community is an example of a particularly comprehensive framework for university-community cooperation.
- The university needs to define what it can offer and then make sure this responds to what the local community defines as its needs. For example, the Swedish-speaking minority in Finland is not underprivileged economically, even if some members of this group are far from affluent and are living in rural areas. It is, however, faced with the challenge of preserving and developing its specific culture and language as a small minority whose members need to interact intensively with the Finnish-speaking majority. Social advancement and political and economic influence require Swedish speakers also to be fluent in Finnish since communication outside of the minority community is mostly in Finnish because relatively few native Finnish speakers are fluent in Swedish. Therefore, Åbo Akademi University plays an important role in maintaining and

developing the specific Finnish-Swedish culture and language, and it does so on a basis of a solid academic record.

- Student involvement in cooperation with the local community is beneficial to both the students and the local community, and it is, perhaps, particularly effective when it is part of a university program or course, and if it gives students credits (in Europe, typically ECTS credits) for their involvement. The University of Iceland Teddy Hospital and the Volunteering Center at Palacký University in Olomouc are examples.

- The effect of university-community cooperation may be almost immediate, as in the case of legal clinics offering free legal advice, as at the University of Malta. The benefits may, however, also be more long term and not only help the target group but also develop attitudes and competences that students will deploy in their later lives as professionals and citizens. The "Night Outdoors" program in Hradec Králové is particularly focused on assisting as well as developing empathy with a particularly vulnerable group: the homeless.

- Universities are centers of competence in many areas, not the least of which is culture. Universities can play an important general education role in broader society, which, in the Nordic countries, is often referred to as enhancing the cultural horizons of the broader public.[72] Several of the University of Iceland's outreach activities are examples, as is the University of Malta's "University of the Third Age."

- University-community cooperation needs to take account of the specific circumstances of each community. These may be historic and social, as in Queen's working with its immediate, loyalist working-class neighborhood. They may also be geographic, a good example of which is the University of the Aegean's extensive local community with university campuses on six islands. Samisk høgskole/ Sámi allaskuvla conducts teaching and research entirely in Sámi and caters to a very small minority population, the membership of which is not entirely easy to define, spread out over a considerable area. Because of the small size of its target community, the institution offers courses and expertise in only a few academic areas, and these are the ones seen as particularly important to this specific community. In San Marino and Iceland, it may be difficult to identify what is local, what is regional, and what is national, but that is ultimately less important than identifying what the university can do for its community.

Local communities are, of course, not static, and new members may arrive with special needs for support, but they also may arrive with competences that can help the local community if only they are able to deploy their competences and skills.[73] It is to this issue that we now turn in the next chapter, which explores the EQPR.

8

European and Local

The European Qualifications Passport for Refugees

Context

In 2015, Europe faced a situation for which it was badly prepared. In the course of a few weeks, the number of refugees arriving in Europe increased drastically, and most of them came from the Middle East. Seventy-five percent of those who arrived came from just three countries: Syria, Iraq, and Afghanistan. In all, more than nine hundred thousand refugees arrived in Europe in the course of the year, and at least thirty-five hundred died before they could reach European shores—shores because, rather than overland, the majority arrived in makeshift embarkations. Tragedies marked 2015, such as the drowning of more than six hundred refugees on a single day in the Mediterranean when their boat capsized, the death of seventy-one migrants in a refrigeration truck in Austria, and, what became perhaps the most powerful image of the refugee crisis, the body of a four-year-old Syrian refugee, Aylan Kurdi, washed up on a Turkish shore.[1]

But it was also a year of hope. Governments, local communities, and individual citizens mobilized to welcome refugees. Germany, Austria, Sweden, and several other countries decided not to close their borders when faced with a massive increase in the number of refugees arriving. Local communities organized reception centers and other measures to welcome refugees, and volunteers met them at stations. German chancellor Angela Merkel's response became legendary. *Wir schaffen das*—we will manage this—became something of an equivalent to President Barack Obama's *Yes, We Can*.[2] The local response was, in many cases, overwhelming, and community members from many backgrounds and walks of life chipped in.

Most refugees are not just people in need; they also have formidable skills and competences that they could use for the benefit of their new host communities. In particular, for refugees with higher education qualifications, having these recognized is an important obstacle, and finding ways to overcome the obstacle is important to making refugees a resource and not "just" a problem. It is essential to the overall effort of integrating refugees in their new communities for universities to work with their local communities not only to identify what qualifications refugees have, even when these cannot be documented, but also to find good ways of enabling refugees to use their qualifications.

This is important because even though the initial response to the refugee crisis was largely positive, it was not unanimously so. For example, Chancellor Merkel's readiness to welcome refugees was contested within Germany, in particular, from the right wing of her own party the CDU and its Bavarian sister party CSU,[3] and it gave a boost to AfD, a fairly new right-wing party.[4] The European populist right, led by the governments of Hungary and Poland, took a highly restrictive approach to receiving refugees from the Middle East and claimed to be protecting their countries against foreign—especially Muslim—"invasion" (Schultheis 2018). The number of Syrian refugees in all other European countries, however, pales in comparison with those of Turkey, which had by mid-January 2023 received some 3.5 million. Contrary to popular perception in Europe, other countries of the Middle East—but not the Gulf States[5]—also received significant numbers. Lebanon stands out by hosting more than eight hundred thousand refugees[6] within a total population of some 6.7 million[7] and a very volatile political, economic, and societal situation even before the latest crisis in the Middle East.

By 2021, the number of new refugees arriving in Europe had diminished considerably, to 123,000. The 2021 figure was 29 percent higher than the one for 2020,[8] the year in which Europe felt the full impact of COVID-19, but it was at approximately the same level as the figure for 2019, which was the last pre-COVID-19 year. In 2022, Europe experienced a new refugee crisis, as large numbers of Ukrainians fled the Russian invasion of their country. As of mid-January 2023, almost eight million Ukrainian refugees had been registered across Europe, and, of these, almost five million had been registered for Temporary Protection or similar national protection schemes in Europe. In the course of 2023, numbers dropped somewhat as some refugees returned home even as others left. Ukraine's neighbors to the west received a very significant share of these refugees, with Poland, Germany, the Czech Republic, and Romania among those receiving the most.[9] Moldova received more than one hundred thousand refugees from Ukraine even if the population of Moldova is only about 2.6 million. This figure is all the more impressive in view of the fact that Moldova is one of Europe's poorest countries, is strongly divided between pro-European and pro-Russian factions, and itself feels threatened by Russia due to the long-standing presence of Russian troops in Transnistria, which is a de facto breakaway part of the country lacking international recognition (Deleu 2005; Bocancea and Carp 2016). Some of the countries that had been extremely reluctant to receive refugees from the Middle East changed their position when it came to refugees from Ukraine, with Poland as the main example. Only Hungary has still maintained its antirefugee position in the new crisis. Orbán's government remained closer to Russia than any other government in the EU, has consistently tried to block both EU sanctions on Russia and aid to Ukraine, and—in the end unsuccessfully—also tried to prevent the opening of membership negotiations for Ukraine and Moldova.[10]

Refugees and Education: Toward a Council of Europe Response

Refugees come from all backgrounds and range from those with minimal formal education to those holding advanced degrees and having held academic positions in their home country. Many refugees were students or higher education graduates in their home country. In the case of refugees from Syria, the classic student age cohort was overrepresented among refugees not only because it is easier for younger people to flee but because escaping military service was a strong motivation for many. The Assad regime is in essence waging a war against large parts of its own population, and young men forced into military service ran a substantial risk not only of death or injury but also of being forced to fight against their own kin.[11]

The first initiative within the Council of Europe came from Greece. At the Ministerial Conference organized in Bruxelles in April 2016,[12] the then Greek alternate minister for education approached us informally and asked if the Council of Europe could help with a summer academy for refugee students.[13] This academy would have a double purpose: helping prepare refugee students to study at Greek universities and bringing together refugee and Greek students. The Council of Europe contributed to the program, in particular, on education for democracy.

The summer academy was a success, but we believed it would be preferable to undertake more specific activities to help refugees continue their education at European universities. Some European countries had experience with this, and the Council was approached by the ENICs of Norway and the

United Kingdom. Norway, in particular, had started developing methods to assess qualifications that refugees claimed but could not document, and both ENICs thought this experience needed to be developed further and be applied at a European level. They had first approached the European Commission, but the Commission had showed little enthusiasm for the project. It is not quite clear why the Commission was unenthusiastic, but I would venture to guess that at least two factors played a role. First, the initiative came from a non-EU country and one that was soon to leave the EU through Brexit. Second, a few countries had developed less advanced assessment methods in their own national contexts on the basis of which they issued what was known as "background documents." In addition to being based on a less advanced methodology, these documents had little potential use outside of the country in which they were issued. Denmark was one of the countries that had developed its own background document and ultimately proved to be the one most strongly opposed to the idea of a qualifications passport, and the person responsible for recognition issues in the Commission at the time was seconded from the Danish Ministry of Education.

Recognizing Refugees' Qualifications: The Lisbon Recognition Convention

It quickly became clear that the idea of developing an EQPR[14] had great potential, and the Council of Europe decided to develop a project. European universities had already established many measures to help refugees, and the EUA had gathered these in a Refugees Welcome Map.[15] The Council of Europe had set up a small group to look at what we could do to help refugee students, in which the EUA also participated.

There was little reason for the Council to duplicate other initiatives, and our work soon came to focus on developing the EQPR. We had a good basis for doing so because of the Lisbon Recognition Convention (Chapter 1). In 1994–1997, when the convention was developed and adopted, there was a refugee crisis in Europe. Many people had to flee their homes because of the wars in former Yugoslavia, and, in particular, in Bosnia and Herzegovina. We, therefore, managed to include an article in the convention by which parties commit to taking "all feasible and reasonable steps within the framework of its education system and in conformity with its constitutional, legal, and regulatory provisions to develop procedures designed to assess fairly and expeditiously whether refugees, displaced persons and persons in a refugee-like situation fulfil the relevant requirements for access to higher education, to further higher education programmes or to employment activities, even in cases in which the qualifications obtained in one of the Parties cannot be proven through documentary evidence" (Council of Europe and UNESCO 1997: Article VII).

Since 1997, however, Europe had not seen another continent-wide refugee crisis until 2015. Most countries had, therefore, failed to take national measures to put the so-called Article VII into practice. A survey conducted in 2015 and published a year later showed that only eight of the more than fifty states party to the convention had national regulations on procedures for recognition of qualifications held by refugees and displaced persons without documentary evidence of their qualifications. In another six countries, it was the competent recognition authorities—in most cases the national information centers—that regulated the recognition of refugees' qualifications,[16] and some of these were quite advanced. Norway was singled out as having the most comprehensive system, and, in 2014, it had introduced a Recognition Procedure for Persons without Verifiable Documentation (UVD-procedure)[17] that used some of the methods that were later developed further in the EQPR. All of thirty-five countries, however—70 percent of the respondents—reported that they had no regulations to facilitate the recognition of refugees' qualifications (Council of Europe and UNESCO 2016: 57–63).

We decided to take two measures to improve the recognition of refugees' qualifications, one legal and the other practical. The legal measure was a recommendation that was ultimately adopted by the Lisbon Recognition Convention Committee at an extraordinary meeting at Council of Europe Headquarters in Strasbourg in November 2017 (Council of Europe and UNESCO 2017).[18] The recommendation reiterates the principle already included in the Lisbon Recognition Convention that refugees who cannot adequately document their qualifications or periods of study are entitled to having these assessed for the purpose of gaining admission to a study program or seeking employment. It also says that competent recognition authorities "should take adequate measures in this respect within the limits of each Party's constitutional, legal and regulatory provisions" (para. 9). The recommendation then outlines measures that countries should take to facilitate this kind of recognition. In some cases, they need to review and amend their national regulations and legislation (para. 14). While neither the recommendation nor the explanatory memorandum[19] could identify specific problem cases, it was said at the time that, in one country, its national security legislation made it difficult to recognize nondocumented qualifications.

The part of the recommendation dealing with the assessment proper (paras. 15–17) makes it clear that the assessment of inadequately documented qualifications should aim to establish whether applicants are likely to hold the qualifications they claim as well as the value of those qualifications within the education system of the host country. It also suggests that the assessment of inadequately documented qualifications be based on information gathered from reliable public sources as well as from the person applying for recognition of their qualifications and that this could be supplemented by interviews with the applicant, examinations, and any other appropriate assessment methods. This provision is key to the EQPR, which was developed in parallel to the recommendation.

The EQPR was, however, not the only game in town, and it was in its early stages. Rather than spell out how the EQPR could be used, we, therefore, had to refer to background documents generally and stipulate that these "should give an authoritative description of the qualifications or periods of study applicants are considered likely to have obtained or completed with all available documents and supporting evidence. The background document does not in itself constitute an act of recognition" (para. 18). The recommendation also outlines the kind of information that should be included in background documents (para. 19) as well as its main functions (para. 20). All of these provisions are perfectly well adapted to the EQPR, and we were able to highlight the EQPR in the explanatory memorandum (p. 15). I have vivid memories of one meeting of the Bureau of the Convention Committee, where the Council had to insist with force that the EQPR not only needed to be included among the examples but should be given pride of place, over examples of national background documents.

It may seem obvious that refugees need information about the possibilities that are available to them for obtaining recognition of their qualifications, but this was not so obvious that it could be left unstated in the recommendation. The text outlines the kind of information refugees should receive (para. 23) and, equally importantly, stipulates that this information should be provided as soon as possible after refugees arrive in their host country (para. 24). For most refugees, the first few weeks after they flee are particularly difficult, and it is important to use this time to prepare their transition into their host community—which may or may not be in the country where they first arrive—and also to show them that possibilities exist. In a situation where refugees have lost almost everything they had, it is essential to give hope and motivation.

Recognition: The Difference between a Vicious and a Virtuous Cycle

Therefore, it is important to recognize refugees' qualifications.[20] If refugees arrive in their new host country with their diplomas or other documents proving their qualifications, credentials evaluators know what to do. They can assess these qualifications in the same way as they would assess any other application supported by adequate documentation (Council of Europe and UNESCO 2017: para. 3). If, however, the refugees cannot document their qualifications, the recommendation and the EQPR provide a good solution.

To understand why recognition is essential, we should try to put ourselves in the shoes of the refugees. On arrival in their new host countries, most are placed in camps or other forms of temporary accommodation. Even if the bare necessities of life are provided for, most camps and most national authorities give refugees very limited opportunities to lead an active life and feel useful to their new community. If refugees see no possibility to use the skills and competences[21] they have from their home countries, the message they will receive is that their host societies have no confidence in them and that their hosts are willing to feed them, but that they do not believe the refugees can be useful to their host communities and find a place there. This can easily become a self-fulfilling prophecy. Qualifications are not like riding a bike or—a natural example for a Nordic—skiing. Once you have learned to bike or ski, you do not forget it. Your skills may get rusty, but they do not disappear completely. Qualifications are more like speaking a language. If you do not practice it, you forget, and it can take a lot of effort to resuscitate the competence. This can happen even with your native language, especially if you are totally immersed for a long time in an environment where only one language is spoken. After my AFS exchange year in Illinois, English came much more naturally to me than Norwegian, and it took me a few days back in Norway to get back up to speed. Had I returned to Norway only after thirty years, and had I spoken English only during that time, I am not sure my Norwegian would have survived. Today, even if I live outside of my native country, the situation is different because I live in an environment where I use several languages every week and keep up with Norwegian at least by frequent reading.

So, if refugees are kept in passivity with no possibility to use the competences they have, they can easily get stuck in a vicious circle in which they lose their competences because they cannot keep them alive, and where they are told—directly or indirectly—that they are worth less than the native-born members of their host community, who see them as a burden rather than a resource. In the medium to longer term, they will lose not only their competences but their motivation, and, in a few cases, they may even be tempted by extremist politics because they see no other way of changing their status as second- or third-rate citizens. If, on the other hand, refugees are given an opportunity to put their qualifications to use, they will not only maintain but continue to develop these qualifications. The inherent message is that their new host community trusts and appreciates them and believes refugees can contribute to the community and become a part of it. As many of those interviewed for the EQPR also told us, perhaps the most important message is that when refugees are given a chance to use their qualifications and be useful to their host communities, the inherent human dignity of the refugees is recognized.

The difference between condemning refugees to an existence of assistance and passivity, in the vicious circle, or giving them an opportunity to continue to develop their qualifications and both be and feel useful to their new community, in the virtuous circle, is crucial to each refugee. It is also essential to their host community. Can we really afford not to make good use of the competences and potential of all those who live in our community? The difference is also crucial to the refugees' home countries. If and when the refugees can return home, recognizing their qualifications and giving them an opportunity to develop them will put the refugees in a position to help rebuild their home countries after the conflicts and disasters that drove them out in the first place. If, however, refugees return not only with diminished competences and motivation but also with bitterness toward their host countries, it is a recipe for continued strife internally as well as internationally. As Stig Arne Skjerven and I wrote in 2019:

> Recognising refugees' qualifications is not a luxury nor indeed just an option. Refugees who, for good reason, cannot document their qualifications today are unlikely to be able to do so tomorrow. If their qualifications are recognised, refugees can put their talents to use, to their own benefit and that of their host society. They will continue to develop their qualifications, they will feel valued and motivated and they will be well placed to help reconstruct their home countries when they are able to return home. This is a virtuous circle. The alternative is a vicious circle in which host countries effectively tell refugees that their qualifications are of no interest and in which refugees are kept passive and demotivated. And they will lose their qualifications: as we know only too well, qualifications that are not used, will wither away. Whether refugees use or lose their qualifications is of enormous importance to the refugees themselves, but no less so to their host countries and their home countries. (Bergan and Skjerven 2019)

Establishing the EQPR

Recognition of qualifications may sound like a trivial and technical topic, but it can make a huge difference in the lives of people and societies. The recommendation that the Lisbon Recognition Convention adopted in 2017 is an important political statement and encourages European countries to take measures to make recognition possible even when qualifications cannot be adequately documented. Nevertheless, I would argue that the EQPR is the more important of the two measures we took to help countries make recognition a reality.[22]

The project started modestly but we moved relatively fast. As we saw, Greece had already indicated a strong interest in helping refugees pursue their studies, while Norway and, to some extent, the United Kingdom had experience with recognizing undocumented qualifications. Italy was also very positive to the idea and joined the project. Crucially, so did the UNHCR, the UN agency that is responsible for helping most of the world's refugees.[23]

The Council of Europe convened the partners to the first project meeting in the fall of 2016. Thanks to the Greek Ministry of Education and Religious Affairs and, in particular, to the Greek representative in the Council's Education Committee, Maria Fassari,[24] we were able to hold the meeting in Athinai (Athens). In this way, we were able to involve more of the people who would be directly involved on the ground with organizing the first interview sessions. For practical reasons, we decided to focus this pilot project on refugees living in camps in Attika, the Greek region in which Athinai is located. The help of the Greek Ministry, the Greek ENIC, and the local branch of the UNHCR proved crucial in organizing the three interview sessions we were able to conduct in 2017. From the start, the EQPR has been financed largely by voluntary contributions from member states, even if there has also been some funding from the Council of Europe's ordinary education budget. Italy and Norway have been particularly generous funders.

At this meeting, we also agreed on some basic principles for the project, such as limiting participation to candidates who had formal status as refugees or asylum seekers, and we agreed on the outline of the interview sessions. Skjerven and Marina Malgina from NOKUT, the Norwegian ENIC, had experience with the Recognition Procedure for Persons without Verifiable Documentation (UVD-procedure) and were crucial to developing the EQPR methodology. Malgina also took on the role as content coordinator and led the assessment teams during the evaluations.

A Sound Methodology and a Common Format

From the outset, the EQPR had two main objectives. On the one hand, it needed to provide a sound methodology for assessing refugees' qualifications in the absence of adequate documentation. On the other hand, the assessment should be described in a format that would make it possible for the refugees to use the assessment if they moved to a new host country without having to undergo a new assessment. The EQPR brought these two objectives together.

The EQPR provides information on the identity of the holder as well as on the qualification that has been assessed and other relevant information provided by the applicant, such as previous work experience and his or her native language and proficiency in foreign languages.[25] The EQPR also includes an explanation of what the document is, and, importantly, what it is not. The EQPR is not a formal recognition decision or statement, it cannot replace formal identity documents or recognition statements, and it does not guarantee access to higher education and employment. It is a less good option than formal recognition on the basis of a fully documented application, but, for many refugees, that is not an alternative. Those who have to flee their homes at short notice may not think a diploma is the most important thing to take along. They, or those who assess their qualifications, may not be able to contact their home institution to obtain copies of the diplomas or additional information on the study program they followed, either because university files may have been destroyed, because communications are difficult or nonexistent, or because the authorities of their home country may be unwilling to help those who fled. The EQPR may be the second-best option but it is vastly better that the alternative: no recognition and starting from scratch or being condemned to passivity and unemployment. The fact that the EQPR does not guarantee access to studies or employment is anyway a characteristic it shares with all other kinds of assessment. The recognition of qualifications demonstrates that the holders are qualified. It does not guarantee they will be selected.

For the EQPR to be credible, it needs to build on a sound methodology. Each candidate is interviewed by two professional credentials evaluators. In this way, no decision will be based on the assessment and opinion of one person only. To ensure that the decision is based on as broad a background of experience as possible, the two interviewers should come from different countries. All interviewers must also be experienced professionals because they will be faced with assessments that are considerably more challenging than classic recognition cases. For this project, we, therefore, required that all interviewers have at least two years' experience as credentials evaluators. At least one needs to have specialized knowledge and understanding of the education system from which the refugee claims to have qualifications as well as the language used by this system. This is essential for two reasons. The first is that not all refugees are proficient in other languages, and being interviewed by someone who speaks their language will help put the candidates at ease. Interviews may be conducted either in English or in the language of the candidate.[26]

The second reason is one of quality control. An interviewer with good knowledge of the language and education system of the country in which the candidates earned their qualifications will find it easier to identify any attempted fraud. This has overall not been a major problem in the EQPR project, but there have inevitably been some cases, just as there are cases of fraudulent qualifications with what looks like bona fide documents. For classic recognition with a full set of documents, I know of one case where a candidate presented a document that looked credible with a signature by a dean that also looked credible. Upon verification, it turned out that the person who signed had, in fact, been the dean of the faculty from which the student claimed to have earned the qualification, but not at the time the document was supposedly issued. For the EQPR, our most emblematic case of attempted fraud was when the candidate clearly had no clue about the inner workings of the university that she or he claimed to have attended and the name of which (s)he mispronounced. Thanks to an Arabic-speaking interviewer, the attempted fraud was discovered.

Even if the EQPR is used in cases where the refugees cannot present full documentation, this does not mean that there are never any kind of documents available. Even if the refugees have no diplomas, they may be able to produce other documents that can at the very least support their claim that they have been enrolled at the university. Before the interview, applicants also fill out a form, and their answers determine whether the credentials evaluators involved in the project believe their application is likely to succeed.

2017: A Pilot Project

The first interviews were held in March 2017, and they were followed by a further two sessions later in the year. From the outset, it was clear that even if the scope of this pilot project was limited, it would determine whether the project was solid enough to be followed up with a more ambitious version in the years after. Therefore, the stakes were high.

During the pilot project, all interviews were held at premises provided by the Greek Ministry of Education, and all candidates were brought there from camps in Attika, with the help of the UNHCR. All interviewers came from the ENICs of Greece, Italy, Norway, and the United Kingdom, and Malgina provided a training on the first day and also ran a summing-up session on the final day of the week. With my Council of Europe colleagues Samir Hećo and Đana Đafić and Fassari from the Greek Ministry, she also organized the interview sessions. On average, interviews lasted forty-five minutes, after which interviewers compared notes for about fifteen minutes. It was encouraging to see that they reached similar conclusions in most cases and that serious disagreements were very rare.

Over the three interview sessions in 2017, ninety-two candidates were interviewed, of whom seventy-three received the EQPR. The relatively high success rate was due to the fact that the candidates for the interviews were selected on the basis of the written information they had provided through the form referred to earlier, so that candidates who were clearly not qualified for the EQPR were not interviewed. The interviews were nevertheless essential in verifying that those selected were in fact qualified, and, in about 20 percent of the cases, the credentials evaluators concluded that they were not.

We felt it was important to test the methodology through face-to-face interviews, but, from the very beginning, it was clear that this was not a sustainable solution. It is expensive to take credentials evaluators from different parts of Europe to a single location and then to keep them there for a full week. Liberating five days in one go for a pilot project is one thing, but doing so on a regular basis is much more difficult. Therefore, we also wanted to test out online interviews. At the same time, we were not in a simulation game. We were interviewing real refugees who saw the EQPR as an opportunity for a better future. We could not risk having to cut an interview because the technology did not function. Our solution was to conduct some interviews with the candidate and the credentials evaluators sitting in three different rooms in the same building and connecting online. If the connection was broken, we could quickly convert the interview from online to face-to-face. The experiment worked, and, in the end, we decided to interview two candidates fully online. Both passed the interview and were awarded the EQPR.

Both the Greek Ministry and the UNHCR were indispensable to providing information on the EQPR in the refugee camps and identifying candidates. After the first interview session, we decided to ask some of the refugees who had received the EQPR to be our advocates among their peers, and this proved to be an important move. They could explain the EQPR and the interview process to their peers with an insight and a credibility that those of us speaking from an institutional perspective could not match. We also learned from this experience that EQPR holders were the best advocates of the project in other forums, so we started inviting some of them to international meetings. Incidentally, this was something of a challenge because they could not travel between European countries until they obtained formal refugee status in their new host countries.

Mahmoud Alkoko, who moved from Greece to Germany, presented the EQPR very convincingly at a meeting in Strasbourg, while the first EQPR recipient, Anwar al-Horani, proved to be a particularly effective advocate. She relocated to Norway, was accepted at Oslo Metropolitan University, and, eventually, obtained a position in an NGO working with disabled people. Because her original profession, physiotherapy, is regulated, she could not practice it in Norway, but her job is very close to her original profession. I shared a platform with al-Horani at both a high-level event during the UNESCO General Conference in Paris[27] and at the UN Refugee Forum in Genève,[28] and I can attest to both her presentation skills and the fact that even after a relatively short time in her new host country, she spoke excellent Norwegian.

Expanding the EQPR: More Diverse and More Local

By the end of 2017, we were relatively certain we had a sound methodology and a good format for describing the assessment. Nevertheless, we felt we needed to test the EQPR in a broader context and also involve more countries. Several of the ENICs that had been skeptical initially now warmed to the idea of the EQPR, and we used the annual meetings of the ENIC and NARIC Networks to present the project and the results we had obtained. Here, we combined presentations by the Council of Europe Secretariat and the ENICs involved to present the project from different angles.

The second phase of the project, following the first, pilot phase, was launched with a conference in Athinai in March 2018,[29] was broader and more diverse. From the outset, nine countries participated. In addition to the original four countries and the UNHCR, we had Armenia, Canada, France, Germany, and the Netherlands. All were valuable additions. Canada is part of the UNESCO Europe region, and after years of hard work by the Canadian recognition center, especially its longtime director Yves Beaudin, the country ratified the Lisbon Recognition Convention in 2018. France, Germany, and the Netherlands are all large ENICs with considerable influence within the network, and the Netherlands had moved from initial skepticism to wishing to join. Armenia may not appear to be the obvious destination for refugees from the Middle East, and the country has many problems of its own, not least related to the precarious situation of Artsakh (Nagorno-Karabakh). This situation has now been made even more difficult after an Azerbaijani attack on the Armenian population in Artsakh in the second half of September 2023, creating a serious humanitarian situation and further weakening an already thinly stretched Armenian society, plagued by internal political divisions and a faltering economy, which now has to absorb the vast majority of the well over one hundred thousand ethnic Armenians that have left Artsakh.[30] Armenia has to face this situation without the kind of international supports that Ukraine enjoys in the face of the Russian invasion. However, there was a fairly sizable Armenian population in Syria. Deir ez-Zor was the site of camps where Armenians in the Ottoman Empire were sent during the Armenian Genocide,[31] and it hosted an important Armenian community until the early days of the Syrian civil war. At that time, many Syrians from the Armenian community fled to Armenia, where both they and the Armenian authorities found adjustment and integration more difficult than they had foreseen. Many had Arabic as their first language, with limited knowledge of Armenian, and they had grown up in a very different society.

In addition to more than doubling the number of participating countries, we also diversified the interviews. Italy indicated an early interest in both hosting interviews and including new groups. Whereas in Greece, most refugees came from Afghanistan, Iraq, and Syria, and many had higher education qualifications, Italy presented a different picture. Many refugees there came from sub-Saharan Africa, many had French rather than English as their second language, and many claimed secondary school leaving rather than higher education qualifications. In the pilot project, we had required all candidates to have completed at least one year of higher education studies, but now we included those who claimed a secondary school leaving qualification giving access to higher education.

Largely thanks to Italy, this second phase also innovated in another important way. So far, all interviews had been held in Athinai and the interviewers had come from the participating ENICs, which was important for getting the project off the ground. In Italy, we decentralized the interviews to several cities with universities, and, in each case, we involved the local university. We also enlisted the Italian Rectors' Conference. This was possible thanks to the strong involvement of CIMEA, the Italian ENIC,[32] as well as strong support from the Italian ministry responsible for higher education. Decentralizing the interviews, with successive sessions in several cities like Milano, Torino,[33] Palermo, Catania,[34] and Cagliari, enabled us to reach refugees where they lived. Importantly, involving universities demonstrated the value of the EQPR to those responsible for student admissions at their respective institutions.[35] Relatively quickly, close to forty EQPR holders were admitted to Italian universities, and this number has since increased further.

In this second phase, not only did we have a more diversified group of candidates and interviews in more countries, as those in Italy were soon followed up by interviews in France, Germany, and the Netherlands; interview methods were also diversified. Face-to-face interviews remained important, and these sessions allowed the credentials evaluators to meet and exchange experiences, which was important to the further development of the project. At the same time, however, it was important to gain experience with online interviews. These will clearly be the main modus operandi in the longer term. Already, in 2018, we included more online interviews, in the first instance during the weeklong interview sessions that were organized in several countries.[36] It soon turned out that the format of the interviews had no significant impact on the results. From an initial success rate of around 80 percent in the pilot project in 2017, the rate rose to approximately 85 percent during the second phase, and this has remained the success rate ever since, regardless of whether the interviews were conducted face-to-face or online.

In this phase, we also sought to establish closer links with public authorities in cities where candidates were interviewed. In March 2019, we organized a session at the Council of Europe headquarters in Strasbourg, with candidates coming from different parts of France. By then, not only was the French

ENIC closely involved, but we had received a very enthusiastic message from Frédérique Pharaboz, who was responsible for education issues in the French Ministry of the Interior. Her enthusiasm was a boost to the project, and she provided good advice on how to approach the authorities responsible for the reception of refugees. The session in Strasbourg also provided an opportunity to highlight the EQPR with the Permanent Representations[37] of Council of Europe member states.

We decided to organize a public event that would highlight different aspects of the project and also provide an attractive frame for presenting the refugees interviewed with their EQPRs. Thanks to the City of Strasbourg, we were able to hold this event at City Hall, with the participation of the mayor and deputy mayor as well as the head of the UNHCR representation in Strasbourg and the Council of Europe's Director General for Democracy, Snežana Samardžić-Marković, who had been a strong supporter of the project from its inception. Several Permanent Representations also attended the event, which was open to the public.[38] With the launching conference in Athinai in 2018, this event set a precedent that we planned to follow up in other cities. Then COVID-19 hit.

The Impact of COVID-19

COVID-19 came to Europe in early 2020. The effect on higher education was as devastating as it was on most other areas of society (Bergan et al. 2021). Both admissions to higher education and international student mobility—as with almost all other kinds of mobility—came to a near halt, and enrollment of international students dropped dramatically (Skjerven 2021). The ENIC and NARIC Networks undertook a reflection on how they could best help those affected, including by recognizing disrupted learning and exploring possible long-term effects (Council of Europe, European Commission, and UNESCO 2020). National recognition centers were themselves closed, in particular, in the early parts of the pandemic. Staff worked from home but did not always have easy access to their files, many of which contained confidential information provided by applicants.

For the EQPR, the most immediate consequence was that interviews could no longer be carried out face-to-face. In the short term, we had to cancel interview sessions planned for the spring and early summer of 2020. Luckily, however, we already had experience with conducting interviews online, so, even if a hiatus was inevitable as we adjusted to the impact of COVID-19, we were able to move interviews online. This also brought about a change in the format. Rather than scheduling a series of interviews over sessions lasting for a week each and based in a specific city, we now organized individual interviews with the candidate and the interviewers in three different locations. This format is much closer to what will be the norm in the longer term. One reason why we could not revert to online interviews immediately, however, was that even if candidates can be interviewed online, we need to provide a location in which their web connection is stable and secure, and a person of authority needs to be able to verify the candidate's identity. The EQPR needs not only to verify whether candidates are likely to have the qualifications they claim but also whether they are the persons they claim to be. During the initial COVID-19 confinement, this was impossible. During the first confinement in France, you even needed to fill out a form to leave your home, with a list of valid reasons to choose from. Interviewing for the EQPR was not one of them.

Another almost immediate impact of the COVID-19 pandemic was that the health systems of most European countries were overburdened. In many countries, advanced students in health-related disciplines—not only medical and nursing students but also those training to become laboratory technicians and other relevant studies—were enlisted in the effort to face COVID-19. Many health-related professions are regulated, and practicing them requires not only passing an academic examination but also obtaining a professional license.[39] There are good reasons for this: few of us would entrust our health to doctors and nurses without being sure that they are duly qualified.

Even advanced students in health-related disciplines could, therefore, not work independently. Even in a time of crisis, they needed to help out under the supervision of duly licensed health professionals. The Council of Europe and the UNHCR asked why EQPR holders with relevant health qualifications could not do the same. The two organizations pointed out that Europe hosted refugees and asylum seekers with the competences and relevant experience who were willing to get involved and help. We recognized that most health-related professions are tightly regulated, and competent national health authorities need to give the necessary approvals. Even if the EQPR is not a substitute for the necessary professional certificates and licenses, it can help the authorities speed things up by providing some of the background needed. The EQPR can help establish a qualified pool of preassessed refugee health practitioners, enabling the national health authorities to determine how best to deploy refugee resources, if and when needed.[40]

By the spring of 2020, 454 refugees had received the EQPR, and 46 of these had health-related qualifications (Bergan and Skjerven 2020). We also provided several examples of EQPR holders who were already contributing to dealing with COVID-19, and a Ghanaian refugee working in Greece was featured in *Time* magazine.[41] With the UNHCR and our country partners, the

Council of Europe tried to launch subprojects on using the EQPR to inform the COVID-19 response. This was, however, only partly successful. France and Italy were very open to the idea, whereas in Germany and the United Kingdom, the reticence was too great and the weight of the regulated professions too substantial to allow us to advance. Nevertheless, the COVID-19 pandemic clearly showed the potential of enabling refugees to put their qualifications and competences at the service of their host societies and the important role the EQPR could play in this respect.

Toward a More Permanent System for Recognizing Refugees' Qualifications

The COVID-19 pandemic also had the effect of prolonging the second phase of the EQPR project by one year, until the end of 2021. Even if the long-term goal is that assessing refugees' qualifications with a view to granting them the EQPR should become a part of the everyday work of recognition centers, we are not quite there yet. In 2022, the Council of Europe and its partners, therefore, launched a third phase.[42]

As of December 2023, 1,101 refugees had been interviewed, 707 online. Of these refugees, 943 had been awarded the EQPR, and these included 614 awarded to applicants interviewed online.[43] The overall success rate is, therefore, close to 85 percent, and it is still not significantly different depending on the format of the interview. The number of interviews took a hit in 2020 due to the COVID-19 pandemic, and the project still interviews fewer refugees than it did in 2019, before COVID-19.

At the same time, there are several important developments. The original four participating countries have now (August 2024) become twenty-two,[44] and several of these have joined relatively recently. Especially for countries in Central and Eastern Europe, Russia's invasion of Ukraine and the refugee stream it caused demonstrated the need for the EQPR. More than one-third of the states party to the Lisbon Recognition Convention now participate in the EQPR project, and all parties have acknowledged the importance of recognizing refugees' qualifications through their ratification of the convention as well as by adopting the specific recommendation in 2017. Importantly, in 2020 the ministers of the EHEA confirmed that "we commit to reviewing our own legislation, regulations, and practice to ensure fair recognition of qualifications held by refugees, displaced persons and persons in refugee-like situations, even when they cannot be fully documented, in accordance with Article VII of the Lisbon Recognition Convention. We welcome the European Qualifications Passport for Refugees and will support further broadening its use in our systems" (Bologna Process 2020c: 7).

Interviews are increasingly conducted online and organized more flexibly. When refugees ask to have their qualifications assessed and complete the required formalities online, including filling out the questionnaire, the Council of Europe tries to organize interviews as rapidly as possible. Nevertheless, it is important also to continue face-to-face interview sessions, not least because they enable credentials evaluators to exchange experiences and to present the EQPR to local stakeholders, as we did in Strasbourg in March 2019. Online interviews will become increasingly common, but they cannot fully substitute for face-to-face interview sessions, at least not yet.

Interviews have become increasingly professionalized. In the early phase of the project, the participating ENICs selected interviewers from among their most experienced evaluators and made sure they also had specialized knowledge and understanding of the education systems from which the refugees had their qualifications and the languages used in these systems. The cultural and linguistic competences remain important, but evaluators are no longer trained on the job. Thanks to NOKUT (the Norwegian ENIC), and particularly Malgina, there is now an online training course for evaluators consisting of five modules of increasing complexity. These include online sessions gathering all participants and are spread over several months, starting in the fall and ending in the spring of the following year. Credentials evaluators who have not previously participated in the project need to complete at least three of the modules before they can be part of interviews.[45] In addition, the training offer includes specialized modules on specific countries. Soon after the Taliban took power in Afghanistan in August 2021 and drove many Afghans out of their country, my colleagues organized an online training on Afghan qualifications that gathered more than ninety participants.[46]

Refugees need the EQPR because they were unable to take their diplomas and other education documents with them when they had to flee. The early EQPRs were also paper documents, but it was unintentionally ironic that refugees who had lost access to their paper documents would be issued a new set of such documents that they could again lose. From the early stages of the project, developing a secure online system for handling the EQPRs was, therefore, a high priority. Thanks to CIMEA, the Italian ENIC,[47] refugees now apply by creating a personal account on a secure website.[48] Once they are awarded the EQPR, it is stored in their personal account, to which only the refugee and the system administrator have access. The refugees can choose to give others access to their EQPR for a specified period of time, which means they can give access to an admissions officer at a university or a prospective employer for as long as they need access to assess the refugees' qualifications for a specific purpose. The basic principles are that the EQPRs are stored securely, that they cannot be falsified, and that each refugee is in control of how his or her EQPR is used.

Toward a Partnership with Local Actors

Awarding the EQPR is important, but it is not a goal in itself. For each refugee, the EQPR should be a stepping stone toward further studies or employment, and we saw that this was the case for some of the early EQPR holders. More than eighty EQPR holders have by now been accepted at universities,[49] and Italy has also accepted the EQPR as one of the documents that qualifies holders to apply for the university scholarships offered to refugees or international protection holders managed by the Conference of Italian University Rectors (CRUI) with the Italian Ministry of the Interior and the national association of the bodies for the right to higher education (ANDISU) (Finocchietti and Bergan 2021).

The experiences from France and, in particular, Italy point to an important development for the future of the EQPR. In France, the contact to public authorities other than those responsible for education, notably the Ministry of the Interior, has proven very valuable. As just one example, if assessment of refugees' qualifications through online interviews more or less on demand becomes the norm, refugees will still need to be interviewed in a location with secure Wi-Fi connection and where their identities can be verified. At least in France, the Ministry of the Interior could be very helpful in identifying places where this could be done, such as in *préfectures* and *sous-préfectures*.[50] The good contacts established with the City of Strasbourg as well as with the University of Clermont Auvergne are likewise examples of how local involvement can assist refugees. Clermont Auvergne was a key participant in another Council of Europe project aiming to integrate refugees in higher education by recruiting them as part-time teachers and sharing their experience with students.[51]

In Italy, universities were involved in interviewing refugees, and this facilitated their access to universities, simply because these became aware of the EQPR and could see by their own involvement that the methodology is sound. The decentralized interviews enabled several universities to be involved and benefited refugees in all parts of the country. The local involvement was taken one step further in December 2022, when the Council of Europe organized an assessment session in Torino in cooperation with both the University of Torino and the Agenzia Piemonte Lavoro,[52] the regional employment agency. Italy is one of the countries that has shown itself to be open to trying to provide opportunities for refugees with health-related qualifications, and it is interesting to note that most of those interviewed in Torino in December 2022 were refugees from Ukraine, with many looking to find employment in the health field.[53] This is now possible thanks to a decree issued by Italian authorities in March 2022 allowing refugees from Ukraine to work in health-related professions based on the EQPR.[54] Less than a month later, the European Commission adopted a similar recommendation that explicitly mentions both the Lisbon Recognition Convention and the EQPR (European Commission 2022).

Looking to the Future

As we look ahead, some key elements appear for the recognition of refugees' qualifications in accordance with Article VII of the Lisbon Recognition Convention and the 2017 Recommendation, both of which cover cases where refugees for good reasons are unable to document their qualifications.

The EQPR has proved its worth and is in practice the only instrument that provides a sound and proven methodology and a format that can be used across borders. It is also the only instrument that relies on assessment by professional credentials evaluators from many European countries who have undergone specialized training, building on their general competence in recognition matters, and it is the only instrument that provides refugees with a possibility to store their documents safely and also to share their EQPR with persons of their choice—typically admission officers or prospective employers—for a limited time. No national "background document" comes close to offering the same guarantees and advantages.

Assessing refugees with a view to awarding them the EQPR must become a normal part of the work of all national information centers, and interviews should, as far as possible, be organized on demand and online. The Council of Europe should continue to coordinate the EQPR to ensure that quality standards are kept, that all applicants are interviewed by two evaluators from different countries, and that all EQPRs awarded are stored safely online.

While the participation of the national information centers is vital, so is expanding the project to include credentials evaluators at universities, as the experience in Italy has demonstrated very clearly. These will ultimately decide whether EQPR holders are admitted to study programs, and they have strong competence in recognition and admissions issues. They should and will be invited to participate in the training course for EQPR evaluators.

Refugees with pertinent qualifications represent a resource also when it comes to regulated professions, especially in health-related fields of work, as we saw during the most intensive phases of the COVID-19 pandemic. In many countries, public authorities need to be persuaded to let EQPR holders with relevant qualifications work under the supervision of duly licensed professionals, but Italy and France have shown that this is possible. Local authorities and communities, who can most directly benefit from the competence these refugees represent, could play an important role in persuading central authorities.

Not least, the EQPR project should develop even closer ties to local authorities and communities, and this is one of the main objectives of the current, third phase of the project. They should do so in cooperation with universities, as shown in the recent example of the interview session in Torino. Providing refugees who have higher education qualifications, in any academic discipline, with an opportunity to put these qualifications at the service of the local communities is eminently suitable for a strengthened cooperation between universities and their local communities as part of the local democratic mission of higher education.

A further challenge is whether the EQPR could be expanded to include qualifications other than higher education and those giving access to higher education. The short answer is "yes, but." European education systems are quite good at integrating refugee children (and other children who arrive from abroad without a knowledge of the host country and its language); the Encamp secondary school in Andorra[55] is an excellent example. This is done informally, and we should avoid establishing formal systems that may complicate what currently works well. The question of a similar qualifications passport for vocational qualifications is legitimate, and, in principle, the answer should be positive. There are, nevertheless, several important factors that distinguish vocational from higher education qualifications. One is that it is probably easier and also less risky for employers to test vocational qualifications informally without recourse to a diploma-like document. Put bluntly, the consequences of risking a faulty diagnosis of repairs needed on a car are less than those of a faulty diagnosis by health professionals. The second is that international cooperation on the recognition of qualifications is much better developed in higher education, and there is much more experience to share. A third is that vocational qualifications are even more specialized than higher education qualifications, and there is less emphasis on transversal competences.[56]

Lessons Learned

The main lessons learned in this chapter are as follows:

- The influx of refugees, in particular from Syria and Iraq, to Europe as of the summer of 2015 reminded us not only that refugees are in a fragile situation but also that they can be a resource to their new host communities if these are prepared to make good use of the refugees' qualifications.
- Many refugees are unable to take their diplomas or other proof of their qualifications when they flee. Therefore, it is essential to find alternative ways of assessing their qualifications.
- Recognizing refugees' qualifications can make the difference between a vicious and a virtuous circle. If refugees are kept in pas-

sivity with no possibility to use the competences they have, they lose their competences because they cannot keep them alive, and they feel like a burden rather than a resource. In the medium to longer term, they will lose not only their competences but also their motivation. If, on the other hand, refugees are given an opportunity to put their qualifications to use, they will maintain and develop these qualifications, help their new host community, and become a part of it. They will also be prepared to help rebuild their home community if and when they can return.

- The EQPR, developed by the Council of Europe and partners from 2017 onward, provides both a sound methodology for assessing refugees' qualifications when these cannot be documented and a good format for describing the assessment in such a way that the assessment can remain valid even if the refugees move to new host countries.

- While in the early phase of the EQPR project, interviews were conducted face-to-face, they are now increasingly done online. For reasons of costs and time, this will clearly be the standard method in the future.

- Assessing refugees' qualifications with a view to granting them the EQPR must become an integrated part of recognition practice in Europe. In the longer term, it cannot continue as a separate project but must become a standard part of how national recognition centers and universities assess foreign qualifications. This implies coordination at the European level, with the Council of Europe as a contact point with a good overview of the expertise available in different centers, and national centers playing a similar role within their respective countries. It also means maintaining the secure database already established as well as continuing to train credentials evaluators, in particular from universities. It will also require being able to organize online interviews rapidly and flexibly, hopefully retaining the principle that each candidate be interviewed by two credentials evaluators who should come from different countries and at least one of whom should have specialized knowledge and understanding of the education system in which the refugee's qualifications have been earned. Regular exchanges of experience among participating credentials evaluators will remain essential.

- Refugees must be able to make use of their qualifications once they have obtained the EQPR. To ensure improved access for EQPR holders to further higher education studies, it is important to involve universities as closely as possibly in the assessment, as demonstrated by the example of Italy.

- Much work remains to ensure that the EQPR is accepted in the labor market. Public sector employers may be reached through public authorities, and working with local authorities is particularly important. Two Council of Europe bodies could be important: the Congress of Local and Regional Authorities in Europe and the Intercultural Cities Network. Private employers are a highly diverse group and difficult to reach, especially the smaller companies. Nevertheless, there are national employers' associations, and, to the extent local public authorities and individual universities are involved in the project, these could and should be encouraged also to reach out to local private employers.
- The cost per assessment must be reduced as much as possible, in particular through online assessments. There must, however, be acceptance that assessing refugees' qualifications where these cannot be adequately documented will entail higher costs than the classic recognition of well-documented qualifications. In the longer run, these costs must be borne nationally and at each institution rather than primarily through a dedicated Council of Europe project based on voluntary contributions by some member states. The Council of Europe budget must in the medium term cover the costs of the European coordination, the secure website, and the training of new credentials evaluators, as part of the Council of Europe program for the recognition of qualifications.
- In the longer term, a similar qualifications passport for refugees with vocational education qualifications may be explored, but European cooperation in this area is less well developed and the challenges are probably greater than for higher education and general school leaving qualifications.
- At lower education levels, European education systems are quite good at integrating refugee children (and other children who arrive from abroad without knowledge of the host country and its language) informally. We, therefore, should be wary of establishing formal systems that may complicate what currently works well.
- Helping refugees get recognition of and then make good use of their qualifications must become an integral part of the local democratic mission of higher education.

With this, we now turn to look at what lessons can be learned from the European experience and what European universities and their local communities can do to strengthen this aspect of their democratic mission.

9

Conclusions and the Way Forward

Context

This book explores how European universities fulfill their local democratic mission and place it in the context of their overall democratic mission. The fall of the Berlin Wall in November 1989 and the political transformations that made the "fall of the Wall" possible and then brought profound changes to the countries of Central and Eastern Europe gave rise to a great wave of optimism. For quite some time now, this optimism has given way to uncertainty about the future of democracy in Europe. The most recent crisis is Russia's war of aggression against Ukraine, launched on February 24, 2022, but following on from the occupation of Krym and other parts of the territory of Ukraine in 2014. Ukraine has demonstrated remarkable resilience, symbolized by President Zelensky's response to a U.S. offer of evacuation when he reputedly said, "The fight is here; I need ammunition, not a ride."[1] Russia's unmotivated attack has brought most European countries closer together in near unanimous support of Ukraine. The only European country to support the war is Belarus, whose dictator Lukashenka has aligned with Russia, and all decisions in the Council of Europe, concerning first the suspension of Russia's right of participation and then exclusion, were made with the overwhelming support of its members. At the same time, there is some opposition to supporting Ukraine from the extreme right as well as from the extreme left, and Hungary has done its best—or worst—to reduce EU support. Luckily, Hungary's efforts have been largely unsuccessful, but they have caused some delays. There is also concern about whether and how rising energy prices, caused at least in part by the war, may affect public opinion in European countries in the longer run. On the other hand, Europe has not reacted adequately to Azerbaijan's attacks on and treatment of the ethnic Armenian population in Artsakh (Nagorno-Karabakh). This can only be considered a moral as well as a political failure.

The growth of populism—which is found mostly on the extreme right but also on the far left—combines with distrust of public authorities, polarization of public debate, and the growth of conspiracy theories, which was seen not least during the COVID-19 crisis (Lynas 2020; Birchall and Knight 2022). Some actors question whether societal decisions need to be based on facts, search for "alternative truths," and pretend that democracy can be illiberal. These developments, along with the increasing reluctance many citizens show to engage in public space and a tendency to limit any such engagement to single-issue politics, contribute to what the Council of Europe has termed backlash of democracy (Council of Europe 2021).

Many of these tendencies represent educational challenges. Education is not the answer to all societal problems but many of them cannot be solved without education, and in particular higher education, playing a key role. And we need education, not just training. We are probably training more highly qualified specialists than ever before. I am, however, less convinced we are good at educating intellectuals, by which I mean people with a solid knowledge and understanding of their chosen academic field but also with the ability and will to place their own field in a broader societal context, ask critical questions, and find answers to those questions. European universities are, therefore, faced with the double challenge of strengthening public trust in higher education and research and playing their proper role as democratic actors. In this book, I argue that the two challenges are linked and that universities need to work with their local communities to fully rise to them.

There is a saying that "charity begins at home." I would argue that democracy also begins at home, in each local community and within each university.[2] Like charity, democracy cannot, however, *end* at home. We cannot and should not choose between engaging locally, nationally, or internationally. Limiting our vision to our immediate surroundings can easily lead to closed minds, which, as the saying goes, are often accompanied by open—or loud—mouths. Several populist leaders illustrate the point; charity prevents me from naming examples.

However, ignoring the local is equally dangerous because it can easily lead the world of higher education to ignore or overlook the concerns of many of those who need its insights and understanding, who rightfully expect higher education to provide solutions to their immediate problems, and who can benefit the most from the competences higher education provides. The university must live in and *with* the local community; the community should not live in the shadow of the university.

The Democratic Mission of Higher Education in Europe: Some Trends

This book has identified some key trends in the ways universities in Europe see and carry out their democratic mission, how public authorities support them, and, especially, how the democratic mission of higher education is carried out at the local level.

Democracy Is Culture, Not Just Institutions

If a generation and more ago, democracy was conceived of in terms of institutions, laws, and elections, there is now broad recognition that none of these will be democratic unless they are underpinned by attitudes and behaviors that help them function democratically. Societies cannot be democratic unless they are imbued with what the Council of Europe has come to call "democratic culture" (Council of Europe 2005b). We cannot develop and maintain democratic culture except through education (Council of Europe 2018b, 2018c, 2018d), and higher education needs to play an essential role (Council of Europe 2020d).

Preparing for Democracy Is One of Higher Education's Key Missions

While the economic mission of higher education was the focus of policymakers and also many higher education leaders in Europe a generation ago, they have now developed a more sophisticated and nuanced view that gives equal importance to the democratic mission of higher education. The Council of Europe has identified four main missions:

- Preparation for the labor market
- Preparation for life as active citizens in democratic societies
- Personal development
- Development and maintenance of a broad and advanced knowledge base (Bergan 2005b; Council of Europe 2007)

Influenced by the Council of Europe's work, ministers responsible for higher education recognize, in the framework of the EHEA, the need "to ensure that our HEIs have the necessary resources to continue to fulfil their full range of purposes" and that these include preparing students for life as active citizens in a democratic society (Bologna Process 2007: I.4).

We must hope that these clear statements by public authorities, which in Europe play an important role in developing the framework for higher education policy, will make it easier for universities to give priority to their democratic mission. It is nevertheless largely up to the higher education community itself to ensure that this mission will hold center stage.

The Local Democratic Mission of Higher Education Is Alive and Diverse

The examples in Chapter 7 show that European universities rely on a combination of committed leadership and enthusiastic volunteers in cooperating with their local communities. The cooperation can concern almost any topic of interest to both the university and the local community but initiatives that stimulate participation, broaden and deepen knowledge and understanding, improve economic and societal opportunities for local residents, and consider the local community as a true partner rather than just an object of study or recipient of assistance should be given priority by both universities and the local community. In particular, universities do not need to fulfill their local democratic mission at the expense of other missions. They can be local, national, and international all at the same time, just as they contribute to economic development and foster democratic culture.

The examples also show that universities from all over Europe already work not only *in* but also *with* their local communities. Local communities are mostly the cities or metropolitan areas in which the universities are located, but they may also be a neighborhood, a region, or even a country. Regardless of the size of the local community, the local democratic mission of higher education cannot be top down. It is not a question of a university working *in* its local community but working *with* it. Democracy cannot be practiced by an individual or an institution alone. Democracy can only be a community venture. It requires participation and deliberation. Democracy also requires competences,[3] and universities have an important mission in helping develop the competences of members of the local community.

This book cannot provide anything near a complete overview of how European universities work with and serve their local community, but it attempts to show the diversity of their local democratic mission.

The Economic Mission Can Be Democratic

The Jagiellonian University of Kraków illustrates how universities can both help the development and innovation of local economies and help develop competences and improve the employment prospects of residents, all of which gives democracy better conditions to thrive. Many of the competences developed through higher education that are appreciated in the labor market are also highly useful to democracy.

Societal Outreach

The broader societal mission of higher education is illustrated by three examples:

- The University of Iceland has a broad societal outreach mission, including measures to increase public interest in and understanding of research and academic work and to reach groups that may otherwise not consider higher education an option.
- A selection of universities in the Czech Republic demonstrates the importance of student engagement and outreach through examples ranging from open lectures to demonstrate the importance of research and fact-based decision-making through social work to providing training in information technology.
- The University of San Marino has developed a comprehensive model for cooperation with the broader society, through what is known as a territorial pact.

The Local Community Can Be Spread Out

The University of the Aegean challenges our notion of what a local community may be, as it is spread out over six islands and also serves islands in the region that do not host a campus. In this challenging setting, the university helps its local community address social problems and also contributes to highlighting and disseminating the cultural heritage that is key to Greek identity. It has also decided to cater to refugees.

The Engaged University

By definition, the engaged university embeds public engagement into its work,[4] and engagement goes beyond improving access to higher education and students' possibilities to complete their studies with success.

- DCU works to improve the cultural and educational offers available to the residents of its immediate neighborhood through initiatives such as programs to help people who have been away from formal education prepare to enroll at the university. DCU also runs a center for engaged research.
- Queen's has many similar activities, with the added dimension of working in a deeply divided society that still feels the impact of the

long period of community strife known as the Troubles. It strives to make both of the major groups in Northern Ireland—Catholics and Protestants—feel welcome on campus as well as to motivate young people from a nearby working-class neighborhood to aim for higher education and to give them the competences required to do so.

Higher Education Serving Ethnic and Linguistic Minorities

Europe is home to many minorities, and some of them speak languages different from that of the majority in their country.

- Samisk høgskole/Sámi allaskuvla[5] in the far north of Norway conducts teaching and research entirely in Sámi, a language spoken by some twenty thousand to thirty thousand people,[6] in areas of immediate concern to the Sámi community.
- Åbo Akademi University serves the Swedish-speaking community of Finland, which today comprises some 5 percent of the population and is part of a broader Swedish-speaking community centered on Sweden. Åbo Akademi University is well connected within the Nordic countries as well as more broadly.
- The University of Malta plays a key role in maintaining Malta as a bilingual society (Maltese and English). Beyond fostering the Maltese language, its outreach activities serve an underprivileged area close to the capital Valletta, it provides courses for older residents in several locations throughout the country, and it works with immigrants.

The Democratic Mission of Higher Education Is Strengthened by Global Cooperation

The Council of Europe's work on the democratic mission of higher education started as a transatlantic cooperation with U.S. partners in the International Consortium. The OAS and the IAU have now joined the project, which has become the Global Cooperation for the Democratic Mission of Higher Education.

Each partner could possibly have undertaken similar activities on their own, but they would have forgone the inspiration and mutual learning that is a key part of the cooperation. European universities can certainly learn much from their U.S. counterparts, for example, when it comes to seeing themselves as democratic actors in the broader society as well as at a local level, with a democratic and social responsibility. U.S. universities can learn from the way students, faculty, and staff are partners in university governance in Europe. Latin America, through the OAS, and the rest of the world, through the IAU, provide further impetus not only to the practical cooperation but to the very understanding of the democratic mission.

Regular conferences, known as Global Fora, and organized every two to three years, are the mainstay of the cooperation. Books in the Council of Europe Higher Education Series and articles published regularly in various journals bring the experience of the Global Cooperation to a broader section of the higher education community beyond those who can participate in the Global Fora. Statements, most recently on academic freedom, institutional autonomy, and the future of democracy (Bergan, Gallagher, and Harkavy 2020: 251–255), suggest important elements for policy development on the basis of the shared experience of the Global Cooperation.

The Local Democratic Mission of Higher Education Needs a European Platform

If making the overall democratic mission of higher education a reality requires international cooperation, so does furthering its *local* democratic mission. The AITF provides inspiration for several parts of the world, not least South Africa. It also provided the impetus for the Council of Europe's work to establish European cooperation focusing specifically on the local dimension of the overall democratic mission.

Following preparations through three invitational seminars, and on the basis of a proposal by a working group, the Council of Europe has decided to establish a European Platform on the Local Democratic Mission of Higher Education. At least in the initial period, the suggestion is that the platform be composed of representative higher education organizations like the IAU, EUA, and EURASHE as well as of Council of Europe bodies like Congress of Local and Regional Authorities in Europe[8] and the Intercultural Cities Network.[9] Some universities should also be involved from the start, and more should be invited to join as the work on the platform gets underway.

The platform will have four main activities: advocacy, policy development, identifying examples of promising practices, and undertaking studies or other work on specific issues. It could also help in the further development of the EQPR, described in Chapter 8, and stimulate university-community cooperation in providing EQPR holders an opportunity to put their competences at the service of their new host communities.

Even if it is still uncertain how and when the platform will be launched, it is possible to suggest that its immediate priorities should be:

- Defining and agreeing on the role and tasks of members, to make the platform fully functional
- Organizing a first event relatively soon after the platform is launched, preferably at Council of Europe headquarters
- Presenting the local democratic mission of higher education at other events in Europe
- Developing work on a limited range of specific topics

Longer-term priorities could include:

- Expanding the membership of the platform
- Developing more extensive projects demonstrating how universities and local communities can and do work together on specific issues
- Developing policy recommendations
- Helping communities in crisis, for example, in war-torn areas like Ukraine or Nagorno-Karabakh/Artsakh or in areas hit by natural disasters, such as the earthquake in the southeast of Turkey in early February 2023, where universities are victims but also represent a significant potential for healing and reconstruction.

Lessons Learned: Toward a European Approach to the Local Democratic Mission of Higher Education

This brief summary has no pretense of exhausting the possibilities for and variety of university-community cooperation in Europe. I hope, however, to have identified the most important elements required to develop the local democratic mission as part and parcel of what universities in Europe do and should do.

I suggest the key lessons learned from this book include:

- The local democratic mission must be a political priority for universities, which means the university leadership must make it a priority. This includes making their local democratic mission part of their institutional mission statements and strategies, and quality assurance agencies—which are very different from ranking bodies—should include an assessment of the degree to which universities fulfill their mission in their overall quality assurance of higher education.
- Through advocacy and policy development, higher education will need to convince leaders and policymakers in national and local

public authorities as well as in civil society that developing democracy locally is part of what universities should do.

- Local authorities and civil society must see universities as a source of knowledge and understanding, of relevance and help—and, why not, pride—to their communities.
- Universities must work *with* and not just *in* their communities, and the communities must work with universities. They must speak *with* and not *at* or *past* one another.
  - University-community cooperation is beneficial not only to the community but also to the university. The University of the Aegean, Åbo Akademi University, and the University of Iceland are highly considered by the communities they are a part because they are seen as serving those communities.
- The relationship must be one of mutual respect where both universities and local communities recognize each other's potential and competences.
- Therefore, cooperation is key—internationally as well as locally. Partners need to be convinced and buy in—cooperation imposed is not real cooperation. Queen's needed to convince both its own staff and students and the Sandy Row neighborhood that the university had something to offer and that its intentions were sincere.
  - *International* cooperation is also key. Even if the local democratic mission of higher education is by definition carried out in specific local contexts, it benefits from an exchange of ideas and good practices. Those wishing to work in a local community will often find strength both in being able to argue that other universities' communities in other countries are working along the same lines and in showing that an international organization has provided political support for their ideas. This is an important part of the rationale behind the proposed Council of Europe Platform, and both the Global Cooperation for the Democratic Mission of Higher Education and the EHEA are examples of ideas and policy guidelines developed through international cooperation and then implemented nationally or locally.
- In the European context where ministries responsible for higher education play an important role in devising policies and funding criteria for the education system, these must recognize the local democratic mission as one of the criteria according to which universities will be assessed and funded.
- I do not have sufficient faith in rankings to plead that they adapt to take account of the local democratic mission. Rather, the local democratic mission provides one more reason for disregarding

rankings and not using them as a basis for public policy or funding decisions.

- Broader political and societal developments are important. European cooperation, as it is today, arises from the profound changes in Europe following the fall of Communism that made European cooperation in the true sense of the word possible and not just a dream. But higher education needs to rise to the occasion and make good use of the opportunities offered. The EHEA would not have come about had institutions and their organizations not seen the opportunities and tried to make the best of them. At the same time, higher education can play a role in shaping international developments, as is shown in the support many European institutions, scholars, and students are providing for their colleagues in Ukraine, both those who have had to flee and those who have been able to remain. The contribution of higher education will be essential in rebuilding Ukraine.

- European cooperation is essential to giving the local democratic mission a "European accent." We cannot duplicate what others do in different circumstances, but we can and should learn from others with greater experience in furthering the local democratic mission, such as the U.S. AITF.

- Higher education has a responsibility to the broader society. Academic freedom and institutional autonomy are essential values of democratic societies, universities and their members need to be free to define their priorities in research and teaching, and the main task of universities cannot be to find solutions to every immediate problem society may face. But the need for critical distance does not mean disengagement. To the contrary, our societies need a critical and engaged higher education community, and no fear of "politicization" should hold it back.

- Academic knowledge and its application in society may well be one of the major political battles of the coming years. Again, higher education must engage, and those arguing against "politicized higher education" are often those whose positions do not withstand scrutiny based on academic knowledge and understanding.

- A culture of democracy is essential to our local communities as well as to our countries, to Europe, and to the world. However important democratic institutions and laws are, they will not be democratic in practice unless they build on a culture of democracy: a set of attitudes and behaviors that is largely developed through education—including higher education—and that rely on both theoretical knowledge and understanding and the will and ability to put these into practice. This culture of democracy cannot be fully developed unless higher education contributes.

- Not least, higher education *matters*. Our societies cannot develop as we would wish them to develop unless the higher education community of institutions, faculty, students, and staff engage, unless they believe they can make a difference, and unless they are willing to look beyond their campus and their discipline.

Exchanging experience, developing policies, devising and running joint projects, conducting further research on the local democratic mission, and arguing its importance with public authorities and civil society are a quintessential European undertaking. That is why the proposed Council of Europe Platform for the Local Democratic Mission should be established and made operational as a matter of urgency. The basis has been prepared but the engine must be started.

In the aftermath of World War II, the Council of Europe was established on the assumption that close cooperation between countries and peoples could prevent further wars. The EU was founded on the assumption that economic cooperation could prevent future wars. Neither assumption has held up entirely, but there can be little doubt that the European cooperation built up from the late 1940s onward and expanded with the political changes of the late 1980s to early 1990s has been hugely important in making Europe a continent where, for the most part, life is meaningful. We have, of course, seen wars in the former Yugoslavia and the South Caucasus, Ukraine is now under attack from Russia, and the Armenian population of Artsakh has been driven out by Azerbaijan.

Cooperation between universities and local communities will not prevent all kinds of violence but it will help build the kind of trust that makes future armed conflict more difficult, and it will provide local communities with the kind of knowledge, understanding, and resources required to improve the lives of its residents and make local communities more democratic and inclusive. Universities need to respond to the suggestion made by the then president of the University at Buffalo, William R. Greiner, that "the great universities of the twenty-first century will be judged by their ability to help solve our most urgent social problems" (quoted in Benson et al. 2017: 144). I would add that universities must help solve not only our social but also our societal and civilizational challenges. Making the local democratic mission a European priority will help cooperation and reduce the potential for strife across borders. It will help countries like Ukraine and Armenia rebuild when they suffer aggression.

Not least, making the local democratic mission European will help us all understand that the kind of education we need must help us prepare the kind of societies we want for ourselves, our children, and our grandchildren.[10] John Aubrey Douglass asks whether universities are followers or leaders (Douglass 2021: 34). My answer is clear: universities must be democratic leaders, locally as well as nationally and globally.

Appendix 1

European Cooperation: A Brief Glossary

Committee of Ministers: The Council of Europe's statutory decision-making body, made up of the Ministers for Foreign Affairs of member states. Ministers meet once a year, but the statutory decision-making powers are exercised on their behalf by the Committee of Ministers' Deputies, made up of the Permanent Representative (Ambassador) of each of the forty-six member states to the Council of Europe. The Committee of Ministers' Deputies meets in Strasbourg, generally on a weekly basis.

Available at https://www.coe.int/en/web/cm

Council of Europe: An intergovernmental organization devoted to democracy, human rights, and the rule of law. After the exclusion of Russia in March 2022, in response to its invasion of Ukraine, the Council of Europe has forty-six member states. It was established in 1949, is headquartered in Strasbourg, and is particularly well known for the European Convention on and Court of Human Rights. It also has a strong education program.

Available at https://www.coe.int/en/web/portal/
Education: available at https://www.coe.int/en/web/education

Council of the European Union: The intergovernmental arm of the EU, with headquarters in Bruxelles. It provides the framework within which the ministers of EU member states meet to conduct EU business.

Available at https://www.consilium.europa.eu/en/council-eu/

ERASMUS+ Program: EuRopean Community Action Scheme for the Mobility of University Students; now Erasmus+, established in 1987, is a very comprehensive EU program furthering student and staff mobility.

Available at https://erasmus-plus.ec.europa.eu/

European Commission: The executive branch of the EU, with headquarters in Bruxelles. Among other things, it oversees a very extensive education program.

Available at https://commission.europa.eu/index_en
Education: available at https://commission.europa.eu/education_en

European Convention on Human Rights: The main legal text protecting human rights in Europe, developed in the framework of the Council of Europe and overseen by the European Court of Human Rights. All Council of Europe member states must have ratified the European Convention on Human Rights, and nonmember states cannot be a party to it. Adopted in 1950, it has since been supplemented by sixteen protocols.

Available at https://www.coe.int/en/web/human-rights-convention

European Court of Human Rights: A Council of Europe body overseeing the implementation of the European Convention on Human Rights, with headquarters in Strasbourg. Any resident of a Council of Europe member state may bring a case against his or her government to the European Court of Human Rights provided the case falls under the European Convention on Human Rights and the possibilities of appeal have been exhausted within the country's own legal system.

Available at https://www.echr.coe.int/

European Court of Justice: Formally, the Court of Justice of the European Union is the judicial branch of the EU, with competence to rule in cases concerning EU legislation, based in Luxembourg.

Available at https://curia.europa.eu/jcms/jcms/j_6/en/

European Cultural Convention: The text providing the legal basis of the Council of Europe's programs in education and culture. Adopted in 1954, it is open to ratification by European nonmember states of the Council of Europe, subject to approval by the Committee of Ministers. Currently, fifty states have ratified the European Cultural Convention: all Council of Europe member states as well as Belarus, the Holy See, Kazakhstan, and Russia. Being a party to the European Cultural Convention is one of the requirements for accession to the EHEA.

Available at https://www.coe.int/en/web/conventions/full-list?module=treaty-detail&treatynum=018

European Higher Education Area: A sui generis intergovernmental process (not an organization) providing the most important framework for higher education cooperation and reform in Europe. Launched as the Bologna Process in 1999 with twenty-nine member states, it became the EHEA in 2010 and now has forty-nine member states, of which two—Russia and Belarus—have at the time of writing (August 2024) been suspended because of their role in the war on Ukraine. The European Commission is also a member of the EHEA, whereas eight intergovernmental and nongovernmental organizations—including the Council of Europe—are consultative members. The EHEA is independent of any other international cooperation framework. For a country to accede to the EHEA, it needs to be a party to the European Cultural Convention and to commit in writing to implementing the goals and policies of the EHEA as defined in its successive ministerial communiqués.

Available at https://www.ehea.info/

European Parliament: The legislative body of the EU, whose members have been elected directly since 1979. The European Parliament meets once a month in plenary session in Strasbourg but holds committee meetings in Bruxelles, and its Secretariat is based in Luxembourg.

Available at https://www.europarl.europa.eu/portal/en

European Union: A sui generis supranational political, legal, and economic union of twenty-seven European countries (twenty-eight until the United Kingdom left in 2020 [Brexit]). Its predecessor was the European Coal and Steel Community and, more immediately, the European Economic Community set up by six countries in 1957 through the Treaty of Rome.

Available at https://european-union.europa.eu/index_en

Global Cooperation for the Democratic Mission of Higher Education: A framework for international cooperation furthering the role of higher education in developing and maintaining democracy. Originally launched by the Council of Europe and the International Consortium in 1999, it now also comprises the OAS and the IAU.

Available at https://www.internationalconsortium.org/
Available at https://www.coe.int/en/web/higher-education-and-research/democratic-mission-of-higher-education#{%2234135905%22:[]}

Parliamentary Assembly of the Council of Europe: A consultative assembly made up of representatives of the parliaments of the forty-six Council of Europe member states. It normally meets four times a year in Strasbourg; its committees may meet more frequently and elsewhere.

Available at https://pace.coe.int/en/

Appendix 2

Competences for Democratic Culture

Appendix 2 presents one competence from each of the four major clusters of the Reference Framework of Competences for Democratic Culture and illustrates each competence with an example of a descriptor at basic, intermediate, and advanced level. A full overview of descriptors can be found in the second volume of the RFCDC (Council of Europe 2018b).

VALUES

Competence
Valuing cultural diversity

Examples of Descriptors
Promotes the view that one should always strive for mutual understanding and meaningful dialogue between people and groups who are perceived to be "different" from one another (*basic*)
Expresses the view that the cultural diversity within a society should be positively valued and appreciated (*intermediate*)
Argues that intercultural dialogue should be used to develop respect and a culture of "living together" (*advanced*)

ATTITUDES

Competence
Tolerance of ambiguity

Examples of Descriptors

Shows that he or she can suspend judgments about other people temporarily (*basic*)

Deals with uncertainty in a positive and constructive manner (*intermediate*)

Expresses a desire to have his or her own ideas and values challenged (*advanced*)

SKILLS

Competence

Analytical and critical thinking skills

Examples of Descriptors

Uses evidence to support his or her opinions (*basic*)

Shows that he or she thinks about whether the information he or she uses is correct (*intermediate*)

Can use explicit and specifiable criteria, principles, or values to make judgments (*advanced*)

KNOWLEDGE AND CRITICAL UNDERSTANDING

Competence

Knowledge and critical understanding of language and communication

Examples of Descriptors

Can explain how tone of voice, eye contact, and body language can aid communication (*basic*)

Can explain how social relationships are sometimes encoded in the linguistic forms that are used in conversations (e.g., in greetings, forms of address, use of expletives) (*intermediate*)

Can explain why people of other cultural affiliations may follow different verbal and nonverbal communicative conventions that are meaningful from their perspective (*advanced*) © Council of Europe, 2018. Reproduced with permission.

Notes

PREFACE

1. There is no shortage in Europe of organizations whose name includes the word "council," and we meet some of them in this book. It does not help that most of them simply go by "the Council." When I use "the Council," it refers to the Council of Europe. Similarly, the Commission, with a capital C, will be used to refer to the European Commission.

2. What is today AFS Intercultural Programs was originally established as the American Field Service by U.S. volunteer ambulance drivers during World War I and again during World War II. The high school exchange program was launched in 1947 to develop better understanding among peoples and thereby try to prevent further wars. From the 1970s onward, the AFS program went from being a bilateral exchange between the United States and other countries to a truly global program, where students could as easily go from Japan to Chile as from Norway to the United States. More information is available at https://afs.org/, accessed February 2, 2024. I should declare an interest: my oldest daughter, my wife, and I were all AFS exchange students—from France to Tulsa, Oklahoma; from Chile to Decatur, Illinois; and from Norway to Alton, Illinois, respectively.

ACKNOWLEDGMENTS

1. This oft quoted line is from John Donne's *Devotions* (1624). The full text of the poem is freely available, e.g., at https://www.poemhunter.com/poem/no-man-is-an-island/, accessed August 12, 2024.

INTRODUCTION

1. The law uses the adjective *vitskapeleg*, the noun for which is *vitskap/vitenskap* (the form of the word depends on the variety of Norwegian used), the same concept as the German *Wissenschaft* or the Slavic *nauka*, and has a broader semantic field than the English

"science." Depending on the context, these terms can also be translated as "academic" or "scholarly."

2. Launched as the Bologna Process by twenty-nine countries in 1999 and initially focused primarily on structural reforms, the EHEA now provides the framework for broad cooperation between forty-nine European countries. The EHEA is described in greater detail in Chapter 1.

3. In Europe, the minister of education is the equivalent of the U.S. secretary of education. It should, however, be noted that in European countries public authorities play a greater role in developing higher education policy than does the U.S. Department of Education.

4. For a brief, critical discussion, see Gelman (2011). Speaker O'Neill is often credited with the phrase and certainly used it, but its origins seem to go further back, possibly to 1932, see Barry Popik, "All Politics Is Local," dated June 13, 2009, available at https://www.barrypopik.com/index.php/new_york_city/entry/all_politics_is_local/, accessed on February 2, 2024.

5. See the website of the AITF, available at https://www.margainc.com/aitf/, accessed February 2, 2024.

6. See the website of Penn's Netter Center, available at https://www.nettercenter.upenn.edu/, accessed February 2, 2024.

7. Alsatian is a distinct variety of German, very similar to the variety spoken across the border, in the German State (*Land*) of Baden-Württemberg. How well other speakers of German understand Alsatian depends on where they come from. People from the south of Germany, Luxembourg, or Switzerland understand it quite well, whereas those from the north or east of Germany understand it less well. Unlike Luxemburgish, which is also an Alemannic dialect of German, Alsatian has not been codified or given official status as a language.

8. The phrase is generally attributed to Senator Daniel Patrick Moynihan.

9. Armed conflict was not entirely absent. The Warsaw Pact invasion of Hungary in 1956 and of (then) Czechoslovakia in 1968 as well as the Turkish invasion of Cyprus in 1974 are examples.

10. Referred to as Artsakh by Armenia.

11. See, for example, Helene Skjeggestad and Sondre Moen Myhre, "Det meste går Putins vei" [Most things are going Putin's way], Aftenposten, January 1, 2024, available at https://www.aftenposten.no/verden/i/jlWbvz/det-meste-gaar-putins-vei-hva-skjedde, accessed February 2, 2024.

12. See "Slovakia's September 2023 Election," National Democratic Institute, available at https://www.ndi.org/publications/slovakias-september-2023-election, accessed February 2, 2024.

13. For an account of the AfD, see Pittelkow and Riedel (2022).

14. See "Zwei Wahlen und fünf Botschaften an Berlin" [Two elections and five messages for Berlin], Tagesschau, available at https://www.tagesschau.de/inland/innenpolitik/landtagswahl-bayern-hessen-erkenntnisse-100.html, accessed October 12, 2023.

15. See "Warum die CDU-Brandmauer zur AfD so bröckelt" [Why the CDU firewall against AfD is crumbling], ZDF Heute, available at https://www.zdf.de/nachrichten/politik/afd-cdu-zusammenarbeit-brandmauer-100.html, accessed February 2, 2024.

16. For an updated overview covering the whole education system, see the dedicated website, Save Schools in Ukraine, available at https://saveschools.in.ua/en/, accessed February 2, 2024.

17. Personal information provided during a visit to Almaty and Astana in October 2022.

18. For a brief recent contribution, dated September 26, 2023, see Alpaslan Özerdem's blog, "Reconstruction of Ukraine's Higher Education," available at https://www.wilson center.org/blog-post/reconstruction-ukraines-higher-education, accessed February 2, 2024.

19. For an overview of ongoing efforts, see the website of the European University Association (EUA), available at https://www.eua.eu/issues/32:european-support-to-ukrai nian-higher-education-community.html, accessed February 2, 2024.

20. The Council for Mutual Economic Assistance (Russian: Совет Экономической Взаимопомощи/Sovét Ekonomícheskoy Vzaimopómoshchi), established in 1949 under the leadership of the Soviet Union and dissolved in 1991, was considered as the Eastern bloc response to the Marshall Plan and the organization that developed into the Organization for Economic Cooperation and Development (OECD).

21. The phrase was popularized by Lev Trotsky and is variously translated as "trash heap," "garbage heap," "ash heap," or "dustbin." Arguably, Trotsky himself ended up on it.

22. The "EuRopean Community Action Scheme for the Mobility of University Students," but the fact that the acronym spells out the name of a famous philosopher from Rotterdam is no coincidence.

23. The European Cultural Convention (Council of Europe 1954), adopted in December 1954, provides the legal framework for the Council of Europe's programs in education and culture. It has by now been ratified by fifty countries. See European Cultural Convention (ETS No. 018), available at https://www.coe.int/en/web/conventions/full-list ?module=treaty-detail&treatynum=018, accessed February 2, 2024.

24. Inhabitants of Alsace, the region of eastern France where the author has been living for the past three decades. The two Alsatian *départements* are the Bas-Rhin and the Haut-Rhin, and there is some rivalry between the two.

25. In some cases, the latter condition may be dispensed with.

26. See the Council of Europe news item, available at https://www.coe.int/en/web/por tal/-/russia-ceases-to-be-party-to-the-european-convention-on-human-rights, accessed February 2, 2024.

27. The term "competence" is much used in education policy in Europe. It designates the ability to do something well (or of being competent) and is often developed through education. It is broader than either 'knowledge" or "skill," as indicated by the Council of Europe's *Common European Framework of Reference for Languages* (CEFR): "The general competences of language learners or users (see section 5.1.) consist in particular of their knowledge, skills and existential competence and also their ability to learn" (Council of Europe 2001a: 11), which also notes that "skills and know-how (savoir-faire . . .) whether it be a matter of driving a car, playing the violin or chairing a meeting, depend more on the ability to carry out procedures than on declarative knowledge, but this skill may be facilitated by the acquisition of 'forgettable' knowledge and be accompanied by forms of existential competence (for example relaxed attitude or tension in carrying out a task)" (Council of Europe 2001a: 11). The Council of Europe's RFCDC defines "competence" as "the ability to mobilise and deploy relevant values, attitudes, skills, knowledge and/ or understanding in order to respond appropriately and effectively to the demands, challenges and opportunities that are presented by a given type of context" (Council of Europe 2018b: 32). It further states: "It should be noted that, according to the Framework, competences include not only skills, knowledge and understanding but also values and attitudes" (Council of Europe 2018b: 33).

28. With some variations, such as the U.K. vice chancellor or the Irish and French president, this is the term generally used in Europe to designate a university president.

29. As noted earlier, the European Cultural Convention is the framework for the Council of Europe's Education program. In 1999, forty-seven countries had acceded to the Cultural Convention; the current number is fifty. The countries that joined later are Serbia in 2001 (then as the State Union of Serbia and Montenegro, to which Serbia is considered as the successor state), Montenegro in 2006 (after it declared independence from the State Union), and Kazakhstan in 2010. For an overview of signature and ratifications, see the chart of signatures and ratifications of Treaty 018, available at https://www.coe.int/en/web/conventions/full-list?module=signatures-by-treaty&treatynum=018, accessed February 2, 2024.

30. See the website of Penn's Netter Center, available at https://www.nettercenter.upenn.edu/, accessed February 2, 2024.

31. See the website of the AITF, available at https://www.margainc.com/aitf/, accessed February 2, 2024.

32. As is explored in Chapter 6, the platform will serve as a forum for the exchange of ideas and good practices. It will also engage in advocacy, make policy proposals, and undertake thematic studies.

33. See the website of the IAU, available at https://www.iau-aiu.net/, accessed February 2, 2024.

34. See the website of the EUA, available at https://www.eua.eu/, accessed February 2, 2024.

35. See the website of EURASHE, available at https://www.eurashe.eu/, accessed February 2, 2024.

36. See the Refugees Welcome Map on the website of the EUA, available at https://www.eua.eu/our-work/projects/eua-projects/refugees-welcome-map.html, accessed August 9, 2024.

37. Physiotherapy is a regulated profession. As is explained in Chapter 8, this presents specific challenges in terms of accepting refugees' qualifications on the basis of the EQPR.

CHAPTER 1

1. Originally the European Credit Transfer System, hence the acronym ECTS, but now the European Credit Transfer and Accumulation System, with the same acronym. See the European Commission website for the ECTS, available at https://education.ec.europa.eu/education-levels/higher-education/inclusive-and-connected-higher-education/european-credit-transfer-and-accumulation-system, accessed February 2, 2024.

2. See the European Commission website for the European Strategy for Universities, available at https://education.ec.europa.eu/document/commission-communication-on-a-european-strategy-for-universities, accessed February 2, 2024.

3. See Francis Brochet, "Les défis d'une Union européenne à 36 États" [The challenges of a European Union of 36 countries], Dernières Nouvelles d'Alsace, January 22, 2024, available at https://www.leprogres.fr/elections/2024/01/22/les-defis-d-une-union-europeenne-a-36-etats, accessed August 9, 2024.

4. For an overview of the results, see the one provided by the BBC, available at https://www.bbc.co.uk/news/politics/eu_referendum/results, accessed February 2, 2024.

5. "Yes, it is Europe, from the Atlantic to the Urals, it is Europe, it is the whole of Europe, that will decide the fate of the world," in a speech "to the people of Strasbourg," November 23, 1959.

6. A metropolitan power is the parent state of a colony. In the colonial era, Spain was the metropolitan power of most of Latin America (with Brazil as a major exception, for

which the metropolitan power was Portugal), and the United Kingdom was the metropolitan power of the original thirteen American colonies.

7. There are reasons for considering both Winston Churchill's Iron Curtain speech delivered in Fulton, Missouri, in March 1946, and the Communist coup in Czechoslovakia in February 1948 as the starting dates for this division.

8. For a brief overview, see the Council of Europe brochure, available at https://edoc
.coe.int/en/an-overview/6966-the-council-of-europe-an-overview.html, accessed February 2, 2024.

9. This is the Belarusian form of his name; he is also referred to with the Russian form Aleksandr Lukaschenko. Moreover, the ending -enko is typical of Ukrainian origin family names.

10. See the World Population Review website, available at https://worldpopulationre
view.com/country-rankings/countries-that-recognize-kosovo, accessed February 2, 2024.

11. European Cultural Convention (ETS No. 018), available at https://www.coe.int/en
/web/conventions/full-list?module=treaty-detail&treatynum=018, accessed February 2, 2024.

12. Russia and Belarus were suspended from participation in its work program and governing bodies, in April 2022, in response to the role of both countries in the war on Ukraine.

13. Uvalić-Trumbić at the time worked at UNESCO's higher education center for Europe, known as CEPES (Centre Européen pour l'Enseignement Supérieur), which was established in București, in 1972, as a UNESCO higher education center that also included North America and Israel When CEPES was set up, its location in București was seen as important to East-West cooperation, and it was without a doubt also a nod to Ceasceşcu's perceived independence within the Soviet bloc, at a time when North America and Europe were still relatively unaware of the truly brutal character of his regime. Within CEPES, Uvalić-Trumbić was, among other things, responsible for recognition issues and was the UNESCO cosecretary of the ENIC Network. CEPES was discontinued in 2011.

14. NUFFIC is the Netherlands organization for international cooperation in higher education. It is an independent nonprofit organization based in Den Haag. The abbreviation stands for Netherlands Universities Foundation for International Cooperation, but the full name is never used.

15. The full formal name of the Lisbon Recognition Convention is the Convention on the Recognition of Qualifications concerning Higher Education in the European Region (ETS 165), available at https://rm.coe.int/168007f2c7, accessed on February 2, 2024. We had to use the English name for the capital of Portugal when referring to the convention.

16. Chart of signatures and ratifications of Treaty 165, available at https://www.coe
.int/en/web/conventions/full-list?module=signatures-by-treaty&treatynum=165, accessed February 2, 2024.

17. EuRopean Community Action Scheme for the Mobility of University Students (the C of Community is, however, not taken up in the abbreviation).

18. "In 2020, at least 20% of those graduating in the European Higher Education Area should have had a study or training period abroad."

19. See the European Commission website for the Erasmus+ program, available at https://erasmus-plus.ec.europa.eu/programme-guide/part-a/priorities-of-the-erasmus
-programme/budget, accessed February 2, 2024.

20. For an overview of agencies, see the European Commission website for the Erasmus+ program, available at https://erasmus-plus.ec.europa.eu/contacts/national-agencies, accessed February 2, 2024.

21. See the overview on the European Commission website for the Erasmus+ program, available at https://erasmus-plus.ec.europa.eu/contacts/national-erasmus-offices, accessed February 2, 2024.

22. See the European Commission website for the Erasmus+ program, available at https://erasmus-plus.ec.europa.eu/programme-guide/part-a/priorities-of-the-erasmus-programme/objectives-features, accessed February 2, 2024.

23. See the website of the Erasmus Student Network, available at https://esn.org/about-esn, accessed February 2, 2024.

24. See the Erasmus generation blog, available at https://blog.erasmusgeneration.org/, accessed February 2, 2024.

25. See the Erasmus generation blog, available at https://blog.erasmusgeneration.org/students-helping-students, accessed February 2, 2024.

26. For a reference to this debate in Norway, see Mats Arnesen, "Krever at utenland-ske ansatte lærer seg norsk innen tre år" [They demand that foreign faculty learn Norwegian within three years], Krono, June 14, 2023, available at https://www.khrono.no/krever-at-utenlandske-ansatte-laerer-seg-norsk-innen-tre-ar/788919, accessed February 2, 2024.

27. See the overview on the University of Latvia website, available at https://www.lu.lv/en/science/programmes-and-projects/international-programmes/nordplus/, accessed February 2, 2024.

28. A cooperation agreement between the EU and Iceland, Liechtenstein, and Norway.

29. Austria joined the EU in 1994.

30. For somewhat diverging views on Kosovo, see Judah (2000) and Malcolm (1998).

31. See the CEEPUS website, available at https://www.ceepus.info/content/about, accessed February 2, 2024.

32. Allègre was himself a fairly prominent geochemist. After his spell as minister of education, he gained notoriety as one of France's leading climate skeptics.

33. At the time close to its final planning stage, as the Euro was introduced on January 1, 2002. The United Kingdom chose not to adopt the Euro.

34. For the full text, see Bologna Process 1999.

35. Russia and Belarus were suspended from participation in the governing bodies and work program in April 2022, at my final meeting of the BFUG, because of their role in the invasion of Ukraine. At their meeting in May 2024, EHEA ministers decided to prolong the suspension of both countries.

36. In alphabetical order, BusinessEurope (which represents employers), the Council of Europe, Education International (which represents higher education staff), ENQA (the European Association for Quality Assurance in higher education, which started out as a network, hence the N), the European Association of Institutions in Higher Education (EURASHE, which represents professional higher education institutions), ESU (the European Students Union), the EUA, and UNESCO.

37. See the first Bologna Process Stocktaking report presented to ministers in 2005, available at https://www.ehea.info/media.ehea.info/file/WG_Stocktaking/96/1/BPStocktaking9May2005_578961.pdf, accessed February 2, 2024.

38. The 2018 report is the most recent complete report because for the 2020 ministerial conference, it was decided to focus the report on a long-term overview of key developments. The next Implementation Report will be presented to the ministerial conference to be held in Tirana in May 2024.

39. A qualifications framework describes all qualifications in an education system with stipulated generic learning outcomes and also indicates how students can move from one

qualification to another. A brief overview is available at http://www.ehea.info/page-qual
ification-frameworks, accessed February 2, 2024.

40. The Magna Charta Universitatum, which should not be confused with the Bologna Declaration or the Bologna Process, was adopted by European rectors (the most commonly used term for university presidents) when they gathered to celebrate the nine hun-
dredth anniversary of the University of Bologna in September 1988. The Magna Charta
Observatory was later set up to oversee the Magna Charta Universitatum and is hosted
by the University of Bologna. In 2020, a new text was adopted to update and supplement—
but not replace—the 1988 Magna Charta Universitatum. Both texts as well as information on the activities of the observatory may be found on its website, available at https://
www.magna-charta.org/, accessed February 2, 2024.

41. Ministers were informed and consulted by their BFUG representatives, and in many
countries, the foreign ministries were also consulted.

42. For an overview of developments in Belarus, see Wilson (2021).

43. The highest court competent to rule on alleged violations of EU legislation. This
court is based in Luxembourg and should not be confused with the European Court of
Human Rights, which is part of the Council of Europe, based in Strasbourg, and rules
on alleged violations of the European Convention on Human Rights.

44. For a timeline of developments with regard to the CEU, with several useful links,
see the timeline of events posted on the CEU website, available at https://www.ceu.edu
/istandwithceu/timeline-events, accessed February 2, 2024. CEU's then provost Liviu Matei kept me updated on developments and provided much useful information. See also
Matei (2020).

45. See the Academics for Peace website, available at https://barisicinakademisyenler
.net/node/1, accessed February 2, 2024.

46. See the Amnesty International press release of January 15, 2016, available at https://
www.amnesty.org/en/latest/press-release/2016/01/turkey-detention-of-academics-inten
sifies-crackdown-on-freedom-of-expression/, accessed February 2, 2024.

47. Followers of the Islamic preacher and scholar Muhammed Fethullah Gülen, who
was once an ally of Recep Tayyip Erdoğan. Erdoğan has been the strongman of Turkey,
as prime ministers and president, since at least 2003, when he started his first term as
prime minister. Gülen fell out with Erdoğan and lived in self-imposed exile in Pennsylvania from 1999 until his death in October 2024, but alleged adherents of his movement
were influential in Turkey for years after that. Erdoğan accused Gülen of having mas-
terminded the failed coup.

48. Ali Kucukgocmen, "Turkey Hands Suspended Jail Sentences to Three Academics
over Kurdish Letter: Lawyers," Reuters, February 23, 2018, available at https://www.yahoo
.com/news/turkey-hands-suspended-jail-sentences-three-academics-over-142057392.html
?guccounter=1&guce_referrer=aHR0cHM6Ly93d3cuZ29vZ2xlLmNvbS8&guce_referrer
_sig=AQAAAK8_1rnBUHvyOl29nDEERd6cJL5_0T8blm_fZODxKB_N5vXCDi09fYWS
wfRxDIyjBy-Vu_SZ5COfmes4rPhYPDBbIHi_5flyuENiIu9qBV1-QpCwROD1HYhL2Qh
XJypxeKai37IjjIb8oMt2DcX7T40nVmB8SlCyaD9J4OLtars, accessed August 9, 2024.

49. "Poland's New PM Donald Tusk Sworn In, Completing Transition of Power," Euronews, December 13, 2023, available at https://www.euronews.com/2023/12/13/polands
-new-pm-donald-tusk-sworn-in-completing-transition-of-power, accessed February 2,
2024.

50. On populism, see Müller (2017).

51. See the European Commission Education website, available at https://education
.ec.europa.eu/, accessed February 2, 2024.

52. See the presentation at the EQAR website, available at https://www.eqar.eu/about /projects/deqar-project/about-deqar/, accessed February 2, 2024.

53. See the European Commission Communication on a European Strategy for Universities, available at https://education.ec.europa.eu/sites/default/files/2022-01/communication-european-strategy-for-universities-graphic-version.pdf, accessed February 2, 2024.

54. In the interest of transparency: I am the main external expert in this project.

CHAPTER 2

1. Incidentally, few, if any, European languages make the distinction between policy and politics/political that is found in English, at least not without recourse to the recent loanword "policy."

2. Even if modern English is quite far removed from its Germanic roots, in particular, in its vocabulary.

3. See the website for the European Charter for Regional or Minority Languages, available at https://www.coe.int/en/web/european-charter-regional-or-minority-languages, accessed February 2, 2024.

4. Chart of signatures and ratifications of Treaty 148, available at https://www.coe.int /en/web/conventions/full-list?module=signatures-by-treaty&treatynum=148, accessed August 9, 2024.

5. See the Eurostat website, available at https://ec.europa.eu/eurostat/statistics-explained/index.php?title=Foreign_language_skills_statistics#Number_of_foreign_languages_known, accessed February 2, 2024.

6. So, including the United Kingdom, which had not yet left the EU.

7. See the ECML's website for the European Day of Languages, available at https://edl .ecml.at/Home/tabid/1455/language/en-GB/Default.aspx, accessed February 2, 2024.

8. Both the Council of Europe and the EU prefer "plurilingualism" to "multilingualism," since plurilingualism, in addition to proficiency in several languages, includes the notion of linguistic tolerance.

9. Corresponding to high school in the United States.

10. See "What Languages Are Studied the Most in the EU?" Eurostat, September 24, 2021, available at https://ec.europa.eu/eurostat/fr/web/products-eurostat-news/-/edn-20 210924-2, accessed February 2, 2024.

11. See the website of the Congress of Local and Regional Authorities in Europe, available at https://www.coe.int/en/web/congress, accessed February 2, 2024.

12. Giuseppe Garibaldi, one of the artisans of Italian independence, with Torino-born Camilo Cavour, was born in Nice.

13. The imposition of French as the language spoken by all parts of the population started with the French Revolution and was achieved largely through the extension of schooling with a strongly centralized curriculum. Several regional languages, like Alsatian, Breton, Catalan, Flemish, Occitan, and Provençal, are still spoken to varying degrees in different parts of France, even if they lack official status. The French Constitution (available at https://www.conseil-constitutionnel.fr/le-bloc-de-constitutionnalite/texte -integral-de-la-constitution-du-4-octobre-1958-en-vigueur, accessed February 2, 2024) states, in its Article 2, that "the language of the Republic is French," and this has generally been interpreted to mean that regional languages can have no legal or official status. France claims not to have national minorities and has refused to accede to the Council of Europe Charter on Regional and Minority Languages.

14. For a history of Bohuslän up until its integration into Sweden, see Andersson (2021).

15. See the World Population Review website, available at https://worldpopulationre view.com/country-rankings/countries-that-recognize-kosovo, accessed February 2, 2024.

16. See the overview of members of the International Monetary Fund on its website, available at https://www.imf.org/external/np/sec/memdir/memdate.htm, accessed February 2, 2024.

17. See the overview of members of the World Bank on its website, available at https://www.worldbank.org/en/about/leadership/members, accessed February 2, 2024.

18. See the overview of members of the Venice Commission on its website, available at https://www.venice.coe.int/WebForms/members/countries.aspx?lang=EN, accessed February 2, 2024.

19. See the overview of members of the Council of Europe Development Bank on its website, available at https://coebank.org/en/about/member-countries/, accessed February 2, 2024.

20. Catalunya is the Catalan spelling; the Spanish is Cataluña. English tends to use Catalonia.

21. "Últimas noticias sobre la formación del nuevo gobierno de Pedro Sánchez, 19 de noviembre | El PSOE reconoce que se enfrenta a una legislatura 'compleja' y acusa al PP de ser 'un partido de destrucción'" [The latest news on the formation of Pedro Sánchez's new government, November 19. The PSOE recognizes it faces a "complex" legislative period and accuses the PP of being "a party of destruction"], El Pais, available at https://elpais.com/espana/2023-11-19/ultimas-noticias-sobre-la-formacion-del-nuevo-gobierno -de-pedro-sanchez-en-directo.html, accessed February 2, 2024. PSOE, Spanish Socialist Party (Partido Socialista Obrero Español); PP, Spanish conservative party (Partido Popular).

22. "Consulta aquí los resultados del referéndum en Catalunya" [Look up the results of the referendum in Catalunya here], La Vanguardia, October 26, 2017, available at https://www.lavanguardia.com/referendum/index.html, accessed February 2, 2024. For an overview of Catalan nationalism, see Balcells (2004), which for obvious reasons does not include the most recent developments. For a proindependence argument, see Carreras (2015), for an anti-independence argument, see Kamen (2014).

23. BBC News, available at https://www.bbc.co.uk/news/events/scotland5-decides /results, accessed February 2, 2024.

24. See the Electoral Commission website, last updated September 25, 2019, available at https://www.electoralcommission.org.uk/who-we-are-and-what-we-do/elections-and -referendums/past-elections-and-referendums/eu-referendum/results-and-turnout-eu -referendum/eu-referendum-results-region-scotland, accessed February 2, 2024.

25. "Supreme Court Rules against Scottish Parliament Holding New Independence Referendum," The Guardian, November 23, 2022, available at https://www.theguardian .com/politics/2022/nov/23/scottish-independence-supreme-court-scottish-parliament -second-referendum-indyref2, accessed February 2, 2024.

26. For a good overview of the history of Alsace, see Vogler (1993, 1995) as well as Vogler and Hau (1997).

27. Gaston Thorn (1981–1985), Jacques Santer (1995–1999), and Jean-Claude Juncker (2014–2019).

28. See the Luxembourg government website, available at https://luxembourg.public .lu/fr/societe-et-culture/population/demographie.html, accessed February 2, 2024.

29. Romanians and Hungarians are historical adversaries, and many Romanians are not convinced Hungary has given up all claims on what is now Romanian territory with

a sizable Hungarian minority. The Orbán government has done little to discourage their skepticism, cf. Matthew Holroyd, "Viktor Orbán Criticised for Wearing Scarf with 'Greater Hungary' Map," Euronews, November 22, 2022, available at https://www.euronews.com/2022/11/22/viktor-orban-criticised-for-wearing-scarf-with-greater-hungary-map, accessed February 2, 2024.

30. The references to "education" and "school" follow the terms as used in the survey, which does not explain why it uses "education" only for those who stayed in school until they were at least twenty years old. One possible explanation is that this is an implicit reference to higher education.

31. At this point, the survey does distinguish between those still undertaking education and those who have completed their education.

32. For example, surveys conducted in late July 2024 show that the far-right AfD had the second-highest score of any German party, behind the CDU/CSU but ahead of the Social Democrats (SPD), the party of the current German chancellor, and the Green Party, see the ZDF Politbarometer/Forschungsgruppe Wahlen, available at https://www.forschungsgruppe.de/Aktuelles/Politbarometer/, accessed August 9, 2024.

33. Marine Le Pen (populist right), who proceeded to the second round, Eric Zeymour (to the right of Le Pen), and Nicolas Dupont-Aignan (sovereignist).

34. Jean-Luc Mélenchon (populist left), Fabien Roussel (Communist), Philippe Poutou, Nathalie Arthaud (both far left).

35. All figures are taken from the official website of the French Ministry of the Interior, available at https://www.interieur.gouv.fr/Elections/Les-resultats/Presidentielles/elecresult__presidentielle-2022/(path)/presidentielle-2022/FE.html, accessed February 2, 2024.

36. For an analysis of the Macron presidency by one of the foremost French political analysts, see Duhamel (2023).

37. See the Eurobarometer website, available at https://europa.eu/eurobarometer/surveys/detail/2273, accessed February 2, 2024.

38. "Many Europeans want climate action—but less so if it changes their lifestyle, shows poll," *The Guardian*, May 2, 2023, available at https://www.theguardian.com/environment/2023/may/02/many-europeans-want-climate-action-but-less-so-if-it-changes-their-lifestyle-shows-poll, accessed February 2, 2024.

39. See the Norddeutsche Rundfunk website, available at https://www.ndr.de/ratgeber/verbraucher/Heizungsgesetz-tritt-2024-in-Kraft-Was-aendert-sich,geg102.html#:~:text=K%C3%BCnftig%20muss%20jede%20neu%20eingebaute,die%20Regelung%20fr%C3%BChestens%20ab%202026, accessed February 2, 2024.

40. "Ampel streitet über Zeitplan für Heizungsgesetz" ["The coalition fights over the heating law"], Tagesschau, May 18, 2023, available at https://www.tagesschau.de/inland/innenpolitik/heizungsgesetz-koalition-streit-100.html, accessed February 2, 2024.

41. Jan D. Walter: "Europe's Pension Systems: How Do They Compare with France?" Deutsche Welle, April 24, 2023, available at https://www.dw.com/en/europes-pension-systems-how-do-they-compare-with-france/a-65108034, accessed February 2, 2024.

42. Romain Herreros: "Réforme des retraites: Comment les Républicains ont piégé Élisabeth Borne" [Pension reform: How the Republican trapped Élisabeth Borne], Huffington Post, French edition, March 17, 2023, available at https://www.huffingtonpost.fr/politique/article/reforme-des-retraites-comment-les-republicains-ont-piege-elisabeth-borne_215356.html, accessed February 2, 2024.

43. "Jimmie Åkesson vill riva moskéer i Sverige" [Jimmie Åkesson wants to tear down mosques in Sweden], Aftonbladet, November 25, 2023, available at https://www.aftonbladet.se/nyheter/a/0QadvB/jimmie-akesson-riv-moskeer, accessed February 2, 2024.

44. For a brief overview, see "Sweden Hit by 'Unprecedented' Levels of Gang Violence," *The Guardian*, September 13, 2023, available at https://www.theguardian.com/world/2023/sep/13/sweden-gang-violence-shootings-explosions, accessed February 2, 2024. See also Amalie Bernhus Årtun: "Gjengkriminaliteten i Sverige: Tar dette på stor [*sic*] alvor" [Gang crime in Sweden: Is taking this very seriously], Dagbladet, October 12, 2023, available at https://www.dagbladet.no/nyheter/tar-dette-pa-stor-alvor/80337564, accessed February 2, 2024.

45. "Rawa Majid och Foxtrot Nätverket" [Rawa Majird and the Foxtrot network], Krimfup website (a Swedish website specialized in crime news), April 21, 2023, available at https://www.krimfup.se/articles/rawa-majid-och-foxtrot-natverket, accessed February 2, 2024.

46. France was an exception in 2017–2022, with a solid majority for President Macron's movement La République en Marche Hungary is another exception, with a clear majority for the right nationalist prime minister Viktor Orbán.

47. Multiperspectivity is very different from subjective relativism. The historical facts are not in doubt, and actions that violate the values upon which European societies build—democracy, human rights, the rule of law—cannot be justified even if we need to understand the motivation behind them to prevent similar atrocities in the future. See also the following discussion.

48. Links to the series may be found on the ZDF website, available at https://www.zdf.de/dokumentation/terra-x/deutschland-saga-152.html, accessed February 2, 2024.

49. See the Council of Europe's education website, available at https://www.coe.int/en/web/history-teaching, accessed February 2, 2024.

50. See the Council of Europe's education website, available at https://www.coe.int/en/web/observatory-history-teaching/home, accessed February 2, 2024. The Observatory is an Enlarged Partial Agreement, which is a specific structure within the Council of Europe. Its budget is provided by the countries that are members of the Partial Agreement (eighteen members as of February 2024), and its activities are restricted to these countries.

51. See the Council of Europe's education website, available at https://www.coe.int/en/web/observatory-history-teaching/observatory-in-the-media, accessed February 2, 2024.

52. Vidkun Quisling was the leader of the Norwegian collaborationist party Nasjonal Samling (National Unity), the instigator of an attempted coup on the day Norway was invaded by Nazi Germany on April 9, 1940, and the head of a Norwegian government operating under German tutelage from 1942 to 1945. The literature covering this period is very considerable, but I find Dahl 2015 particularly interesting in that it explores the networks on which Quisling relied. Lorentzen (2022) takes an interesting approach by exploring Quisling through his travels and the influences on him.

53. "Emil Nolde und die Nazis" [Emil Nolde and the Nazis], Die Welt, March 2, 2014, available at https://www.welt.de/regionales/frankfurt/article125350098/Emil-Nolde-und-die-Nazis.html, accessed February 2, 2024.

CHAPTER 3

1. The sixteenth- and seventeenth-century wars with a strong Catholic/Protestant confessional dimension may have been felt, at least by many contemporaries, to have been largely about ideologies or belief systems, even if the dividing lines were not clear-cut. See, for example, Pieper and Saltzwedel (2013).

2. See the NATO website, available at https://www.nato.int/, accessed February 2, 2024.

3. Better known as West Germany, to distinguish it from the Communist-ruled East Germany, whose official name was the German Democratic Republic. Where it is important to distinguish the two, West Germany will be designated as the BRD (Bundesrepublik Deutschland), and East German as the DDR (Deutsche Demokratische Republik). Germany was reunified on October 3, 1990, formally as the Federal Republic of Germany.

4. The history of the EU is considerably more complex, but exploring this history is not our purpose here.

5. See the website of the European Commission, available at https://commission.eu ropa.eu/index_en, accessed February 2, 2024.

6. See the website of the Council of the European Union, available at https://www.con silium.europa.eu/en/, accessed February 2, 2024.

7. See the website of the European Court of Justice, available at https://curia.europa .eu/jcms/jcms/j_6/en/, accessed February 2, 2024.

8. See the website of the European Parliament, available at https://www.europarl .europa.eu/portal/en, accessed February 2, 2024.

9. See the note on the European Parliament: historical background, available at https:// www.europarl.europa.eu/ftu/pdf/en/FTU_1.3.1.pdf, accessed February 2, 2024.

10. UN: Universal Declaration of Human Rights, available at https://www.un.org/en /about-us/universal-declaration-of-human-rights, accessed February 2, 2024.

11. See the website of the Council of Europe, available at https://www.coe.int/en/web /portal, accessed February 2, 2024.

12. See the website of the Council of Europe's Education Department, available at https:// www.echr.coe.int/Pages/home.aspx?p=basictexts&c=, accessed February 2, 2024.

13. See the website of the European Court of Human Rights, available at https://www .echr.coe.int/, accessed August 9, 2024.

14. On neoliberalism, see Harvey (2005), Brown (2019), and Gerstle (2022).

15. Convention for the Protection of Human Rights and Fundamental Freedoms (ETS No. 005), available at https://www.coe.int/en/web/conventions/full-list?module=treaty -detail&treatynum=005, accessed February 2, 2024.

16. Protocol No. 13 to the Convention for the Protection of Human Rights and Fundamental Freedoms, concerning the abolition of the death penalty in all circumstances (ETS No. 187), available at https://www.coe.int/en/web/conventions/full-list?module=treaty -detail&treatynum=187, accessed February 2, 2024.

17. Protocol No. 12 to the Convention for the Protection of Human Rights and Fundamental Freedoms, concerning a general prohibition of discrimination (ETS No. 177), available at https://www.coe.int/en/web/conventions/full-list?module=treaty-detail&trea tynum=177, accessed February 2, 2024.

18. Council of Europe Convention on preventing and combating violence against women and domestic violence (CETS No. 210), available at https://www.coe.int/en/web/con ventions/full-list?module=treaty-detail&treatynum=210, accessed August 9, 2024.

19. Council of Europe Convention on Action against Trafficking in Human Beings (CETS No. 197), available at https://www.coe.int/en/web/conventions/full-list?module =treaty-detail&treatynum=197, accessed August 9, 2024.

20. This rule is not absolute, but the exceptions are few and concern cases where exhausting all possibilities in the national system would present a real danger to the appellant.

21. Protocol to the Convention for the Protection of Human Rights and Fundamental Freedoms as amended by Protocol No. 11, available at https://rm.coe.int/168006377c, accessed February 2, 2024.

22. The guide covers the principle of the right to education (paras. 1–15), restrictions on access to education (paras. 16–45), and discrimination in access to education (paras. 46–58). All quotes from the guide are indicated with the paragraph number, as are other direct references.

23. Specifically, the guide to the court case law says that "since Article 2 of Protocol No. 1 to the Convention applies to higher education, any State setting up such institutions will be under an obligation to afford an effective right of access to them" (para. 13).

24. It would, for example, be difficult to imagine an institution established in a European country and being considered a part of the education system of that country not undergoing quality assurance, but this was an issue in Chile with some of the private institutions set up in the 1980s in anticipation of the demise of the Pinochet regime (Mönckeberg 2005). There is also an issue with online provision that is not a part of any education system.

25. A chronological overview of the Council of Europe's membership can be found at the website of the Council of Europe's office in Tbilisi, available at https://www.coe.int/fr/web/tbilisi/the-coe/objectives-and-missions, accessed May 10, 2024.

26. Chechnya, a republic within the Russian Federation, waged two wars aiming to establish its independence, in 1994–1996 and 1999–2000. Both wars led to widespread destruction and to Chechnya remaining a part of the Russian Federation. Chechnya is now ruled by the pro-Moskva Kadyrov regime, which is judged responsible for atrocities within Chechnya as well as in the war on Ukraine, to which it contributes soldiers.

27. See the report on the Ninth Council of Europe Conference of Ministers responsible for Youth (Saint Petersburg, September 23–25, 2012) submitted to the Council of Europe's Committee of Ministers, available at https://rm.coe.int/16807072ef, accessed February 2, 2024.

28. A recommendation is a legal text adopted by the government of the Council's member states through the Committee of Ministers. It is not legally binding and outlines a set of measures that the Committee of Ministers encourages member states to undertake. Some of the measures may also be directed at actors other than public authorities. A convention, on the other hand, is a legal treaty between the states that ratify it, and its provisions are legally binding on the states party.

29. Recommendation CM/Rec(2022)5 of the Committee of Ministers to member states on passing on remembrance of the Holocaust and preventing crimes against humanity, available at https://search.coe.int/cm/Pages/result_details.aspx?ObjectID=0900001680a5ddcd, accessed February 2, 2024.

30. See the Council of Europe's official announcement, available at https://www.coe.int/en/web/portal/war-in-ukraine, accessed February 2, 2024.

31. Anushka Asthana and Rowena Mason, "UK Must Leave European Convention on Human Rights, Says Theresa May," *The Guardian*, April 25, 2016, available at https://www.theguardian.com/politics/2016/apr/25/uk-must-leave-european-convention-on-human-rights-theresa-may-eu-referendum, accessed February 2, 2024.

32. See, for example, Nick Eardley, "Tories Could Campaign to Leave European Human Rights Treaty if Rwanda Flights Blocked," BBC, August 9, 2023, available at https://www.bbc.com/news/uk-politics-66438422, accessed February 2, 2024.

33. The British Institute of Human Rights, available at https://www.bihr.org.uk/get-informed/legislation/the-council-of-europe-versus-the-european-union, accessed February 2, 2024.

34. Christopher Jarvis, "The Rise and Fall of Albania's Pyramid Schemes," *Finance and Development* 37, no. 1 (March 2000), available at https://www.imf.org/external/pubs

/ft/fandd/2000/03/jarvis.htm, accessed February 2, 2024. For an overview of modern Albanian history, see Abrahams (2015) and Vickers (1997).

35. Dernières Nouvelles d'Alsace, "Loi immigration: Borne consulte tous azimuts pour sauver ce qui peut l'être" [Immigration law: Borne consults all over to save what can be saved], December 14, 2023, available at https://c.dna.fr/politique/2023/12/14/loi-immi gration-borne-consulte-tous-azimuts-pour-sauver-ce-qui-peut-l-etre, with web links to previous related articles, accessed February 2, 2024.

36. Dernières Nouvelles d'Alsace, "Loi immigration: La majorité présidentielle fracturée comme jamais" [Immigration law: The majority divided like never before], December 20, 2023, available at https://c.dna.fr/politique/2023/12/20/la-majorite-presidentielle -fracturee-par-l-adoption-de-la-loi-sur-l-immigration, accessed February 2, 2024.

37. France info Radio France, "Projet de loi immigration: La ministre de l'enseignement supérieur Sylvie Retailleau a présenté sa démission, qui a été refuse" [Proposed immigration law: The minister for higher education Sylvie Retailleau tendered her resignation, which was refused], December 21, 2023, available at https://www.francetvinfo.fr/politique /gouvernement-d-elisabeth-borne/loi-immigration-la-ministre-de-l-enseignement-super ieur-sylvie-retailleau-a-presente-sa-demission-qui-a-ete-refusee_6258624.html, accessed February 2, 2024.

38. Frank Buchy, "Un populisme sans frontière" [A populism without borders], Dernières Nouvelles d'Alsace, December 20, 2023, available at https://c.dna.fr/politique /2023/12/19/un-populisme-sans-frontiere, accessed February 2, 2024.

39. Communiqué by the French Rectors' Conference on the proposed law on immigration, December 20, 2023, available at https://franceuniversites.fr/actualite/commu nique-des-presidentes-et-des-presidents-duniversite-relatif-au-projet-de-loi-immigration/, accessed February 2, 2024.

40. See https://home-affairs.ec.europa.eu/policies/migration-and-asylum/new-pact -migration-and-asylum_en, accessed February 2, 2024.

41. European Commission, "Policy Briefing on the Assessment of Skills and Recognition of Qualifications of Refugees and Migrants in Europe," available at https://migrant -integration.ec.europa.eu/library-document/policy-briefing-assessment-skills-and-rec ognition-qualifications-refugees-and-1_en. See also OECD, "Migration Policy Debates," no. 3, December 2014, available at https://www.oecd.org/els/mig/migration-policy-debates -3.pdf, both accessed February 2, 2024.

42. OECD, "Indicators of Immigration Integration 2023: 3. Immigrant Skills and Labour Market Integration," available at https://www.oecd-ilibrary.org/social-issues-mi gration-health/indicators-of-immigrant-integration-2023_93d393c3-en, accessed August 9, 2024. In this context, "Europe" refers to the European countries that are members of the OECD.

43. Each member state holds this rotating presidency for six months, normally from November to May or May to November. In principle, the order of presidencies follows the English alphabetical order, but members may agree among themselves to change the order, subject to the agreement of the Committee of Ministers. Typically, EU countries often ask to change the order if their presidency of the Committee of Ministers would coincide with their EU presidency, and Iceland has done so to avoid overlap with its presidency of the Nordic Council of Ministers.

44. For an overview, see Lorélie Carrive, "L'attentat contre Charlie Hebdo, minute par minute, par ceux qui l'ont vécu" [The attack on Charlie Hebdo, minute by minute, by those who lived through it], France Inter, August 23, 2020, available at https://www.radio

france.fr/franceinter/l-attentat-contre-charlie-hebdo-minute-par-minute-par-ceux-qui
-l-ont-vecu-1558972, accessed February 2, 2024.

45. Twenty-Fifth Session of the Council of Europe Standing Conference of Ministers
of Education, Council of Europe's Education website, available at https://www.coe.int
/en/web/education-minister-conference, accessed February 2, 2024.

46. The term "competence" is widely used in education policy in Europe. It designates
the ability to do something well (or of being competent) and is often developed through
education. It is broader than either "knowledge" or "skill," as indicated by the Council
of Europe's *Common European Framework of Reference for Languages*: "The general competences of language learners or users . . . consist in particular of their knowledge, skills
and existential competence and also their ability to learn" (Council of Europe 2001a: 11),
which also notes that "skills and know-how (savoir-faire . . .) whether it be a matter of
driving a car, playing the violin or chairing a meeting, depend more on the ability to carry
out procedures than on declarative knowledge, but this skill may be facilitated by the acquisition of 'forgettable' knowledge and be accompanied by forms of existential competence (for example relaxed attitude or tension in carrying out a task)" (Council of Europe
2001a: 11). The Council of Europe's RFCDC defines "competence" as "the ability to mobilise and deploy relevant values, attitudes, skills, knowledge and/or understanding in
order to respond appropriately and effectively to the demands, challenges and opportunities that are presented by a given type of context" (Council of Europe 2018b: 32). It further
states: "It should be noted that, according to the Framework, competences include not only
skills, knowledge and understanding but also values and attitudes" (Council of Europe
2018b: 33).

47. For an overview, see the Council of Europe's Education website, available at https://
www.coe.int/en/web/education, accessed February 2, 2024.

48. See the website of the EHEA, available at http://www.ehea.info/index.php, accessed
February 2, 2024.

49. See the section on language policy, Council of Europe's Education website, available at https://www.coe.int/en/web/language-policy/history, accessed February 2, 2024.

50. See the section on language policy, Council of Europe's Education website, available at https://www.coe.int/en/web/language-policy/cefr, accessed February 2, 2024.

51. The systematic destruction of Armenian people and identity in the final years of
the Ottoman Empire, generally considered to have been launched on April 24, 1915. Referring to the Armenian Genocide as such is unlawful in Turkey. For a history, see Suny
(2015).

52. The Association for Historical Dialogue and Research, available at https://www
.ahdr.info/about-us, accessed February 2, 2024.

53. The Council of Europe's budget is adopted by the Committee of Ministers, normally in late November or early December. Since 2012, budgets have been adopted for
two years, but they can be adjusted at the end of the first year. The ordinary budget covers the programs and activities in which all member states and states party to the Council's conventions participate. Many conventions, such as the European Cultural Convention, are open to nonmember states, who pay a contribution to the activities under the
conventions to which they are party. Partial Agreements focus on a specific area of activity, such as language education or history education. Their budget is paid by the states
party to a given Partial Agreement, and the activities are open only to these countries.

54. See the website of the ECML, available at https://www.ecml.at/, accessed August
92, 2024.

55. ECML's website for the European Day of Languages, available at https://edl.ecml .at/Home/tabid/1455/language/en-GB/Default.aspx, accessed February 2, 2024.

56. See the website of the Observatory on History Teaching in Europe, available at https://www.coe.int/en/web/observatory-history-teaching/home, accessed February 2, 2024.

57. Kosovo, whose independence is not recognized by all Council of Europe member states, is not a Council member or a party to the European Cultural Convention. The Council of Europe is nevertheless able to run projects in Kosovo, mostly financed by the EU, and has a project office in Prishtina. Council of Europe's office in Prishtina, available at https://www.coe.int/en/web/pristina/home, accessed May 10, 2024.

58. See the Council of Europe's Education website, available at https://www.coe.int /en/web/learning-resources, accessed February 2, 2024.

59. See the Council of Europe's Education website, available at https://www.coe.int /en/web/education/best-practice-programme-in-promoting-academic-integrity, accessed February 2, 2024.

60. Council of Europe's Platform on Ethics, Transparency and Integrity in Education (ETINED), available at https://www.coe.int/en/web/ethics-transparency-integrity-in-ed ucation/home, accessed February 2, 2024.

61. For an overview, see the website for the Fourth Summit of Heads of State and Government of the Council of Europe, available at https://www.coe.int/en/web/cm/reykjavik -summit, accessed February 2, 2024.

62. Council of Europe Standing Conference of Ministers of Education, "The Transformative Power of Education: Universal Values and Civic Renewal," document MED-26(2023)06 final September 29, 2023, available at https://rm.coe.int/resolutions-26th -session-council-of-europe-standing-conference-of-mini/1680abee7f, accessed February 2, 2024.

63. Council of Europe's Education website, section on the Steering Committee for Education (CDEDU: Comité Directeur de l'Education), available at https://www.coe.int/en /web/education/cdedu, accessed February 2, 2024.

64. At the time of writing, because of their role in the war on Ukraine, Russia and Belarus are not invited to meetings.

65. At the time of writing, the NGOs that work primarily or exclusively in higher education and that are observers with the committee are the European Association of Institutions in Higher Education (EURASHE, which presents professional higher education institutions), European Students' Union, EUA, IAU, and Scholars at Risk Europe. Education International represents education staff at all levels and areas of education, but its representative in the committee has generally come from the higher education sector.

66. Technically, the Steering Committee for Education (CDEDU: Comité Directeur de l'Education)—steering committees are responsible for a specific area of activity within the Council of Europe and report to the Committee of Ministers.

67. For a recent discussion, see Anne-Camille Beckelynck, "Conseil de l'Europe: Des ambitions et des doutes pour la préparation du prochain Sommet" [Council of Europe: Ambitions and doubts in the preparation of the next Summit], January 28, 2023, available at https://c.dna.fr/politique/2023/01/28/sommet-du-conseil-de-l-europe-des-ambi tions-et-des-doutes (in French), accessed February 2, 2024. It should nevertheless be acknowledged that in late 2023, the Committee of Ministers for the first time in seventeen years adopted a budget for the Council of Europe that implies a real increase in the means at the organization's disposal. A real increase means an increase that is higher than the estimated inflation rate.

CHAPTER 4

1. In the French original: *adapter aux métiers d'après-demain et à l'esprit d'entreprise*.

2. General Agreement on Trade in Services. See World Trade Organization, "The General Agreement on Trade in Services (GATS): Objectives, Coverage and Disciplines," available at https://www.wto.org/english/tratop_e/serv_e/gatsqa_e.htm, accessed February 2, 2024.

3. The Council of Europe had a separate committee for higher education until 2012.

4. The 2007 London Communiqué uses the wording, "Our aim is to ensure that our HEIs have the necessary resources to continue to fulfil their full range of purposes. Those purposes include: preparing students for life as active citizens in a democratic society; preparing students for their future careers and enabling their personal development; creating and maintaining a broad, advanced knowledge base; and stimulating research and innovation" (Bologna Process 2007: para. 1.4).

5. In spite of low or no tuition fees in most European countries, the subsistence cost during the three to five years it takes to earn a degree as well as other costs related to the studies, like computers and study materials, are substantial.

6. Phrased differently: "If it is accepted that VET mainly attracts pupils from less advantaged classes with low and intermediate occupational position, it is thus more likely that VET tracks reproduce rather than reduce pre-existing social inequalities and discriminations" (Tsakarissianos 2008: 35).

7. "European Network of Graduate Tracking," European Commission website, available at https://education.ec.europa.eu/education-levels/higher-education/relevant-and-high-quality-higher-education/about-relevant-high-quality-higher-education/european-network-of-graduate-tracking, accessed February 2, 2024.

8. It could be argued that if education is seen as essential to developing societies, it is perhaps not surprising that policymakers focus on its role in remedying what they see as the greatest challenges their societies face. In this sense, the focus of many European policymakers on the economic mission of higher education may be read as an indication that they have greater confidence in the state of democracy in their countries than in the state of their economies.

9. Book 3. The Republic is easily available on the web, see for example http://faculty.smcm.edu/jwschroeder/Web/ETHR1002/Global_Jutice_Readings_files/3.PlatoRepblic.pdf, accessed August 9, 2024.

10. For an overview of how the purpose of education has been described in Norwegian legislation, see the background note produced for the Bostad Committee appointed to review the purposes of education in Norway. The note is available at https://www.regjeringen.no/globalassets/upload/kd/vedlegg/bostadutvalget/formalsparagrafens-historie2.doc and the report by the committee is available at https://www.regjeringen.no/conten tassets/8d208e2fb15c4b01ab344eb29c8c1be3/no/pdfs/nou200720070006000dddpdfs.pdf, both in Norwegian and accessed February 2, 2024.

11. As noted in Chapter 3, "Tuning educational structures" in Europe was a project coordinated by the Universities of Deusto (Spain) and Groningen (Netherlands) "to understand curricula and to make them comparable." The presentation note on the Tuning project is available at http://www.ehea.info/media.ehea.info/file/Tuning_project/89/3/Tun ing-Educational-Structures-Europe-executive-summary_575893.pdf, accessed February 2, 2024.

12. The Overarching Framework of Qualifications of the EHEA uses the generic terms first, second, and third degrees. These degrees will have different names in different systems. For example, in France, a bachelor's degree is a *license*.

13. "A History of Spanish at Oxford," Faculty of Medieval and Modern Languages, University of Oxford, available at https://www.mod-langs.ox.ac.uk/spanish/history-spanish-oxford#:~:text=In%20December%201848%2C%20F.H.,became%20Professor%20of%20Comparative%20Philology, accessed February 2, 2024.

14. INALCO website, available at http://www.inalco.fr/institut/presentation/histoire, accessed February 2, 2024. A story has it that a proposal to emphasize modern languages when the institute got its present name in 1971 was rejected because "modern languages" translates as *langues vivantes* in French, so the acronym would be INALCOV. This was thought to be too explicit and *osé* in the immediate aftermath of 1968.

15. Nordic Africa Institute, available at https://nai.uu.se/, accessed February 2, 2024.

16. Nordic Institute of Asian Studies, available at https://nias.ku.dk/, accessed February 2, 2024.

17. Nordic Institute of Latin American Studies, available at https://www.su.se/nordic-institute-of-latin-american-studies/, accessed February 2, 2024.

18. Espen Løkeland Stai: "Nordisk Asia-institutt legges ned.—Et betydelig tap" [The Norwegian Asia Institute is closed—A serious loss], available at https://khrono.no/nordisk-asia-institutt-legges-ned-et-betydelig-tap/806496, accessed February 2, 2024.

19. The elected legislative assembly is responsible for legislation, see later. This is a public body; whether it is also a public authority is perhaps up for discussion.

20. The formulation follows the statement adopted by the EHEA ministerial conference in May 2024 (Bologna Process 2024a).

21. Before the development of national qualifications frameworks in Europe, the reference was to degree systems.

22. The American College of Greece, founded in 1875 and relocated to Greece in 1923, is, for example, accredited by the New England Commission of Higher Education. See the institution's website, available at https://www.acg.edu/about-acg/key-facts/, accessed February 2, 2024.

23. The full list of fundamental values as adopted by the ministers of the EHEA: academic freedom and integrity, institutional autonomy, student and staff participation in higher education governance, and public responsibility for and of higher education (Bologna Process 2018). While these may appear to be four values, I argue that they are in fact six because academic freedom and academic integrity are two distinct values, as are the public responsibility *for* and the public responsibility *of* higher education. The statement adopted by EHEA ministers in 2024 (Bologna Process 2024a), also takes this view.

24. See the website of the ENIC and NARIC Networks, available at https://www.enic-naric.net/page-homepage, accessed February 2, 2024. Among other things, this site provides links to each national information center. I was the Council of Europe official responsible for recognition issues, among several other things, from 1991 to 2009.

25. The NARIC Network (Network of National Academic Recognition Information Centres).

26. There are some slight differences. The ENIC Network has an advisory function in relation to the Lisbon Recognition Convention, strictly speaking in its composition limited to the ENICs of countries having ratified the convention, whereas the NARIC Network advises the Commission on recognition issues in relation to EU programs and legislation.

CHAPTER 5

1. Rudi Dutschke was severely wounded but lived until 1979.

2. For an overview of the French student movement, see Fischer (2000).

3. The Ceaușescu regime in Romania refused to participate in the invasion.

4. See the website of Penn's Netter Center, available at http://www.nettercenter.upenn.edu/, accessed February 2, 2024.

5. In spite of his position as an academic, Ostrowski was appointed as a member of the committee representing the Polish Ministry of Education and, hence, as a governmental member.

6. See the website of the Council of Europe Treaty Office, available at https://www.coe.int/en/web/conventions/full-list?module=treaty-detail&treatynum=018. An overview of signatures and ratifications of this convention, including the date on which a given country ratified it, is available at https://www.coe.int/en/web/conventions/full-list?module=signatures-by-treaty&treatynum=018. Both sites accessed February 2, 2024.

7. To my knowledge, Andorra is the only country that joined the Council of Europe during the past generation without first being a party to the Cultural Convention. Belarus ratified the Cultural Convention in 1993, but its progress toward Council of Europe membership was put on hold when the reality of the Lukashenka regime became clear. Lukashenka first became president of Belarus in 1994.

8. The Council of Europe Secretariat has undergone several reorganizations over the years. Mazza was the director of School, Out-of-School, and Higher Education and then of Education and Languages.

9. "Legislative Reform Programme in Higher Education and Research 1991–2000. Final Report," Document CC-HER (2000) 40, available at https://rm.coe.int/1680746a5b, accessed February 2, 2024.

10. In European terms, this would be leadership by rectors.

11. Until the two committees were merged in 2012, the Education Committee was responsible for the Council's projects concerning all parts of the education system except those concerning higher education and research, which—unsurprisingly—were carried out under the responsibility of the Higher Education and Research Committee.

12. These were: the Catholic University of America, Clark-Atlanta University, University of Denver, Florida International University, University of Georgia, University of Iowa, University of Kentucky, Rutgers University–Camden, San Francisco State University, State University of New York at Buffalo, Swarthmore College, Trinity College in Hartford, CT, University of Texas at El Paso, and Wheaton College in Wheaton, IL.

13. The original intention was to have equal participation from both sides of the Atlantic, but one U.S. and three European universities dropped out.

14. These were from Albania (Tirana), Bosnia and Herzegovina (Tuzla), France (Cergy-Pontoise), Greece (Thessalia), Italy (Milano-Bicocca), Lithuania (Vytautas Magnus), North Macedonia (Skopje) (then labeled "the former Yugoslav Republic of Macedonia"), Norway (Bergen), Russia (Samara), Turkey (Ankara), Ukraine (Tavrichesky National University), and United Kingdom/Northern Ireland (Queen's University Belfast).

15. It is worth noting that the collaborating researcher at San Francisco State University was Dr. Brian Murphy, who went on to become the president of De Anza College and in this capacity has been a strong contributor to the project described in this chapter.

16. In France, a "new city" (*ville nouvelle*) designates an urban community established by political decision and located in the periphery of a major city such as Paris or Lyon. The greater Paris area saw many "new cities" established from the 1960s onward, and Cergy-Pontoise is one of them. See the Éduscol website, available at http://geoconfluences.ens-lyon.fr/glossaire/villes-nouvelles, accessed February 2, 2024.

17. See the website of the EHEA, available at http://www.ehea.info/index.php, accessed February 2, 2024.

18. The entry into force of a convention means that the convention becomes effective and acquires legal status. The text of the convention will normally stipulate that this happens on the Nth (e.g., fifth) ratification.

19. Convention on the Recognition of Qualifications concerning Higher Education in the European Region (ETS No. 165), available at https://www.coe.int/en/web/conventions/full-list?module=treaty-detail&treatynum=165, accessed February 2, 2024.

20. See the website of the International Consortium, available at https://www.internationalconsortium.org/about/, accessed February 2, 2024.

21. For a timeline, see "The International Consortium for Higher Education, Civic Responsibility, and Democracy (IC) in cooperation with the Council of Europe, the Organization of American States and the International Association of Universities. Timeline 1999–2021," available at https://bpb-us-w2.wpmucdn.com/web.sas.upenn.edu/dist/f/335/files/2021/06/International_Consortium_Timeline_1999-2021.pdf, accessed February 2, 2024.

22. The American Association for Higher Education that was part of the U.S. Steering Committee was dissolved in 2005. Another association with the same name is still active.

23. See the website for the Council of Europe's Higher Education Series, available at https://www.coe.int/en/web/higher-education-and-research/publications, accessed February 2, 2024.

24. See the website for the Council of Europe's Higher Education Series, available at https://www.coe.int/en/web/higher-education-and-research/publications, accessed February 2, 2024.

25. See the website for the 2006 Global Forum, available at https://www.coe.int/en/web/higher-education-and-research/forum-the-responsibility-of-higher-education-for-a-democratic-culture-2006-, accessed February 2, 2024.

26. A member of the U.K. Parliament and of the Council of Europe's Parliamentary Assembly, Terry Davis was the secretary-general of the Council from September 2004 until August 2009.

27. Then known officially in international contexts as "the former Yugoslav Republic of Macedonia."

28. See the website for the 2008 Global Forum, available at https://www.coe.int/en/web/higher-education-and-research/invitational-forum-on-converging-competences-diversity-higher-education-and-sustainable-democracy-2008-, accessed February 2, 2024.

29. Known as ESIB (the European Students Information Bureau) when Klemenčič was its secretary-general.

30. See the website of the European Wergeland Centre, available at https://theewc.org/, accessed February 2, 2024.

31. See the website for the 2011 Global Forum, available at https://www.internationalconsortium.org/2011/06/27/invitational-global-forum-norway/, accessed February 2, 2024.

32. See the website of the Norwegian Institute of International Affairs, available at https://www.nupi.no/en/, accessed February 2, 2024.

33. Utøya is now both a memorial site and a learning center labeled a democracy workshop, with learning activities run in cooperation with the European Wergeland Centre. See the website of the Utøya memorial site, available at https://utoya.no/, accessed February 23, 2023.

34. See the website for the 2014 Global Forum, available at https://www.internationalconsortium.org/2015/06/25/invitational-global-forum-belfast-northern-ireland-2/, accessed February 2, 2024.

35. A period of political violence between 1968 and 1995 on the background of a bitter conflict between the Catholic and Protestant communities.

36. See the website for the 2017 Global Forum, available at https://www.international consortium.org/2017/06/13/invitation-global-forum-rome-italy/, accessed February 2, 2024.

37. See the website of LUMSA University, available at https://www.lumsa.it/, accessed February 2, 2024.

38. See the website for the 2019 Global Forum, available at https://www.coe.int/en /web/education/globalforum, accessed February 2, 2024.

39. The declaration is also available online at the Council of Europe's Education website, available at https://rm.coe.int/global-forum-declaration-global-forum-final-21-06 -19-003-/16809523e5, accessed February 2, 2024. References are to the printed version in the book cited.

40. See the news item posted on the Council of Europe's Education website, available at https://www.coe.int/en/web/education/-/education-committee-meets-online, accessed February 2, 2024.

41. See the COVID-19 subsection of the Council of Europe's Education website, available at https://www.coe.int/en/web/education/covid-19, accessed February 2, 2024.

42. See the Council of Europe's Education website, available at https://www.coe.int /en/web/education/-/conference-of-ministers-of-education-response-to-pandemic-crisis, accessed February 2, 2024.

43. See the website of Campus Engage Ireland, available at https://www.campusen gage.ie/, accessed February 2, 2024.

44. See the website for the 2022 Global Forum, available at https://www.dcu.ie/en gagement/global-forum-2022, accessed February 2, 2024.

CHAPTER 6

1. For an account of the dissolution of the union between Denmark and Norway, see Glenthøj (2012).

2. See the University of Bergen website, overview of the history of the university, available at https://www.uib.no/om/73873/universitetet-i-bergens-historie, accessed February 2, 2024.

3. See the København University website, overview of the history of the university, available at https://om.ku dk/profil/historie/, accessed February 2, 2024.

4. The Danish Technical University traces its roots to a polytechnical institute established in 1829, but it got university status as recently as 1994. See the description of the profile of the university at its website, available at https://www.dtu.dk/om-dtu/profil, accessed February 2, 2024.

5. See the AITF website, available at https://www.margainc.com/aitf/, accessed February 2, 2024.

6. See the website of Penn's Netter Center, available at http://www.nettercenter.upenn .edu/, accessed February 2, 2024.

7. See the website of the Congress of Local and Regional Authorities, available at https:// www.coe.int/en/web/congress, accessed February 2, 2024.

8. See the AITF website, available at https://www.margainc.com/aitf/, accessed February 2, 2024.

9. Some European countries, like Albania, Azerbaijan, Bosnia and Herzegovina, and Turkey, are either majority Muslim, or Muslims are a long-established and significant part of the national community.

10. See the presentation of the floods in June 2016 on the specialized website La Chaine Météo, available at https://actualite.lachainemeteo.com/actualite-meteo/2018-06-06/retour-sur-la-crue-de-la-seine-en-juin-2016-47527, accessed February 2, 2024.

11. "Transports, pétrole, déchets . . . le point sur les grèves avant l'Euro 2016" [Transportation, gas, garbage . . . update on the strikes prior to the 2016 Euro], Les Échos, available at https://www.lesechos.fr/2016/06/transports-petrole-dechets-le-point-sur-les-greves-avant-leuro-2016-207732, accessed February 2, 2024; the 2016 Euro was the European soccer championship tournament.

12. The Spiritual Family The Work.

13. At the time, its formal name was the Steering Committee for Educational Policy and Practice (CDPPE).

14. It rhymes in Norwegian: *når Djevelen ville at intet skulle skje, oppnevnte han den første komité.*

15. "coLAB—A Laboratory for New Forms of Collaboration," Council of Europe's Education website, available at https://pjp-eu.coe.int/en/web/charter-edc-hre-pilot-projects/colab-a-laboratory-for-new-forms-of-collaboration, accessed February 2, 2024.

16. See the website of the Institute for the Development of Education (IDE), available at https://en.iro.hr/, accessed February 2, 2024.

17. There is a joint website for both projects, available at https://en.iro.hr/2022/05/12/steering-higher-education-for-community-engagement/, accessed August 10, 2024.

18. See the website of the European Platform for Community Engagement in Higher Education, available at https://community-engagement.eu/, accessed February 2, 2024.

19. See the website of the European Universities initiative, available at https://education.ec.europa.eu/education-levels/higher-education/european-universities-initiative, accessed February 2, 2024.

20. See the website of CIVICA—The European University of Social Sciences, available at https://www.civica.eu/who-we-are/about-civica, accessed February 2, 2024.

21. See the website of the European Science Engagement Association, available at https://eusea.info/, accessed February 2, 2024.

22. See the website of the European Science Engagement Association, available at https://eusea.info/platform/about-this-platform/about/, accessed February 2, 2024.

23. See the European Commission's website for the Smart Specialisation Platform, available at https://s3platform.jrc.ec.europa.eu/, accessed February 2, 2024.

24. See the website of the Copernicus Alliance, available at https://www.copernicus-alliance.org/, accessed February 2, 2024.

25. See the overview of members on the website of the Copernicus Alliance, available at https://www.copernicus-alliance.org/ca-members, accessed February 2, 2024.

26. See the presentation by the IAU of its initiative on Higher Education and Research for Sustainable Development (HESD), available at https://iau-aiu.net/HESD, accessed February 2, 2024.

27. The committee was renamed the Steering Committee for Education (CDEDU) as of 2022.

28. The report was finalized before the Russian invasion of Ukraine, and, as noted, Russia and Belarus are at present not invited to meetings under the Cultural Convention. Whether and when they can return will be a political decision by the Council's member states, and this will depend on developments in Ukraine.

29. See the presentation of the Council of Europe Platform on Ethics, Transparency and Integrity in Education (ETINED), available at https://www.coe.int/en/web/ethics-transparency-integrity-in-education, accessed February 2, 2024.

30. The Group wished to avoid the term "examples of good (or best) practice."

31. EURASHE, which represents professional higher education institutions. See its website, available at https://www.eurashe.eu/, accessed February 2, 2024.

32. See the website of the Congress of Local and Regional Authorities, available at https://www.coe.int/en/web/congress, accessed February 2, 2024.

33. See the website of the Council of Europe's Intercultural Cities program, available at https://www.coe.int/en/web/interculturalcities, accessed February 2, 2024.

34. See the Council of Europe's Education website, available at https://www.coe.int/en/web/education/-/council-of-europe-education-department-launches-new-initiative-to-revitalise-democracy-through-higher-education, accessed August 10, 2024.

CHAPTER 7

1. See the website of the National Co-ordinating Centre for Public Engagement, available at https://www.publicengagement.ac.uk/introducing-public-engagement, accessed February 2, 2024.

2. See the website of the Guild of European Research-Intensive Universities, available at https://www.the-guild.eu/, accessed February 2, 2024.

3. See the website of the Jagiellonian University of Kraków, available at https://en.uj.edu.pl/en_GB/international-cooperation/networks, accessed February 2, 2024.

4. See https://en.uj.edu.pl/en_GB/about-university/history, accessed August 10, 2024.

5. This refers to the Stalinist period in Poland; it started in 1927 in the Soviet Union.

6. All information and quotes from the CITTRU website, available at https://www.sciencemarket.pl/?lang=en, accessed February 2, 2024.

7. For a brief overview of the university's history, see the University of Iceland website, available at https://english.hi.is/node/17089, accessed February 2, 2024.

8. See the Study in Iceland website, available at https://study.iceland.is/, accessed February 2, 2024.

9. I am indebted to Una Strand Viðarsdóttir of the Icelandic Ministry of Higher Education and Research for the numbers which indicate full-time equivalents. Personal communication, October 13, 2022.

10. See the overview of University of Iceland community projects, available at https://english.hi.is/collaboration/community_projects, accessed February 2, 2024.

11. In Norwegian, the term is quite literally "illuminating the people," *folkeopplysning*.

12. See the University of Iceland website, available at https://english.hi.is/news/the_university_in_society, accessed February 2, 2024.

13. See the web post on this initiative Vísindi á mannamáli, available at https://www.hi.is/samfelagsverkefni_hi/visindi_a_mannamali (in Icelandic), accessed February 2, 2024.

14. See the website of the Children's Culture Festival, available at https://reykjavik.is/en/childrens-culture-festival, accessed February 2, 2024.

15. See the website for this initiative, available at https://ung.hi.is/is, (in Icelandic), accessed February 2, 2024.

16. See the website for this initiative, available at https://www.visindavefur.is/ (in Icelandic), accessed February 2, 2024.

17. See the website for this initiative, available at https://english.hi.is/sprettur, accessed February 2, 2024.

18. Samples available at https://www.youtube.com/playlist?list=PLoc0mU0QB6h45yg4TJL6wQsGZE-jn4OQC, accessed February 2, 2024.

19. A modern Icelander can, with some practice, read the old Norse sagas, most of whose authors were Icelandic, without too much difficulty, even if modern translations are also available. Speakers of modern Danish, Norwegian, and Swedish, on the other hand, are entirely dependent on modern translations unless they have studied Old Norse. Personally, largely thanks to Old Norse in high school and Old English at university, I can get the gist of most Icelandic texts, at least as long as I know the subject area.

20. See the website for the University of Iceland dentistry service, available at https://www.hi.is/tannlaeknadeild/tannlaeknathjonusta (in Icelandic), accessed February 2, 2024.

21. See the overview of the history of the Palacký University Olomouc on its website, available at https://www.upol.cz/en/university/basic-information/university-history/#c3126, accessed February 2, 2024.

22. Robert Taite, "Pro-western Petr Pavel Sweeps to Landslide Win in Race for Czech Presidency," *The Guardian*, January 28, 2023, available at https://www.theguardian.com/world/2023/jan/28/petr-pavel-wins-landslide-victory-in-czech-presidential-elections, accessed February 2, 2024.

23. The quote is from the Volunteering Center website, available at https://dobrovolnici.upol.cz/en/about-us/, accessed February 2, 2024.

24. See the Masaryk University website, available at https://www.muni.cz/en/masaryk-helps-ukraine, accessed February 2, 2024.

25. In Europe, regulated professions are those that, in addition to an academic degree, require a professional license, which again normally requires that the student undergo professional practice and training either as a part of the study program or after graduation but before the professional license is granted. Exactly which professions are regulated varies considerably from one country to another. Within the EU, the recognition of qualifications required for the exercise of regulated professions is governed by directives binding on all EU member states. To simplify, we may say that regulated professions are those in which malpractice may cause great and immediate harm, with the exception of the teaching profession (regulated in some but not all EU countries), in which the potential damage is possibly even greater but longer term. Information on recognition of professional qualifications in the EU is available at https://single-market-economy.ec.europa.eu/single-market/services/free-movement-professionals/recognition-professional-qualifications-practice_en, accessed February 2, 2024.

26. See the website of the University of San Marino, available at https://www.unirsm.sm/ (in Italian), accessed February 2, 2024.

27. See the website of the Sammarinese National Assembly, available at https://www.consigliograndeegenerale.sm/contents/instance18/files/document/17135603TDPdLL.QuadroIst.pdf (in Italian), accessed February 2, 2024.

28. Information provided to the EHEA Working Group advising San Marino on the implementation of the roadmap accompanying its accession to the EHEA at the meeting of the group on February 14–15, 2023.

29. Personal communication from Paula Cenci, February 24, 2023.

30. See the information on the Observatory on Youth on the University of San Marino website, available at https://www.unirsm.sm/osservatorio-giovani/ (in Italian), accessed February 2, 2024.

31. See the University of the Aegean website in English, available at https://www.aegean.edu/, accessed February 2, 2024, and a more complete website in Greek, available at https://www.aegean.gr/, accessed February 2, 2024.

32. Lemnos, Lesvos, Samos, Chios, Syros, and Rhodos (Rhodes).

33. Country sheet for Greece, available through the website of the World Travel and Tourism Council, available at https://wttc.org/research/economic-impact, accessed February 2, 2024.

34. Example mentioned by Spyros Syropolous in a conference presentation.

35. Facebook posts by Spyropolous, January 2023.

36. Available at https://www.dcu.ie/civic-engagement/news/2023/sep/summer-school -2022, accessed February 2, 2024.

37. See the DCU website on civic engagement, available at https://www.dcu.ie/engage ment/news/2022/may/bridge-education-course-starts-21st-february-2022, accessed February 2, 2024.

38. See the announcement on the DCU website on civic engagement, available at https://www.dcu.ie/engagement/news/2022/may/community-organisation-management -course-starts-february-2022, accessed February 2, 2024.

39. See the Student Volunteer Ireland website, available at https://www.studentvol unteer.ie/, accessed February 2, 2024.

40. See the presentation on the DCU website, available at https://www.dcu.ie/bar retstown, accessed February 2, 2024.

41. See the presentation on the DCU website, available at https://www.dcu.ie/engage ment/news/2021/apr/centre-engaged-research, accessed August 10, 2024.

42. See the website of the International Consortium, available at https://www.inter nationalconsortium.org/, accessed February 2, 2024.

43. The point was made by Gallagher at one of the three invitational conferences that led the Council of Europe to launch a project on the local democratic mission of higher education (Chapter 6).

44. For the role of universities in the Peace Process that led to the Good Friday Agreement, see Jack (2023).

45. See the announcement of the launch of the Social Charter of Queen's, available at https://daro.qub.ac.uk/social-charter-2017, accessed February 2, 2024.

46. Community-engaged research initiatives creating connections between students at Queen's and community organizations across Northern Ireland. See the presentation of the Queen's University Science Shop, available at https://www.qub.ac.uk/sites/Science Shop/, accessed February 2, 2024.

47. See the presentation of the Queen's University Communities and Place initiative, available at https://www.qub.ac.uk/social-charter/equality/qcap/qcap-about/?utm_source =Facebook&utm_medium=Post&utm_campaign=Social%2520Charter&utm_content =Video, accessed February 2, 2024.

48. See the website of the Market Development Association, available at https://mar ketbelfast.org/, accessed February 2, 2024.

49. See the website of the Association for Historical Dialogue and Research, available at https://www.ahdr.info/, accessed February 2, 2024.

50. In pronunciation, syntax or vocabulary: an example of the latter is the use of *kruh* (Croatian) or *hleb* (Serbian) for "bread."

51. Sámi designates the ethnic group and its members, whereas Sápmi designates the cultural and geographic area in which they live. The traditional term "Lapp"—and by extension Lapponia or Lappland—is considered derogatory and is no longer used, at least not benevolently.

52. For a brief history in English, see Kent (2018).

53. In linguistic terms, there are no absolute criteria for distinguishing between a dialect and a language. Alsatian may well be considered an Alemannic variety of Ger-

man. Luxemburgish, which is spoken some 200 kilometers to the north of Alsace, is linguistically a Moselle-Franconian variety of German but has language status as the official language of the Grand Duchy of Luxembourg, a status it shares with French and (High) German. A reasonably fluent Alsatian speaker can understand Luxemburgish quite well, and vice versa.

54. Cf. the overview article in Store Norske Leksikon, available at https://snl.no/Alta -saken (in Norwegian), accessed February 2, 2024.

55. Literally the Sámi Higher School; the first version of the name is Norwegian and the second Sámi. See the institution's website, available at https://samas.no/nb (Sámi, Norwegian, and English), accessed February 2, 2024.

56. For an overview of the history of the Swedish part of Finnish history and culture, see Hårdstedt (2023).

57. The history is somewhat more complex, notably during the period when Finland was part of the Russian Empire between 1809 and 1917, but this does not change the overall situation of the Swedish-speaking minority.

58. Swedish is part of the Nordic subgroup of Germanic languages, and Danish, Norwegian, and Swedish speakers can understand each other reasonably well, at least with some exposure to the other languages. Finnish is a Finno-Ugric rather than an Indo-European language, with Estonian as its closest linguistic relative. A Finnish speaker will not understand Swedish without studying the language, and vice versa.

59. See the Åbo Akademi University website, available at https://www.abo.fi/, accessed February 2, 2024. The website is available in English, Finnish, and Swedish.

60. See the presentation of the Åbo Akademi University on its website, available at https://www.abo.fi/om-abo-akademi/, accessed February 2, 2024.

61. See the overview of the Åbo Akademi University study programs, available at https://www.abo.fi/utbildningsprogram/sprak/ (in Swedish), accessed February 2, 2024.

62. See the presentation of the initiative on the Åbo Akademi University website, available at https://www.abo.fi/vad-sager-vetenskapen/ (in Swedish), accessed February 2, 2024.

63. See the University of Malta website, available at https://www.um.edu.mt/about/, accessed February 2, 2024.

64. See the presentation of the University of Malta Cottonera Resource Centre, available at https://www.um.edu.mt/services/resourcecentres/crc/aboutus/, accessed February 2, 2024.

65. Available at https://www.um.edu.mt/services/resourcecentres/crc/aboutus/, accessed February 2, 2024.

66. At the time of writing, the last year for which an activities report is available through the website.

67. See the presentation of the Maltese University of the Third Age (U3A), available at https://www.um.edu.mt/services/u3a/ourcentres/, accessed February 2, 2024.

68. This Swiss city should not be confused with the city of Freiburg in the southwest of Germany, which also has a well-known university.

69. Spoken as a native language by about 0.5 percent of the population, in the southeast of Switzerland, and also known as Rumantsch or Rumantsch Grischun. Despite its official status, the language is under pressure, see "Studie: Amtssprache Rumantsch Grischun im Alltag gescheitert" [Study: Rumantsch Grischun fails as an everyday official language], Tagblatt, May 31, 2019, available at https://www.tagblatt.ch/newsticker/schweiz /studie-amtssprache-rumantsch-grischun-im-alltag-gescheitert-ld.1123661, accessed February 2, 2024.

70. In the Gettysburg Address, see the Abraham Lincoln online website, available at https://www.abrahamlincolnonline.org/lincoln/speeches/gettysburg.htm, accessed February 2, 2024.

71. See the "Compass: Manual for Human Rights Education with Young People" web page, on the Council of Europe website, available at https://www.coe.int/en/web/compass/democracy, accessed February 2, 2024.

72. Folkeopplysing, in Norwegian.

73. As noted in the Introduction, the term "competence" is much used in education policy in Europe. It designates the ability to do something well (or of being competent) and is often developed through education. It is broader than either "knowledge" or "skill," as indicated by the Council of Europe's CEFR. A full explanation can be found in the notes to the Introduction.

CHAPTER 8

1. All figures from the UNHCR, available at https://www.unhcr.org/news/stories/2015/12/56ec1ebde/2015-year-europes-refugee-crisis.html, accessed February 2, 2024.

2. In the fall of 2022, Chancellor Merkel—who had by then left office—received the UNHCR Nansen Award honoring individuals and organizations that have distinguished themselves by working to make refugees' situation less difficult, see the UNHCR press release, available at https://www.unhcr.org/news/press/2022/10/6331702ef/angela-merkel-receive-unhcr-nansen-refugee-award-protecting-refugees-height.html, accessed February 2, 2024.

3. Respectively, Christlich Demokratische Union Deutschlands (The Christian Democratic Union of Germany) and Christlich-Soziale Union in Bayern (The Christian Social Union in Bayern). The CDU has no branch in Bayern and CSU has no branches outside of Bayern.

4. Alternative for Germany, established in 2013 as a Euroskeptic (in the double sense of skeptical to the EU and to the euro, which in 2001 replaced the German mark) and right liberalist party. It was relatively rapidly taken over by right-wing populists and has gone through several schisms. Today, the AfD is presented in the German national as well as several regional parliaments, but the mainstream parties have so far been unwilling to cooperate with the AfD. At least important parts of the AfD have links to the right-wing anti-Islamic movement Pegida, which in German is characterized as *identitär* (i.e., emphasizing national identity). For an account of the AfD, see Pittelkow and Riedel (2022).

5. In 2021, the United Arab Emirates, which include Dubai and Abu Dhabi, hosted 1,355 refugees, according to the World Bank, available at https://data.worldbank.org/indicator/SM.POP.REFG?locations=AE, accessed February 2, 2024.

6. All figures from the UNHCR, available at https://data.unhcr.org/en/situations/syria, accessed February 2, 2024.

7. See the Worldometer website available at https://www.worldometers.info/world-population/lebanon-population/, accessed February 2, 2024.

8. See the UNHCR 2021 Global Report, the section on Europe, available at https://reporting.unhcr.org/globalreport2021/europe, accessed February 2, 2024.

9. See the UNHCR overview, available at https://data.unhcr.org/en/situations/ukraine, accessed February 2, 2024. According to the same site, the number of refugees had fallen to just below 6 million. The situation is fluid and numbers uncertain as refugees are returning home for various reasons even as others leave. More information is available at https://visitukraine.today/blog/1825/why-ukrainian-refugees-are-returning-home

-important-reasons, accessed February 4, 2024. Russia is indicated as having received almost 2.8 million refugees from Ukraine (the number of "border crossings" is 2.8 million) but the figures are not comparable. Russia invaded Ukraine, and most of those who moved from Ukraine to Russia are either ethnic Russians from the east of the country or forcibly displaced Ukrainians. See the Center for Strategic and International Studies, available at https://www.csis.org/analysis/update-forced-displacement-around-ukraine, accessed February 4, 2024. See also the Centre for Economic Strategy, available at https://ces.org.ua/en/refugees-from-ukraine-final-report/, accessed February 4, 2024.

10. See this news item as reported by Euronews, available at https://www.euronews.com/my-europe/2022/12/06/eu-ministers-delay-key-votes-on-tax-deal-and-ukraine-aid-over-hungary-impasse, and CNN, available at https://edition.cnn.com/2023/12/14/europe/eu-council-accession-talks-ukraine-intl/index.html, both accessed February 4, 2024.

11. On the Syrian civil war, see Baczko, Doronsorro, and Quesnay (2016).

12. Among other things, this conference adopted the model of the RFCDC (Chapter 3). See the Council of Europe website for the Twenty-Fifth Session of the Council of Europe Standing Conference of Ministers of Education, available at https://www.coe.int/en/web/education-minister-conference, accessed February 2, 2024.

13. See the call published by the Greek Ministry of Education, Research, and Religious Affairs, available at https://www.minedu.gov.gr/publications/docs2016/SUMMER_SCHOOL_Call_for_Participants_July2016_2.pdf, accessed February 2, 2024.

14. Detailed information on the EQPR is available at https://www.coe.int/en/web/education/recognition-of-refugees-qualifications, an overview of news articles, available at https://www.coe.int/en/web/education/eqpr-newsroom; several presentation videos, available at https://www.coe.int/en/web/education/eqpr-multimedia; and a presentation folder, available at https://rm.coe.int/leaflet-eqpr-eng/1680a6d734. The best information video may be found, in long and short versions, available at https://www.coe.int/en/web/education/documentary-on-project-european-qualifications-passport-for-refugees. All sites accessed February 2, 2024.

15. See the Refugees Welcome initiative of the EUA, available at https://eua.eu/101-projects/541-refugees-welcome-map.html, accessed February 2, 2024.

16. The formal terminology is "qualifications held by refugees, displaced persons, and persons in a refugee-like situation." In general, the shorthand "refugees' qualifications" is used.

17. See the information published by the Norwegian Directorate for Education and Skills, available at https://hkdir.no/en/foreign-education/education-from-outside-of-norway/recognition-of-foreign-higher-education-bachelor-master-and-phd/about-the-recognition-higher-education/recognition-procedure-for-applicants-without-verifiable-documentation-uvd, accessed February 2, 2024.

18. See the news item published on the Council of Europe's Education website, available at https://www.coe.int/en/web/education/-/new-recommendation-on-recognition-of-qualifications-held-by-refugees, accessed February 2, 2024.

19. An explanatory memorandum explains the reasoning behind the provisions of a recommendation and may also provide elaboration and examples, which a legal text does not. Contrary to a recommendation, an explanatory memorandum does not have legal force or status. A convention may have a similar explanatory text, which is in this case referred to as an explanatory "report" rather than "memorandum." The explanatory memorandum to the recommendation on the recognition of refugees' qualifications is available in Council of Europe and UNESCO 2017.

20. The Lisbon Recognition Convention defines a higher education qualification as "any degree, diploma or other certificate issued by a competent authority attesting the successful completion of a higher education programme" (Article I).

21. As noted previously, the term "competence" is much used in education policy in Europe. It designates the ability to do something well (or of being competent) and is often developed through education. It is broader than either "knowledge" or "skill," as indicated by the Council of Europe's CEFR. A full explanation is found in the notes to the Introduction.

22. I oversaw the development of the EQPR from its inception until my retirement from the Council of Europe in February 2022. The colleagues directly involved in the project were the head of our Cooperation and Capacity Building Division, Sarah Keating, with two colleagues from this division: Hećo and Đafić. Later Marjorie Mantulet, a junior professional, and Gloria Manazzu, a communications specialist, also contributed, and we were able to recruit Malgina on a temporary contract in 2021–2022. All were based in Strasbourg, except Đafić, who was based at the Council's Sarajevo office. Hećo's background is particularly relevant for this project, as he arrived in France as a refugee from Bosnia and Herzegovina in the 1990s.

23. See the UNHCR website, available at https://www.unhcr.org/. The UN Relief and Works Agency for Palestine Refugees is responsible for relief and works programs for Palestine refugees in the Middle East, available at https://www.unrwa.org/. The International Organization for Migration is the UN agency responsible for migration issues more broadly, available at https://www.iom.int/mission. All three sites accessed February 2, 2024.

24. Fassari was the chair of this committee in 2019–2021 and the vice chair in 2017–2019.

25. For a sample EQPR, see the dedicated Council of Europe website, available at https://rm.coe.int/sample-eqpr-/16809874fb, accessed February 2, 2024.

26. Or, to be exact, in the language of the country in which the candidate obtained his or her qualifications. These are very often one and the same, but there may be cases where they differ, for example, if an applicant from Pakistan or Afghanistan obtained his or her qualification in Syria or Iraq. Before the war, Ukraine hosted some seventy-five thousand students from 155 countries. See the Study in Ukraine website, available at https://studyinukraine.gov.ua/forum-statistic-info/ (in Ukrainian), accessed February 2, 2024.

27. See the news item published on the Council of Europe's Education website, available at https://www.coe.int/en/web/education/-/the-european-qualifications-passport-for-refugees-eqpr-presented-at-unesco-general-conference-high-level-event, accessed February 2, 2024.

28. See the news item published on the UNHCR website, available at https://www.unhcr.org/programme-and-practical-information.html, accessed February 2, 2024.

29. See the news item published on the Council of Europe's Education website, available at https://www.coe.int/en/web/education/-/launch-of-new-phase-of-project-european-qualifications-passport-for-refugees-, accessed February 2, 2024.

30. A tightly reasoned report submitted in early August 2023 by Luís Moreno Ocampo, an Argentinian international lawyer who was the first procurator of the International Court of Justice in Den Haag, accuses the Azerbaijani president and government of being responsible for genocide according to accepted international legal standards of using hunger as a weapon, and this even before the latest armed attack, see website available at https://luismorenoocampo.com/wp-content/uploads/2023/08/Armenia-Report-Expert-Opinion.pdf?utm_source=Web&utm_medium=Landing&utm_campaign=Downloads, accessed February 2, 2024.

31. Generally dated to 1915–1923. For a good history, see Suny (2015).

32. See the CIMEA website, available at https://www.cimea.it/, accessed February 2, 2024.

33. See the news item published on the Council of Europe's Education website, available at https://www.coe.int/en/web/education/-/european-qualifications-passport-for -refugees-in-italy, accessed February 2, 2024.

34. See the news item published on the Council of Europe's Education website, available at https://www.coe.int/en/web/education/-/eqpr-evaluation-session-held-in-palermo -and-catania, accessed February 2, 2024.

35. See the news item published on the Council of Europe's Education website, available at https://www.coe.int/en/web/education/-/italian-universities-start-accepting-the -european-qualifications-passport-for-refugees-for-scholarship-applicatio-1, accessed February 2, 2024.

36. See the news item published on the Council of Europe's Education website, available at https://www.coe.int/en/web/education/-/eqpr-evaluation-session-in-greece-saw -increased-use-of-video-interviews, accessed February 2, 2024.

37. Permanent Representations are similar to embassies but are accredited to international organizations like the Council of Europe or the UN rather than to a country. Hence, France has a Permanent Representation to the Council of Europe and the United States has one to the UN, even though they are the respective host countries to these two organizations. A Permanent Representation is headed by a Permanent Representative, who has ambassadorial rank and presents his or her credentials to the Secretary General of the organization concerned rather than to a Head of State.

38. See the news item published on the Council of Europe's Education website, available at https://www.coe.int/en/web/education/-/the-role-of-education-in-supporting-ref ugees-integration-joint-event-in-strasbourg, accessed February 2, 2024.

39. Which professions are regulated varies between countries, but they are broadly those in which malpractice can have serious and immediate consequences. Typical examples are medicine, dentistry, law, and engineering. Teaching, where malpractice has less immediate but perhaps even more serious consequences, is a regulated profession in several European countries. Within the EU, regulated professions are covered by EU Directives. For an overview, see the European Commission website, available at https:// single-market-economy.ec.europa.eu/single-market/services/free-movement-profession als/recognition-professional-qualifications-practice_en, accessed February 2, 2024.

40. See a joint press release by the Secretary General of the Council of Europe and the UNHCR on April 14, 2020. See the news item published on the Council of Europe' Education website, available at https://www.coe.int/en/web/education/-/council-of-europe -and-unhcr-support-member-states-in-bringing-refugee-health-workers-into-the-fight -against-covid-19, accessed August 10, 2024.

41. See the news item published on the Council of Europe's Education website, available at https://www.coe.int/en/web/education/-/eqpr-featured-in-time-magazine, accessed February 2, 2024.

42. See the news item published on the Council of Europe's Education website, available at https://www.coe.int/en/web/education/-/the-european-qualifications-passport-for -refugees-holds-its-8th-project-co-ordination-group-meeting, accessed February 2, 2024.

43. Personal communication from Heċo, December 19, 2023.

44. Albania, Andorra, Armenia, Bosnia and Herzegovina, Canada, Croatia, France, Georgia, Germany, Greece, Ireland, Italy, Latvia, Moldova, the Netherlands, Norway, Poland, Portugal, Romania, San Marino, Serbia, and the United Kingdom.

45. See the news item published on the Council of Europe's Education website, available at https://www.coe.int/en/web/education/-/european-qualifications-passport-for-refugees-from-theory-to-practice-newly-trained-credential-evaluators-start-evaluating-refugees-qualifications, accessed February 2, 2024.

46. See the news item published on the Council of Europe's Education website, available at https://www.coe.int/en/web/education/-/credentials-evaluators-trained-on-evaluating-qualifications-of-afghan-refugees, accessed February 2, 2024.

47. The key persons in the EQPR project in CIMEA have been its director Luca Lantero as well as Chiara Finochietti, Letizia Brambilla Pisoni, Vera Lucke, and Silvia Bianco.

48. The information may be accessed, for those with a right to access, at the protected website, available at https://wallet.diplo-me.eu/coe/#/auth/login, accessed February 2, 2024.

49. Personal communication from Hećo, December 19, 2023.

50. French administrative subdivisions under the authority of the Ministry of the Interior.

51. See the news item published on the University of Auvergne website, available at https://www.uca.fr/international/accueil-international/etudiants-et-chercheurs-en-exil/le-projet-colab (in French), accessed February 2, 2024.

52. See the website of the Piemonte labor agency, available at https://agenziapiemontelavoro.it/, accessed February 2, 2024.

53. Personal communication from Hećo, January 17, 2023.

54. "Da oggi i medici ucraini potranno esercitare in Italia" [From today, Ukrainian medical doctors may exercise their profession in Italy], ANSA, available at https://www.ansa.it/canale_saluteebenessere/notizie/sanita/2022/03/22/da-oggi-i-medici-ucraini-potranno-esercitare-in-italia_abb14037-2f92-4a07-bfce-91146932ecb1.html (in Italian), accessed February 2, 2024.

55. See the website of the Encamp secondary school, available at http://ad2eenc.educand.ad/ (in Catalan), accessed December 19, 2023.

56. For an explanation of subject specific and transversal competences, see the discussion of the Tuning project in Chapter 3.

CHAPTER 9

1. Sharon Brathwaite: "Zelensky Refuses US Offer to Evacuate, Saying 'I Need Ammunition, Not a Ride,'" CNN, February 26, 2022, available at https://edition.cnn.com/2022/02/26/europe/ukraine-zelensky-evacuation-intl/index.html, accessed February 2, 2024.

2. Here I am building on John Dewey's famous proposition: "Democracy must begin at home, and home is the neighborly community" (cited in Harkavy 2015: 280). Benson et al. (2017: xiii) argue that "today, democracy's home is the engaged neighborly college or university and its local community partners."

3. See the Introduction for an explanation of how this term is used in European education policy.

4. See the "Introducing Public Engagement" web page on the website of the National Co-ordinating Centre for Public Engagement, available at https://www.publicengagement.ac.uk/introducing-public-engagement, accessed February 2, 2024.

5. Literally the Sámi Higher School; the first version of the name is Norwegian and the second Sámi.

6. See the presentation of Sámi on the website of the Norwegian Language Council (Språkrådet), available at https://www.sprakradet.no/Spraka-vare/Spraka-i-Norden /Samisk/ (in Norwegian), accessed February 2, 2024.

7. EURASHE, which represents professional higher education institutions.

8. See the website of the Congress of Local and Regional Authorities, available at https://www.coe.int/en/web/congress, accessed February 2, 2024.

9. See the website of the Council of Europe's Intercultural Cities program, available at https://www.coe.int/en/web/interculturalcities, accessed February 2, 2024.

10. Paraphrased from Tironi (2005).

References

Abrahams, Fred C. 2015 *Modern Albania: From Dictatorship to Democracy in Europe*. New York: New York University Press.

Andersson, Tomas. 2021. *Bohusläns historia: Från järnålder till 1658* [The history of Bohuslän: From the Iron Age until 1653]. Lund: Historiska Media.

Applebaum, Anne. 2018. "A Warning from Europe: The Worst Is Yet to Come." *The Atlantic*, October 2018. Available at https://www.theatlantic.com/magazine/archive/2018/10/poland-polarization/568324/. Accessed February 2, 2024.

Attali, Jacques. 1998. *Pour un modèle européen d'enseignement supérieur* [For a European higher education model]. Available at https://medias.vie-publique.fr/data_storage_s3/rapport/pdf/984000340.pdf. Accessed February 2, 2024.

Baczko, Adam, Gilles Doronsorro, and Adam Quesnay. 2016. *Syrie: Anatomie d'une guerre civile* [Syria: Anatomy of a civil war]. Paris: CNRS.

Balcells, Albert. 2004. *Breve historia del nacionalismo catalán* [A brief history of Catalan nationalism]. Madrid: Alianza Editorial.

Bawa, Ahmed. 2018. "Reimagining the Social Purpose of Universities through Engagement." In Bergan and Harkavy 2018, 163–176.

———. 2019. "Engagement as Transformative: A South African Experience." In Bergan, Harkavy, and Munck 2019a, 124–135.

Benson, Lee, Ira Harkavy, John Puckett, Matthew Hartley, Rita A. Hodges, Francis E. Johnston, and Joann Weeks. 2017. *Knowledge for Social Change: Bacon, Dewey, and the Revolutionary Transformation of Research Universities in the Twenty-First Century*. Philadelphia: Temple University Press.

Benson, Lee, John Puckett, and Ira Harkavy. 2007. *Dewey's Dream: Universities and Democracies in an Age of Education Reform, Civil Society, Public Schools, and Democratic Citizenship*. Philadelphia: Temple University Press.

Bergan, Sjur, ed. 2004. *The University as Res Publica*. Council of Europe Higher Education Series No. 1. Strasbourg: Council of Europe.

———. 2005a. "Bologna Conference on Qualifications Frameworks. Danish Ministry of Science, Technology and Innovation, København, January 13–14, 2005. Report by the General Rapporteur." Available at https://www.ehea.info/media.ehea.info/file/Qual ifications_framework_Copenhagen_2005/27/8/050113-14_General_report_578278 .pdf. Accessed February 2, 2024.

———. 2005b. "Higher Education as a 'Public Good and a Public Responsibility': What Does It Mean?" In Weber and Bergan 2005, 13–28. Available at https://rm.coe.int/the -public-responsibility-for-higher-education-and-research/168075ddd0. Accessed February 2, 2024.

———. 2011. "Reflections on Ranking in Europe." In *Not by Bread Alone*, ed. Sjur Bergan, 159–173. Council of Europe Higher Education Series No. 17. Strasbourg: Council of Europe. Available at https://rm.coe.int/not-by-bread-alone/168075dddd. Accessed February 2, 2024.

———. 2013. "Reimagining Democratic Societies: What Does Education Have to Do with It?" In Bergan, Harkavy, and van't Land 2013a, 45–52.

———. 2015. "Anchor Institutions for Europe? Higher Education Institutions as Community Actors." In Bergan, Gallagher, and Harkavy 2015, 287–302.

———. 2016. "History, Democracy, and Human Rights." In *Crossing Borders: Combining Human Rights Education and History Education*, ed. Claudia Lenz, Sanna Brattland, and Lise Kvande, 53–66. Berlin: Lit Verlag Reihe: Erinnern und Lernen. Texte zur Menschenrechtspädagogik.

———. 2018. "Democracy, Knowledge, and Inclusion versus Post-Truth Politics—Reaffirming the Principles of Higher Education." In Bergan and Harkavy 2018, 19–28.

Bergan, Sjur, and Radu Damian, eds. 2010. *Higher Education for Modern Societies: Competences and Values*. Council of Europe Higher Education Series No. 15. Strasbourg: Council of Europe. Available at https://rm.coe.int/higher-education-for-modern-so cieties-competences-and-values/168075dddb. Accessed February 2, 2024.

Bergan, Sjur, and Ligia Deca. 2018. "Twenty Years of Bologna and a Decade of EHEA: What Is Next?" In *European Higher Education Area: The Impact of Past and Future Policies*, ed. Adrian Curaj, Ligia Deca, and Remus Pricopie, with Sjur Bergan, Ellen Hazelkorn, Liviu Matei, Jamil Salmi, and Hans de Wit (coeditors), 283–306. Also accessible through Springer Open Access: Available at https://link.springer.com/chap ter/10.1007/978-3-319-77407-7_19. Accessed February 2, 2024.

Bergan, Sjur, Eva Egron-Polak, and Sijbolt Noorda. 2020. "Academic Freedom and Institutional Autonomy—What Role in and for the EHEA?" In *Academic Freedom, Institutional Autonomy and the Future of Democracy*, ed. Sjur Bergan, Tony Gallagher, and Ira Harkavy, 41–55. Council of Europe Higher Education Series No. 24. Strasbourg: Council of Europe. Available at https://rm.coe.int/prems-025620-eng-2508-higher -education-series-no-24/1680a19fdf. Accessed February 2, 2024.

Bergan, Sjur, Tony Gallagher, and Ira Harkavy, eds. 2015. *Higher Education for Democratic Innovation*. Council of Europe Higher Education Series No. 21. Strasbourg: Council of Europe.

———, eds. 2020. *Academic Freedom, Institutional Autonomy, and the Future of Democracy* Council of Europe Higher Education Series No. 24. Strasbourg: Council of Europe. Available at https://rm.coe.int/prems-025620-eng-2508-higher-education-series -no-24/1680a19fdf. Accessed February 2, 2024.

Bergan, Sjur, Tony Gallagher, Ira Harkavy, Ronaldo Munck, and Hilligje van't Land, eds. 2021. *Higher Education's Response to the COVID-19 Pandemic: Building a More Sus-

tainable and Democratic Future. Council of Europe Higher Education Series No. 25. Strasbourg: Council of Europe. Available at https://rm.coe.int/prems-006821-eng-2508 -higher-education-series-no-25/1680a19fe2. Accessed February 2, 2024.

Bergan, Sjur, and Ira Harkavy, eds. 2018. *Higher Education for Diversity, Social Inclusion and Community*. Council of Europe Higher Education Series No. 22. Strasbourg: Council of Europe.

Bergan, Sjur, Ira Harkavy, and Ronaldo Munck, eds. 2019a. *The Local Mission of Higher Education: Principles and Practice*. Dublin: Glasnevin.

———. 2019b. "The Way Forward." In Bergan, Harkavy, and Munck 2019a, 137–144.

———, eds. 2023. *Higher Education Leadership for Democracy, Sustainability and Social Justice*. Council of Europe Higher Education Series No. 26. Strasbourg: Council of Europe. Available at https://rm.coe.int/prems-070423-eng-2506-highereducation26 -web/1680ad83d5. Accessed February 2, 2024.

Bergan, Sjur, Ira Harkavy, and Hilligje van't Land, eds. 2013a. *Reimagining Democratic Societies: A New Era of Personal and Social Responsibility*. Council of Europe Higher Education Series No. 18. Strasbourg: Council of Europe.

———. 2013b. "A Word from the Editors." In Bergan, Harkavy, and van't Land 2013a, 13–24.

Bergan, Sjur, and Stig Arne Skjerven. 2019. "Recognising Refugee Qualifications—A Virtuous Circle." University World News, July 8, 2019. Available at https://www.univer sityworldnews.com/post.php?story=20190708095054787. Accessed February 2, 2024.

———. 2020. "A Way to Enable Refugees to Help in the COVID-19 Crisis." University World News, May 2, 2020. Available at https://www.universityworldnews.com/post .php?story=2020050114282238. Accessed February 2, 2024.

Bierce, Ambrose. (1911) 1967. *The Enlarged Devil's Dictionary*. Edited by E. J. Hopkins. Harmondsworth: Penguin American Library.

Birchall, Claire, and Peter Knight. 2022. *Conspiracy Theories in the Time of Covid-19*. London: Routledge.

Bjeliš, Aleksa. 2015. "Universities and Demanding Times." In Bergan, Gallagher, and Harkavy 2015, 201–215.

———. 2018. "Universities and Their Communities in Disruptive Times." In Bergan and Harkavy 2018, 177–191.

Bocancea, Sorin, and Radu Carp, eds. 2016. *Calea europeană a Republicii Moldova* [The Republic of Moldova's European road]. Iași: Adenium.

Bologna Process. 1998. "Sorbonne Joint Declaration Joint Declaration on Harmonisation of the Architecture of the European Higher Education System by the Four Ministers in Charge for France, Germany, Italy and the United Kingdom." Available at https:// www.ehea.info/media.ehea.info/file/1998_Sorbonne/61/2/1998_Sorbonne_Declara tion_English_552612.pdf. Accessed February 2, 2024.

———. 1999. "The Bologna Declaration of 19 June 1999: Joint Declaration of the European Ministers of Education." Available at https://www.ehea.info/Upload/document /ministerial_declarations/1999_Bologna_Declaration_English_553028.pdf. Accessed February 2, 2024.

———. 2001. "Towards the European Higher Education Area: Communiqué of the Meeting of European Ministers in Charge of Higher Education in Prague on May 19th 2001." Available at https://www.ehea.info/Upload/document/ministerial_declarations/2001 _Prague_Communique_English_553442.pdf. Accessed February 2, 2024.

———. 2003. "Realising the European Higher Education Area. Communiqué of the Conference of Ministers Responsible for Higher Education in Berlin on 19 September 2003."

Available at https://www.ehea.info/Upload/document/ministerial_declarations/2003
_Berlin_Communique_English_577284.pdf. Accessed February 2, 2024.

——. 2004. "Further Accessions to the Bologna Process: Procedures for Evaluation of
Applications and Reports from Potential New Members." Document BFUG B3 7, 4
October 2004. Available at https://ehea.info/media.ehea.info/file/20041012-13_Noord
wijk/79/9/BFUG3_7_further_accessions_579799.pdf. Accessed February 2, 2024.

——. 2005a. *A Framework of Qualifications for the European Higher Education Area.*
Bologna Working Group on Qualifications Frameworks. København: Ministry of Science, Technology, and Innovation. Available at https://www.ehea.info/media.ehea
.info/file/WG_Frameworks_qualification/71/0/050218_QF_EHEA_580710.pdf. Accessed February 2, 2024.

——. 2005b. "The Framework of Qualifications for the European Higher Education
Area." Available at http://www.ehea.info/media.ehea.info/file/WG_Frameworks_qual
ification/85/2/Framework_qualificationsforEHEA-May2005_587852.pdf. Accessed
February 2, 2024.

——. 2007. "London Communiqué—Towards the European Higher Education Area:
Responding to Challenges in a Globalised World." Available at http://www.ehea.info
/Upload/document/ministerial_declarations/2007_London_Communique_English
_588697.pdf. Accessed February 2, 2024.

——. 2009. "The Bologna Process 2020—The European Higher Education Area in the
New Decade. Communiqué of the Conference of European Ministers Responsible for
Higher Education, Leuven and Louvain-la-Neuve, 28–29 April 2009." Available at http://
www.ehea.info/Upload/document/ministerial_declarations/Leuven_Louvain_la
_Neuve_Communique_April_2009_595061.pdf. Accessed February 2, 2024.

——. 2012a. "Making the Most of Our Potential: Consolidating the European Higher
Education Area Bucharest Communiqué." Available at http://www.ehea.info/Upload
/document/ministerial_declarations/Bucharest_Communique_2012_610673.pdf.
Accessed February 2, 2024.

——. 2012b. "Meeting of the Bologna Follow-Up Group, Copenhagen, 18–19 January
2012. Draft outcomes of proceedings." Available at https://ehea.info/cid104275/bfug
-meeting-28.html. Accessed February 2, 2024.

——. 2012c. "Mobility for Better Learning: Mobility Strategy 2020 for the European
Higher Education Area (EHEA)." Available at http://www.ehea.info/media.ehea.info
/file/2012_Bucharest/39/2/2012_EHEA_Mobility_Strategy_606392.pdf. Accessed February 2, 2024.

——. 2015a. "Belarus Roadmap for Higher Education Reform." Available at http://www
.ehea.info/media.ehea.info/file/2015_Yerevan/70/9/Roadmap_Belarus_21.05.2015
_613709.pdf. Accessed February 2, 2024.

——. 2015b. *Report for the 2012–15 Working Group on Mobility and Internationalisation.* Available at http://www.ehea.info/media.ehea.info/file/2015_Yerevan/71/7/MI
_WG_Report_613717.pdf. Accessed February 2, 2024.

——. 2015c. *Standards and Guidelines for Quality Assurance in the European Higher
Education Area (ESG) Approved by the Ministerial Conference in May 2015.* Available
at http://www.ehea.info/media.ehea.info/file/2015_Yerevan/72/7/European_Standards
_and_Guidelines_for_Quality_Assurance_in_the_EHEA_2015_MC_613727.pdf. Accessed February 2, 2024.

——. 2015d. "Yerevan Communiqué." Available at http://www.ehea.info/Upload/doc
ument/ministerial_declarations/YerevanCommuniqueFinal_613707.pdf. Accessed
February 2, 2024.

———. 2018. "Paris Communiqué." Available at http://www.ehea.info/Upload/document/ministerial_declarations/EHEAParis2018_Communique_final_952771.pdf. Accessed February 2, 2024.

———. 2020a. "Principles and Guidelines to Strengthen the Social Dimension of Higher Education in the EHEA." Available at http://www.ehea.info/Upload/Rome_Ministerial_Communique_Annex_II.pdf. Accessed February 2, 2024.

———. 2020b. "Rome Ministerial Communiqué. Annex I. Statement on Academic Freedom." Available at http://www.ehea.info/Upload/Rome_Ministerial_Communique_Annex_I.pdf. Accessed February 2, 2024.

———. 2020c. "Rome Ministerial Communiqué. 19 November 2020." Available at http://www.ehea.info/Upload/Rome_Ministerial_Communique.pdf. Accessed February 2, 2024.

———. 2024a. "EHEA Statement on Fundamental Values." Available at https://ehea.info/Immagini/ANNEX-1-EHEA-STATEMENTS-ON-FUNDAMENTAL-VALUES1.pdf, accessed August 9, 2024.

———. 2024b. "Tirana Communique." Available at https://ehea.info/Immagini/Tirana-Communique1.pdf.

Boyd, Julia, and Angelika Patel. 2020. *A Village in the Third Reich: How Ordinary Lives Were Transformed by the Rise of Fascism*. London: Elliott and Thompson.

Boyte, Harry, and Elizabeth Hollander. 1999. "Wingspread Declaration on Renewing the Civic Mission of the American Research University." Available at https://compact.org/resources/wingspread-declaration-on-the-civic-responsibilities-of-research-universities. Accessed August 12, 2024

Brincat, Joseph M. 2021. *Maltese and Other Languages: A Linguistic History of Malta*. Santa Venera: Midsea Books.

Brown, Wendy. 2019. *In the Ruins of Neoliberalism: The Rise of Antidemocratic Politics in the West*. New York: Columbia University Press.

Butenschøn, Nils, Else Grete Broderstad, Anni-Siiri Länsman, Kari Morthensen, Nils Oskal, Per Ravna, Johan Strömgren, and Vera Schwach. 2012. *Langs lange spor–om samisk forskning og høyere utdaning* [Along long paths—On Sámi research and higher education]. Report by a commission established by the Norwegian Ministry of Education. In Norwegian and Sámi, available at https://www.regjeringen.no/globalassets/upload/kd/vedlegg/forskning/rapporter/langs_lange_spor-.pdf. Accessed February 2, 2024.

Campus Compact. 1999. "Presidents' Declaration on the Civic Responsibility of Higher Education." Available at https://compact.org/resources/presidents-declaration-on-the-civic-responsibility-of-higher-education. Accessed February 2, 2024.

Cantor, Nancy, and Peter Englot. 2018. "Higher Education's Promise and Responsibility." In Bergan and Harkavy 2018, 204–215.

Carreras, Albert. 2015. *Volem la independència? Reflexions per al futur immediat* [Do we want independence? Reflections for the immediate future]. Barcelona: Editorial Base.

Cartledge, Paul. 2016. *Democracy: A Life*. Oxford: Oxford University Press.

Chevaillier, Thierry, and Jean-Claude Eicher. 2021. "Higher Education Funding: A Decade of Changes." Available at https://shs.hal.science/halshs-00004954/document. Accessed February 2, 2024.

Coleman, John, ed. 1999. *The Conscience of Europe*. Strasbourg: Council of Europe.

Council of Europe. 1953. *European Convention on the Equivalence of Diplomas Leading to Admission to Universities* (ETS No. 15). Available at https://www.coe.int/en/web/conventions/full-list?module=treaty-detail&treatynum=015. Accessed February 2, 2024.

———. 1954. *European Cultural Convention* (ETS No. 018). Available at https://www.coe .int/en/web/conventions/full-list?module=treaty-detail&treatynum=018. Accessed February 2, 2024.

———. 1997. "Second Summit of Heads of State and Government (Strasbourg, 10–11 October 1997). Final Declaration and Action Plan." Available at https://rm.coe.int/16 8063dced. Accessed February 2, 2024.

———. 1998. *Recommendation No. R(98) 6 of the Committee of Ministers to Member States concerning Modern Languages*. Available at https://rm.coe.int/16804fc569. Accessed August 12, 2024.

———. 1999. "Budapest Declaration for a Greater Europe without Dividing Lines." Available at https://www.internationalconsortium.org/budapest-declaration-for-a-greater -europe-without-dividing-lines/. Accessed February 2, 2024.

———. 2001a. *Common European Framework of Reference for Languages: Learning, Teaching, Assessment*. Cambridge: Cambridge University Press. Available at https://rm.coe .int/1680459f97. Accessed February 2, 2024.

———. 2001b. *Recommendation Rec(2001)15 of the Committee of Ministers to Member States on History Teaching in Twenty-First-Century Europe*. Available at https://rm.coe.int /16804ec22c. Accessed August 12, 2024.

———. 2002. *Recommendation Rec (2002)12 of the Committee of Ministers to Member States on Education for Democratic Citizenship*. Available at https://search.coe.int/cm /Pages/result_details.aspx?ObjectID=09000016804f7b87. Accessed February 2, 2024.

———. 2005a. "Multiperspectivity in Teaching and Learning History: Presentations from Seminars and Workshops Materials." Available at https://rm.coe.int/CoERMPublic CommonSearchServices/DisplayDCTMContent?documentId=0900001680492f87. Accessed February 2, 2024.

———. 2005b. "Third Summit of Heads of State and Government of the Council of Europe (Warsaw, 16–17 May 2005). Action Plan." Available at https://www.coe.int/t/dcr /summit/20050517_plan_action_en.asp. Accessed August 12, 2024.

———. 2006a. "Higher Education and Democratic Culture: Citizenship, Human Rights and Civic Responsibility—Declaration." Available at https://rm.coe.int/declaration -on-the-responsibility-of-higher-education-for-democratic-c/1680779f5b. Accessed February 2, 2024.

———. 2006b. *Recommendation 1762 (2006) by the Parliamentary Assembly on Academic Freedom and University Autonomy*. Available at https://pace.coe.int/en/files/17469/html. Accessed February 2, 2024.

———. 2007. *Recommendation CM/Rec(2007)6 of the Committee of Ministers to Member States on the Public Responsibility for Higher Education and Research*. Available at https://search.coe.int/cm?i=09000016805d5dae. Accessed August 12, 2024.

———. 2009a. *The Use of Sources in Teaching and Learning History: The Council of Europe's Activities in Cyprus*. Vol. 1. Available at https://rm.coe.int/CoERMPublicCom monSearchServices/DisplayDCTMContent?documentId=0900001680492d6b. Accessed February 2, 2024.

———. 2009b. *The Use of Sources in Teaching and Learning History: The Council of Europe's Activities in Cyprus*. Vol. 2. Available at https://rm.coe.int/CoERMPublicCom monSearchServices/DisplayDCTMContent?documentId=0900001680492d6c. Accessed February 2, 2024.

———. 2010. *Recommendation CM/Rec(2010)7 of the Committee of Ministers to Member States on the Council of Europe Charter on Education for Democratic Citizenship and*

Human Rights Education. Available at https://rm.coe.int/16803034e5. Accessed August 12, 2024.

———. 2011a. *Living Together: Combining Diversity and Freedom in 21st-Century Europe—Report of the Group of Eminent Persons of the Council of Europe*. Strasbourg: Council of Europe.

———. 2011b. *A Look at Our Past/ Μια ματιά στο παρελθόν μας/ Geçmişimize bir bakış*. Strasbourg: Council of Europe.

———. 2012. *Recommendation CM/Rec(2012)13 of the Committee of Ministers to Member States on Ensuring Quality Education*. Available at https://www.ecml.at/Portals/1/documents/CoE-documents/CMRec2012-13_quality_EN.pdf?ver=2016-11-29-113145-700. Accessed August 12, 2024.

———. 2014. *Shared Histories for a Europe without Dividing Lines*. Strasbourg: Council of Europe. E-book available at https://www.coe.int/en/web/history-education/an-electronic-e-book. Accessed February 2, 2024.

———. 2018a. *Common European Framework of Reference for Languages: Learning, Teaching, Assessment; Companion Volume with New Descriptors*. Strasbourg: Council of Europe. Available at https://rm.coe int/cefr-companion-volume-with-new-descriptors-2018/1680787989. Accessed February 2, 2024.

———. 2018b. *Reference Framework of Competences for Democratic Culture: Context, Concepts and Model*. Vol. 1. Strasbourg: Council of Europe. Available at https://rm.coe.int/prems-008318-gbr-2508-reference-framework-of-competences-vol-1-8573-co/16807bc66c. Accessed February 2, 2024.

———. 2018c. *Reference Framework of Competences for Democratic Culture: Descriptors of Competences*. Vol. 2. Strasbourg: Council of Europe. Available at https://rm.coe.int/prems-008418-gbr-2508-reference-framework-of-competences-vol-2-8573-co/16807bc66d. Accessed February 2, 2024.

———. 2018d. *Reference Framework of Competences for Democratic Culture: Guidance for Implementation*. Vol. 3. Strasbourg: Council of Europe. Available at https://rm.coe.int/prems-008518-gbr-2508-reference-framework-of-competences-vol-3-8575-co/16807bc66e. Accessed February 2, 2024.

———. 2018e. *Quality History Education in the 21st Century: Principles and Guidelines*. Strasbourg: Council of Europe. Available at https://rm.coe.int/prems-108118-gbr-2507-quality-history-education-web-21x21/16808eace7. Accessed February 2, 2024.

———. 2020a. *Common European Framework of Reference for Languages: Learning, Teaching, Assessment—Companion Volume*. Strasbourg: Council of Europe. Available at https://rm.coe.int/common-european-framework-of-reference-for-languages-learning-teaching/16809ea0d4. Accessed February 2, 2024.

———. 2020b. "Informal Conference of Ministers of Education Organised under the Greek Chairmanship of the Committee of Ministers. The Education Response to the COVID Crisis. Political Declaration 29 October 2020." Available at https://rm.coe.int/the-education-response-to-the-covid-crisis-political-declaration-for-t/16809fee7a. Accessed February 2, 2024.

———. 2020c. *Making the Right to Education a Reality in Times of COVID-19: A Roadmap for Action on the Council of Europe Education Response to COVID-19*. Strasbourg: Council of Europe. Available at https://rm.coe.int/making-the-right-to-education-a-reality-in-times-of-covid-19-a-roadmap/16809fee7b. Accessed February 2, 2024.

———. 2020d. *Reference Framework of Competences for Democratic Culture. Guidance Document for Higher Education*. Strasbourg: Council of Europe. Available at https://

rm.coe.int/rfcdc-guidance-document-for-higher-education/1680a08ee0. Accessed February 2, 2024.

———. 2021. *State of Democracy, Human Rights and the Rule of Law: A Democratic Renewal for Europe—Report by the Secretary General*. Strasbourg: Council of Europe. Available at https://rm.coe.int/annual-report-sg-2021/1680a264a2. Accessed February 2, 2024.

———. 2022a. "The Democratic and Local Democratic Mission of Higher Education: Project Description." Document DGII/EDU/CDEDU (2022) 27.

———. 2022b. *The Importance of Plurilingual and Intercultural Education for Democratic Culture: Recommendation CM/Rec(2022)1 and Explanatory Memorandum*. Strasbourg: Council of Europe. Available at https://rm.coe.int/prems-013522-gbr-2508-cmrec-2022-1-et-expose-motifs-couv-a5-bat-web/1680a967b4. Accessed February 2, 2024.

———. 2022c. "The Local Democratic Mission of Higher Education: A Council of Europe Platform. Policy Brief." Document DGII/EDU/CDEDU (2022) 29.

———. 2022d. *Recommendation CM/Rec(2022)5 of the Committee of Ministers to Member States on Passing on Remembrance of the Holocaust and Preventing Crimes against Humanity*. Available at https://search.coe.int/cm/Pages/result_details.aspx?ObjectID=0900001680a5ddcd. Accessed February 2, 2024.

———. 2023a. "Learners First: Education for Today's and Tomorrow's Democratic Societies—Council of Europe Education Strategy 2024-2030." Available at https://rm.coe.int/education-strategy-2024-2030-26th-session-council-of-europe-standing-c/1680abee81. Accessed February 2, 2024.

———. 2023b. *Pandemics and Natural Disasters as Reflected in History Teaching: Thematic Report by the Observatory on History Teaching in Europe 2022*. Strasbourg: Council of Europe. Available at https://rm.coe.int/prems-011523-gbr-2527-pandemics-and-natural-disasters/1680aa6262. Accessed February 2, 2024.

———. 2024. *OHTE General Report on the State of History Teaching in Europe. Volume 1 Comparative Analysis* Strasbourg: Council of Europe. Available at https://rm.coe.int/2024-05-ohte-general-report-vol-1-provisional/1680afaa22.

Council of Europe, European Commission, and UNESCO. 2020. "Recognition of Foreign Qualifications in Times of COVID-19: A Reflection Document for the ENIC NARIC Networks and Their Stakeholders. Prepared by the Lisbon Recognition Convention Committee Bureau, ENIC Bureau and the NARIC Advisory Board, with Support of the Co-Secretariats." Available at https://www.enic-naric.net/Upload/Documents/Recognition_of_qualifications_in_times_of_COVID19.pdf. Accessed February 2, 2024.

Council of Europe/International Consortium. 2006. "Higher Education and Democratic Culture: Citizenship, Human Rights and Civic Responsibility. Declaration." Document DECS/EDU/HE (2006) 26. Available at https://rm.coe.int/declaration-on-the-responsibility-of-higher-education-for-democratic-c/1680779f5b. Accessed February 2, 2024.

———. 2008. "Forum on Converging Competences: Diversity, Higher Education, and Sustainable Democracy, Strasbourg, October 2–3, 2008—Recommendations and Conclusions." Available at https://rm.coe.int/conclusions-and-recommendations-invitational-forum-on-converging-compe/168075dff2. Accessed June 22, 2023.

Council of Europe and UNESCO. 1997. *The Convention on the Recognition of Qualifications concerning Higher Education in the European Region*. Lisbon Recognition Convention: European Treaties Series No. 165. The text of the convention as well as its explanatory report and an updated list of signatures and ratifications are available at https://www.coe.int/en/web/conventions/full-list?module=treaty-detail&treatynum =165. Accessed February 2, 2024.

———. 2016. *Monitoring the Implementation of the Lisbon Recognition Convention: The Committee of the Convention on the Recognition of Qualifications concerning Higher Education in the European Region—Final Report.* Available at https://www.enic-naric .net/Upload/Documents/Monitoring_Implementation_LRC_Final_Report_ENGLISH .pdf. Accessed February 2, 2024.

———. 2017. *Recommendation on the Recognition of Refugees' Qualifications under the Lisbon Recognition Convention and Explanatory Memorandum: Adopted by the Lisbon Recognition Convention Committee at Its Extraordinary Session on 14 November 2017.* Available at https://www.enic-naric.net/Upload/Documents/Recommendation _Recognition_Qualifications_Refugees_ENGLISH.pdf. Accessed February 2, 2024.

Cutajar, JosAnn, and John Vella. 2018. "Contentious Politics and the Production of Place: The Case of Cottonera." University of Malta. Available at https://www.um.edu.mt/li brary/oar/bitstream/123456789/20223/1/%2804%29%20Cutajar%20and%20Vella.pdf. Accessed February 2, 2024.

Dahl, Hans Fredrik. 2015. *Quislings nettverk* [Quisling's networks]. Oslo: Aschehoug.

Dang, Que Anh, and Takao Kamibeppu. 2020. "Curbing University Autonomy and Academic Freedom in the Name of Quality Assurance, Accountability and Internationalisation in East Asia." In Bergan, Gallagher, and Harkavy 2020, 103–120. Available at https://rm.coe.int/prems-025620-eng-2508-higher-education-series-no-24/1680a 19fdf. Accessed February 2, 2024.

Deleu, Xavier. 2005. *Transnistrie: La poudrière de l'Europe* [Transnistria: Europe's powder keg]. Paris: Hugo.

Douglass, John Aubrey. 2021. "Neo-nationalism and Universities." In *Neo-Nationalism and Universities: Populists, Autocrats, and the Future of Higher Education,* ed. John Aubrey Douglass, 22–42. Baltimore, MD: Johns Hopkins University Press.

Duhamel, Alain. 2023. *Le Prince balafré: Emmanuel Macron et les Gaulois (très) réfractaires* [The scarred prince: Emmanuel Macron and the (very) unmanageable Gauls]. Paris: Editions de l'Observatoire.

Eurobarometer. 2021. *Values and Identities of EU Citizens: Eurobarometer Special Report 508.* Brussels: European Union. Available at https://data.europa.eu/data/datasets /s2230-94-1-508-eng?locale=en. Accessed February 2, 2024.

European Commission. 2022. "Commission Recommendation (EU) 2022/554 of 5 April 2022 on the Recognition of Qualifications for People Fleeing Russia's Invasion of Ukraine." Available at https://eur-lex.europa.eu/legal-content/EN/TXT/?uri=CELEX %3A32022H0554. Accessed August 12, 2024.

European Court of Human Rights. 2022. *Guide on Article 2 of Protocol No. 1 to the European Convention on Human Rights: Right to Education—Updated on August 31, 2022.* Strasbourg: European Court of Human Rights. Available at https://www.echr.coe.int /documents/d/echr/guide_art_2_protocol_1_eng. Accessed February 2, 2024.

European Education and Culture Executive Agency, Eurydice. 2018. *The European Higher Education Area in 2018: Bologna Process Implementation Report.* Brussels: Publications Office. Available at https://data.europa.eu/doi/10.2797/265898. Accessed February 2, 2024.

European Union. 2015. "Declaration on Promoting Citizenship and the Common Values of Freedom, Tolerance and Non-Discrimination Through Education." Available at https://eu.daad.de/medien/eu.daad.de.2016/dokumente/service/auswertung-und -statistik/paris_declaration_2015_en.pdf. Accessed August 9, 2024.

———. 2017. "Council Recommendation of 20 November 2017 on Tracking Graduates (2017/C 423/01)." Available at https://eur-lex.europa.eu/legal-content/EN/TXT/?uri =CELEX%3A32017H1209%2801%29. Accessed August 12, 2024.

Farnell, Thomas, Paul Benneworth, Bojana Ćulum Ilić, Marco Seeber, and Ninoslav Šćukanec Schmidt. 2020. *TEFCE Toolbox: An Institutional Self-Reflection Framework for Community Engagement in Higher Education*. Zagreb: Institute for the Development of Education. Available at https://www.acup.cat/sites/default/files/2023-05/5fc 001621c2973222bea0acf_tefce_toolbox.pdf. Accessed February 2, 2024.

Farnell, Thomas, Ana Skledar Matijević, and Ninoslav Šćukanec Schmidt. 2020. *Linking Universities and (Local) Communities in Europe: Overview of Initiatives and Stakeholders—A Study Prepared for the Council of Europe*. Zagreb: Institute for the Development of Education.

Finocchietti, Chiara, and Sjur Bergan. 2021. "Opening Up Education Opportunities for Refugee Scholars." University World News, March 27, 2021. Available at https://www .universityworldnews.com/post.php?story=20210322124447931. Accessed February 2, 2024.

Fischer, Didier. 2000. *L'histoire des étudiants en France de 1945 à nos jours* [A history of students in France from 1945 to our days]. Paris: Flammarion.

Gallagher, Tony. 2019. "Embedding Engagement: The Example of Queen's University Belfast." In Bergan, Harkavy, and Munck 2019a, 52–62.

Gallagher, Tony, and Jennifer Harrison. 2015. "Civic Engagement in a Divided Society: The Role of Queen's University in Northern Ireland." In Bergan, Gallagher, and Harkavy 2015, 51–62.

Gelman, Andrew. 2011. "All Politics Is Local? The Debate and the Graphs." FiveThirtyEight, January 3, 2011. Available at https://fivethirtyeight.com/features/all-politics-is-local -the-debate-and-the-graphs/. Accessed February 2, 2024.

Gerstle, Gary. 2022. *The Rise and Fall of the Neoliberal Order: America and the World in the Free Market Era*. New York: Oxford University Press.

Géstsdóttir, Steinunn. 2019. "The University of Iceland's Participation in the Local and National Community: Increasing Impact, Widening Access." In *The Local Mission of Higher Education: Principles and Practice*, ed. Sjur Bergan, Ira Harkavy, and Ronaldo Munck, 80–89. Dublin: Glasnevin.

Gitlin, Todd. 1993. *The Sixties: Years of Hope, Days of Rage*. New York: Bantam Books.

Glenthøj, Rasmus. 2012. *Skilsmissen: Dansk og norsk før og efter 1814* [The divorce: Danish and Norwegian before and after 1814]. Odense: Syddansk Universitetsforlag.

Gran, John Willem, Erik Gunnes, and Lars Roar Langslet, eds. 1993. *Den katolske kirke i Norge: Fra kristningen til i dag* [The Catholic Church in Norway: From Christianization until today]. Oslo: Ashehoug.

Guarasci, Richard, and David Maurrasse. 2015. "Higher Education Institutions as Pillars of Their Communities: The Role of Anchor Institutions." In Bergan, Gallagher, and Harkavy 2015, 101–108.

Hainmueller, Jens, and Michael J. Hiscox. 2007. "Educated Preferences: Explaining Attitudes toward Immigration in Europe." *International Organization* 61 (Spring 2007), 399–442. Available at https://www.mit.edu/~jhainm/Paper/EducatedPreferencesIO revised.pdf. Accessed February 2, 2024.

Hall, Martin. 2015. "Connected Learning. Innovation in the Face of Conflict." In Bergan, Gallagher, and Harkavy 2015, 185–200.

Haque, Charles, and Cyrille Pluyette. 2023. "Le naufrage moral de la Russie" [Russia's moral shipwreck]. *L'Express*, no. 3724 (January 26–February 1), 20–21.

Hårdstedt, Martin. 2023. *Finlands svenska historia* [The Swedish history of Finland]. Helsinki/Stockholm: Svenska litteratursällskapet i Finland and Natur och Kultur.

Harkavy, Ira. 2015. "US Higher Education, Community Engagement and Democratic Innovation: A Historical Overview and Suggestions for Moving Forward." In Bergan, Gallagher, and Harkavy 2015, 273–285.

———. 2023. "Dewey, Implementation, and Creating a Democratic Civic University." *The Pluralist* 18, no. 1 (Spring 2023), 49–75.

Harkavy, Ira, and Lee Benson. 1998 "De-Platonizing and Democratizing Education as the Bases of Service Learning." In *Academic Service Learning: Pedagogy and Research*, ed. R. A. Rhoads and J. Howard, 11–19. San Francisco: Jossey-Bass.

Harkavy, Ira, Sjur Bergan, Tony Gallagher, and Hilligje van't Land. 2020. "Universities Must Help Shape the post-COVID-19 World." University World News, April 18, 2020. Available at https://www.universityworldnews.com/post.php?story=2020041315254 2750. Accessed February 2, 2024.

Harris, Jim, and Marcine Pickron-Davis. 2015. "Case Study of Widener University and Chester: A Story about Conflict and Collaboration." In Bergan, Gallagher, and Harkavy 2015, 71–83.

Harvey, David. 2005. *A Brief History of Neoliberalism*. Oxford: Oxford University Press.

Huber, Josef, and Ira Harkavy, eds. 2007. *Higher Education and Democratic Culture: Citizenship, Human Rights and Civic Responsibility*. Council of Europe Higher Education Series No. 8. Strasbourg: Council of Europe.

Jack, Patrick. 2023. "25 Years On: Universities' Role in Northern Ireland Peace Process." *Times Higher Education*, April 24, 2023.

Jagiellonian University. 2021. *The Jagiellonian University 2030 Strategy*. Available at https://en.uj.edu.pl/documents/81541894/148892674/JU-2030-Strategy.pdf/adfd7bfb-eebc-4d3d-a4e0-e010fc577cac. Accessed February 2, 2024.

Judah, Tim. 2000. *Kosovo: War and Revenge*. New Haven, CT: Yale University Press.

Kallendorf, Craig W., ed. and trans 2008. *Humanist Educational Treatises*. Cambridge, MA: Harvard University Press. The I Tatti Renaissance Library.

Kamen, Henry. 2014. *España y Cataluña: Historia de una pasión* [Spain and Catalonia: The history of a passion]. Madrid: La Esfera de los Libros.

Kennedy, Declan, Áine Hyland, and Norma Ryan. 2007. "Writing and Using Learning Outcomes: A Practical Guide." Berlin: Raabe. Available at https://www.researchgate.net/publication/238495834_Writing_and_Using_Learning_Outcomes_A_Practical_Guide. Accessed February 2, 2024.

Kent, Neil. 2018. *The Sámi Peoples of the North: A Social and Cultural History*. London: Hurst.

Kistryn, Stanisław. 2019. "A Traditional University in Its Local Community: The Jagiellonian University in Kraków." In Bergan, Harkavy, and Munck 2019a, 74–79.

Knaus, Gerald. 2020. *Welche Grenzen brauchen wir? Zwischen Empathie und Angst–Flucht, Migration und die Zukunft von Asyl* [What borders do we need? Between empathy and fear-flight, migration and the future of asylum]. München: Piper.

Kommunal- og distriktsdepartementet. 2019. *Meld. St. 31 (2018–2019) Samisk språk, kultur og samfunnsliv* [The Norwegian Ministry of Municipalities and Regions: Parliamentary Report No. 31 (2018–19) on Sámi Language, Cultural, and Society]. Available at https://www.regjeringen.no/contentassets/b3497da7cab1411094b96772d57b8d4e/no/pdfs/stm201820190031000dddpdfs.pdf. Accessed February 2, 2024.

Lorentzen, Trude. 2022. *Quislings koffert: I fotsporene til en forræder* [Quisling's suitcase: In the footsteps of a traitor]. Oslo: Kagge.

LOV-1998-07-17-6. 1998. "Lov om grunnskolen og den vidaregåande opplæringa" [Law on the primary school and on secondary education]. Available at https://lovdata.no/dokument/NL/lov/1998-07-17-61. Accessed February 2, 2024.

LOV-2005-04-01-15. 2005. "Lov om universiteter og høyskoler" [Law on universities and colleges]. Available at https://lovdata.no/dokument/NL/lov/2005-04-01-15. Accessed February 2, 2024.

L'Università ta' Malta. 2019. *Strategic Plan 2020–25*. Valletta: University of Malta. Available at https://www.um.edu.mt/media/um/docs/about/strategy/UMStrategicPlan2020-2025.pdf. Accessed February 2, 2024.

L'Università ta' Malta/Cottonera Resource Centre. 2019. "Academic Report October 2017–September 2018." Available at https://www.um.edu.mt/media/um/docs/services/resourcecentres/crc/CRCAnnualReport2017-20181.pdf. Accessed February 2, 2024.

Lynas, Mark. 2020. "COVID: Top 10 Current Conspiracy Theories." Alliance for Science, April 20, 2020. Available at https://allianceforscience.org/blog/2020/04/covid-top-10-current-conspiracy-theories/. Accessed February 2, 2024.

Magna Charta Observatory. 1988. "Magna Charta Universitatum." Available at https://www.magna-charta.org/magna-charta-universitatum/mcu-1988. Accessed February 2, 2024.

———. 2020. "Magna Charta Universitatum 2020." Available at https://www.magna-charta.org/magna-charta-universitatum/mcu2020. Accessed February 2, 2024.

Malcolm, Noel. 1998. *Kosovo: A Short History*. London: Papermac.

Manners, Paul. 2015. "The Development of Public Engagement with Research Policy Agenda in the United Kingdom." In Bergan, Gallagher, and Harkavy 2015, 169–184.

Matei, Liviu. 2019. "Can International Universities Be Anchor Institutions? Local, Regional, and Global: The Central European University." In Bergan, Harkavy, and Munck 2019a, 90–101.

———. 2020. "Academic Freedom, University Autonomy, and Democracy's Future in Europe." In Bergan, Gallagher, and Harkavy 2020, 29–40. Available at https://rm.coe.int/prems-025620-eng-2508-higher-education-series-no-24/1680a19fdf. Accessed February 2, 2024.

Maurrasse, David. 2019. "What Is an Anchor Institution and Why?" In Bergan, Harkavy, and Munck 2019a, 16–27.

McDonald, Jackie, Nikki Johnston, and Garnet "Buzz" Busby, with Tony Gallagher. 2015. "Community Engagement in Belfast: Queen's University and the Sandy Row Community." In Bergan, Gallagher, and Harkavy 2015, 63–69.

Mönckeberg, María Olivia. 2005. *La Privatización de las Universidades: Una historia de dinero, poder e influencias* [The privatization of universities: A story of money, power, and influence]. Santiago: Copa Rota.

Montague, Andrew. 2023. "Connecting Dublin City University to Its Local Community." In Bergan, Harkavy, and Munck 2023, 193–194.

Müller, Jan Werner. 2017. *What Is Populism?* London: Penguin.

Musil, Caryn McTighe. 2007. "Knee-Deep in Democracy." In *Higher Education and Democratic Culture: Citizenship, Human Rights and Civic Responsibility*, ed. Josef Huber and Ira Harkavy, 119–121. Council of Europe Higher Education 8. Strasbourg: Council of Europe.

National Co-ordinating Centre for Public Engagement. 2019. "The Engaged University." Bristol: National Co-ordinating Centre for Public Engagement. Available at https://www.publicengagement.ac.uk/sites/default/files/2023-06/nccpe_the_engaged_university_report_aug20_final_0.pdf. Accessed February 2, 2024.

Naumescu, Valentin. 2019. *Politica marilor puteri în Europa Centrală și de Est* [Great power policies in Central and Eastern Europe]. București: Humanitas.

Nyland, Jim, and David Davies. 2020. "Academic and Scholarly Freedom: Towards a 'Disputing' University with Critically Engaged Students." In Bergan, Gallagher, and Harkavy 2020, 73–84. Available at https://rm.coe.int/prems-025620-eng-2508-higher-education-series-no-24/1680a19fdf. Accessed February 2, 2024.

OECD (Organisation for Economic Co-operation and Development). 2020. "What Are Europeans' Views on Migrant Integration? An In-depth Analysis of 2017 Special Eurobarometer—'Integration of Immigrants in the European Union.'" Paris: OECD. Available at https://one.oecd.org/document/DELSA/ELSA/WD/SEM(2020)3/En/pdf. Accessed February 2, 2024.

Olstad, Finn. 2019. *Den store forsoningen: Norsk historie 1905–45.* [The great reconciliation: Norwegian history 1905–45]. Oslo: Dreyer.

O'Malley, Brendan. 2021. "Turkish Academics in the Era of Erdoğan." In *Neo-Nationalism and Universities: Populists, Autocrats, and the Future of Higher Education*, ed. John Aubrey Douglass, 141–159. Baltimore, MD: Johns Hopkins University Press.

Ozarowska, Joanna. 2019. "The University and Local Civil Engagement: An Irish Case Study." In *The Local Mission of Higher Education: Principles and Practice*, ed. Sjur Bergan, Ira Harkavy, and Ronaldo Munck, 29–38. Dublin: Glasnevin.

Pasquarella, Lynn. 2018. "Leading in Higher Education in a Post-Truth Era." In Bergan and Harkavy 2018, 39–44.

Paugam, Serge. 2020. "Comment comprendre le mouvement des Gilets jaunes?" [How should the yellow vest movement be understood?]. In *50 questions de sociologie* [50 Questions in Sociology], ed. Serge Paugam, 327–336. Paris: Presses Universitaires de France.

Pew Research Center. 2020. "Majorities in the European Union Have Favorable Views of the Bloc." Available at https://www.pewresearch.org/global/2020/11/17/majorities-in-the-european-union-have-favorable-views-of-the-bloc/. Accessed February 2, 2024.

Pieper, Dietmar, and Johannes Saltzwedel, eds. 2013. *Der Dreissigjährige Krieg: Europa im Kampf um Glaube und Macht 1618–1648* [The Thirty Year War: Europe in the struggle for faith and power 1618–1648]. Munich: Goldmann.

Pittelkow, Sebastian, and Katja Riedel. 2022. *Rechts unten—Die AfD: Intrigen, heimliche Herrscher und die Macht der Geldgeber* [Lower right—The AfD: Intrigues, secret rulers, and the power of the donors]. Hamburg: Rowolt.

Plantan, Frank. 2004. "The University as a Site of Citizenship." In *The University as Res Publica*, ed. Sjur Bergan, pp. 83–128. Council of Europe Higher Education 1. Strasbourg: Council of Europe.

Rauhvargers, Andrejs. 2011. *Global University Rankings and Their Impact*. Bruxelles: EAU. Available at https://eua.eu/downloads/publications/global%20university%20rankings%20and%20their%20impact.pdf. Accessed February 2, 2024.

———. 2013. *Global University Rankings and Their Impact—Report II*. Bruxelles: EAU. Available at https://eua.eu/downloads/publications/global%20university%20rankings%20and%20their%20impact%20-%20report%20ii.pdf. Accessed February 2, 2024.

Repubblica di San Marino. 2023. *Assetto istituzionale ed organizzativo dell'Università degli Studi della Repubblica di San Marino* [Institutional and organizational structure of the University of the Republic of San Marino]. Decreto delegato 1 giugno 2023 no. 90 [Delegated decree June 1, 2023, no. 90]. Available at https://www.bollettinoufficiale.sm. Accessed February 2, 2024. *RicercaBU, and Statuto dell'Università degli Studi della Repubblica di San Marino* [Statute of the University of the Republic of San Marino], Allegato "A" al Decreto Delegato 1 giugno 2023 no. 90 [Appendix A to the delegated decree June 1, 2023, no. 90]. Available at https://www.consigliograndeegenerale.sm. Accessed February 2, 2024.

Sanz, Nuria, and Sjur Bergan, eds. 2002. *The Heritage of European Universities*. Strasbourg: Council of Europe.

Scalisi, Marcello, and Silvia Marchionne. 2020. "Academic Freedom and Institutional Autonomy: Examples and Challenges." In Bergan, Gallagher, and Harkavy 2020, 183–196. Available at https://rm.coe.int/prems-025620-eng-2508-higher-education-series-no-24/1680a19fdf. Accessed February 2, 2024.

Schultheis, Emily. 2018. "Viktor Orbán: Hungary Doesn't Want 'Muslim Invaders,'" Politico, January 8. Available at https://www.politico.eu/article/viktor-orban-hungary-doesnt-want-muslim-invaders/. Accessed February 2, 2024.

Skjerven, Stig Arne. 2021. "Recognition of Foreign Qualifications in the Time of Covid-19." In Bergan, Gallagher, Harkavy, Munck, and van't Land 2021, 241–248. Available at https://rm.coe.int/prems-006821-eng-2508-higher-education-series-no-25/1680a19fe2. Accessed February 2, 2024.

Smith, John H. 2018. "Universities and Their Communities—Role as Anchor Institutions: European Policy Perspectives." In Bergan and Harkavy 2018, 193–199.

Spyropoulos, Spyros. 2019. "When Your Local Community Is Spread Out: The University of the Aegean." In Bergan, Harkavy, and Munck 2019a, 63–73.

Stradling, Robert. 2001. *Teaching 20th-Century European History*. Strasbourg: Council of Europe.

———. 2003. *Multiperspectivity in History Teaching: A Guide for Teachers*. Strasbourg: Council of Europe.

Suny, Ronald Grigor. 2015. *"They Can Live in the Desert but Nowhere Else": A History of the Armenian Genocide*. Princeton, NJ: Princeton University Press.

Taylor Jr., Henry Louis, Gavin Luter, and Pascal Buggs. 2018. "A Possible World and the Right to the University—Reflections on Higher Education in the United States." In Bergan and Harkavy 2018, 217–231.

Teune, Henry (principal investigator), and Frank Plantan (general rapporteur). 2001. *General Report: United States Study Universities as Sites of Citizenship and Civic Responsibility*. Available at https://bpb-us-w2.wpmucdn.com/web.sas.upenn.edu/dist/f/335/files/2023/02/USgeneralreport0401-2.pdf. Accessed February 2, 2024.

Tironi, Eugenio. 2005. *El sueño chileno: Comunidad, familia y nación en el Bicentenario* [The Chilean dream: Community, family, and nation at the bicentennial]. Santiago de Chile: Taurus.

Titlestad, Torgrim. 2012. *Norge i vikingtid: Våre historiske og kulturelle røtter* [Norway in the Viking Age: Our historical and cultural roots]. Stavanger: Sagabok.

Tsakarissianos, Giorgos. 2008. "Social Mobility and VET." In *Modernising Vocational Education and Training Fourth Report on Vocational Education and Training Research in Europe: Background Report*. Vol. 1, ed. Cedefop. Luxembourg: Office for Official Publications of the European Communities (Cedefop reference series). Available at https://www.cedefop.europa.eu/files/02-Tsakarissianos.pdf. Accessed February 2, 2024.

Università degli Studi di San Marino. 2019. *Piano strategico UNIRSM 2021–23* [Strategic plan for the University of the Republic of San Marino 2021–23]. Available at https://www.unirsm.sm/wp-content/uploads/2022/05/Piano-Strategico-UNIRSM-2021-2023.pdf. Accessed February 2, 2024.

van't Land, Hilligje. 2013. "Competences for a Culture of Democracy and Intercultural Dialogue: A Political Challenge and Values." Report from the High-Level Conference

Held in Andorra la Vella February 7–8, 2013. Available at https://rm.coe.int/conclu sions-from-the-andorran-conference-andorra-la-vella-7-8-february/1680994a6c. Accessed February 2, 2024.

Varghese, N. V. 2007. "GATS and Higher Education: The Need for Regulatory Policies." Paris: UNESCO/ International Institute for Educational Planning. Available at https:// unesdoc.unesco.org/ark:/48223/pf0000150689/PDF/150689eng.pdf.multi. Accessed February 2, 2024.

Vickers, Miranda. 1997. *The Albanians: A Modern History*. London: I. B. Tauris.

Vogler, Bernard. 1993. *Histoire culturelle de l'Alsace* [A cultural history of Alsace]. Strasbourg: La Nuée Bleue.

———. 1995. *Histoire politique de l'Alsace* [A political history of Alsace]. Strasbourg: La Nuée Bleue.

Vogler, Bernard, and Michel Hau. 1997. *Histoire économique de l'Alsace* [An economic history of Alsace]. Strasbourg: La Nuée Bleue.

Volkov, Denis, and Andrei Kolesnikov. 2022. "My Country, Right or Wrong: Russian Public Opinion on Ukraine." Washington, DC: Carnegie Endowment for International Peace. Available at https://carnegieendowment.org/files/202209-Volkov_Kolesnikov _War_Opinion1.pdf. Accessed February 2, 2024.

Weber, Luc, and Sjur Bergan. 2005. *The Public Responsibility for Higher Education and Research*. Council of Europe Higher Education Series No. 2. Strasbourg: Council of Europe. Available at https://rm.coe.int/the-public-responsibility-for-higher-education -and-research/168075ddd0. Accessed February 2, 2024.

Weeks, Joann. 2019. "Campus and Community Revitalization in the United States: Penn's Evolution as an Anchor Institution." In Bergan, Harkavy, and Munck 2019a, 39–51.

Wildová, Radka, Tomáš Fliegel, and Barbora Vokšická. 2019. "The Third Mission of Universities: Examples of Good Practice from the Czech Republic." In Bergan, Harkavy, and Munck 2019a, 102–111.

Wilson, Andrew. 2021. *Belarus: The Last European Dictatorship*. New Edition. New Haven, CT: Yale University Press.

Zonta, Claudia A. 2002. "The History of European Universities: Overview and Background." In *The Heritage of European Universities*, ed. Nuria Sanz and Sjur Bergan. Strasbourg: Council of Europe.

Index

Entries are in English alphabetical order, even if some of the language concerned consider letters with diacritical marks separate letters with their own place in the alphabet, such as the Bosnian, Croatian, and Serbian *š*, the Romanian *ş*, the Spanish *ch and ll*, which are considered separate letters in this language, or the Norwegian and Swedish *å*, which in these languages is the last rather than the first letter of the alphabet.

Sjur Bergan is an independent education expert and former Head of the Council of Europe's Education Department. He was instrumental in the development of the Council of Europe's work with U.S. and international partners on the democratic mission of higher education. He is the author of *Not by Bread Alone* and *Qualifications: Introduction to a Concept*.

www.ingramcontent.com/pod-product-compliance
Lightning Source LLC
Chambersburg PA
CBHW020339270326
41926CB00007B/247